# STEPHEN SPENDER
# AND THE THIRTIES

Other books by A. KINGSLEY WEATHERHEAD:

*A Reading of Henry Green*
*The Edge of the Image*
*The Poem* (ed., with Stanley B. Greenfield)

# STEPHEN SPENDER
# AND THE THIRTIES

## A. KINGSLEY WEATHERHEAD

Lewisburg
Bucknell University Press
London: Associated University Presses

© 1975 by Associated University Presses, Inc.


Associated University Presses, Inc.
Cranbury, New Jersey 08512


Associated University Presses
108 New Bond Street
London W1Y OQX, England


**Library of Congress Cataloging in Publication Data**

Weatherhead, Andrew Kingsley, 1923–
  Stephen Spender and the thirties.

  Bibliography: p.
  1. Spender, Stephen, 1909–    2. English poetry—
20th century—History and criticism   I. Title.
PR6037.P47Z95      821'.9'12      73–2891
ISBN 0–8387–1370–4

To the memory of
James W. Hall,
in admiration and gratitude

# Contents

# Preface

This book is an essay mainly about Stephen Spender and his poetry. Until now the poetry has been neglected, mostly, I believe, on account of its purity: large parts of many poems are detached or are straining to become detached from everyday things; and such poems are thus not to be approached in the workaday frame of mind in which one comes in off the street to read the headlines and throw away the bulk mail. Or, to put the matter another way, a poem of Spender's is apt to be art: it is a finished thing, of or tending toward formal perfection. It is not open ended, not continuous with life, but set off, in itself, apart. It does not, therefore, immediately accommodate that widespread contemporary taste which seeks in the poem an extension of waking sensations reported with minimal distortion, and finds the arcane elevation of a stylized art form forbidding or irrelevant. In these pages I want in a minor way to compensate for the neglect and say some things about this poet's work.

We think of Spender mainly as a poet of the thirties, a categorization which he does not resent; and we think of that decade as having been politically minded, because the concerns and interests of men in society, their economics and politics, spread into unwonted areas of intellectual activity, in particular into aesthetic activity. Thus after a brief introductory chapter I have devoted chapter 2 to repeating parts and giving some general sense of the long debate about the interrelationships of politics and poetry.

Chapters 3 to 6 are also intended to supply context by giving samples of the work of other poets who flourished in the thirties and thus create an image of the broad poetic background. These poets are grouped under the rubrics of subject matters and strategies that seem to have been used in common by a number of them during those years, and Spender's position—whether he shared this or that feature or not—is considered. In these chapters I have drawn rather upon the works of minor and uncelebrated writers, not thinking to tell yet again the stories of Auden, Graves, and Thomas; and I have drawn mostly, but not exclusively, from their work in the thirties or early forties. Much of the work of the writers I have brought forward is unknown; some of it is original, but there are no sensational experiments like those being undertaken in the United States during the same period by William Carlos Williams and Wallace Stevens and others. Indeed, for its very conventionality alone, as compared with the manifold departures exercised in American poetry, this body of verse is of some remark. What American in the last forty years would say of rigid poetic forms like the sonnet, that they are "helpful": "They always seem to me to encourage my own writing, and therefore I regard them as free forms."[1] Marianne Moore, perhaps, or John Berryman, or one or two others might have said something to this effect; but it seems to me a characteristically English sentiment. Even though much of the minor verse of the decade is conventional, however, much of it is worth introducing; and there are, of course, occasional fine poems by Ronald Bottrall, Bernard Spencer, Roy Fuller, Geoffrey Grigson, or Norman Cameron—things that don't get into the big

1. Roy Fuller, in *The Poet Speaks,* ed. Peter Orr (New York: Barnes and Noble, 1966), p. 63.

anthologies but that one would as soon see there as "Thirteen Ways of Looking at a Blackbird."

The seventh chapter of this essay considers Spender's poetry as it appeared volume by volume, caring more for the details in the work of the thirties than those later, and also the short stories which, for the features they have in common with the poetry, ought, I believe, to be considered alongside it. And the eighth chapter is an attempt to present the essence of Spender's poetry—the heart of the matter.

# Acknowledgments

Grateful acknowledgment is made to those named below for permission to quote from the works listed:

George Barker, for permission to quote from George Barker's *Collected Poems 1930–1955* (1957).

BARNES & NOBLE BOOKS division of Harper & Row Pub. Inc., for permission to quote from Peter Orr, ed., *The Poet Speaks: Interviews with Contemporary Poets Conducted by Hilary Morrish, Peter Orr, John Press, and Ian Scott-Kilvert* (1966).

Quentin Bell and The Hogarth Press Ltd. for permission to quote from Julian Bell, *Essays, Poems, and Letters,* ed. Quentin Bell (1958), *Work for the Winter and Other Poems* (1936), and *Winter Movement and Other Poems* (1930).

The Bodley Head, Ltd., for permission to quote from Rex Warner, *Poems* (1937).

Jonathan Cape, Ltd, and the Estate of John Cornford, for permission to quote from *John Cornford: A Memoir*, ed. Pat Sloan (excerpt from "To Margot Heinemann" by John Cornford) and to Jonathan Cape Ltd, for permission to quote from C. Day Lewis, *Collected Poems* (1954).

Chatto and Windus, Ltd. and the Author's Literary Estate for permission to quote from C. Day Lewis, *The Buried Day* (1960). Reprinted by permission of A. D. Peters and Company.

Faber and Faber, for permission to quote from Stephen Spender, *The Burning Cactus*, (1936), *Collected Poems: 1928–1953* (1955), *Poems* (1933), *Poems* (1934), *Poems of Dedication* (1947), *Ruins and Visions 1934–1942*, *The Still Centre* (1939), *Trial of a Judge* (1938), *Vienna* (1934), *Edge of Being* (1949). Also for permission to quote from George Barker, *Collected Poems 1930–1955* (1957); from Michael Roberts, *Orion Marches* (1939), *Collected Poems* (1958); from W.H. Auden, *The Orators* (1932) and *Look, Stranger* (1935); from Roy Campbell, *Talking Bronco* (1946); from Charles Madge, *The Disappearing Castle* (1937); and from Louis MacNeice, *The Earth Compels* (1938). All reprinted by permission of Faber and Faber Ltd.

Roy Fuller, for permission to quote from Roy Fuller, *Poems*, published by the Fortune Press (1939); and from *The Middle of a War* (1942) and *A Lost Season*, both published by The Hogarth Press (1944).

Geoffrey Grigson, for permission to quote from the Preface to Geoffrey Grigson's *Collected Poems of 1924–1962* (1963).

David Higham Associates, Ltd., for permission to quote from John Lehmann, *A Garden Revisited and Other Poems*, published by the Hogarth Press (1931) and *The Noise of History*, published by Leonard and Virginia Woolf (1934).

Alan Hodge, Norman Cameron's literary executor, for permission to quote from Norman Cameron, *The Winter House and Other Poems*, Dent (1935).

The Hogarth Press, for permission to quote from Stephen Spender, ed., *Poems for Spain* (excerpts from "Jarama Front," by T. A. R. Hyndman, "Retrospect," by David R. Marshall,

# Acknowledgments

"Looking at a Map of Spain on the Devon Coast," by Jack Lindsay); from Michael Roberts, ed., *New Country: Prose and Poetry by the Authors of New Signatures* (1933); and from Julian Bell, *Essays, Poems, and Letters,* ed. Quentin Bell (1958), *Work for the Winter and Other Poems* (1936), and *Winter Movement and Other Poems* (1930).

Alfred A. Knopf, Inc., for permission to quote from Rex Warner, *Poems* (1937).

Lawrence and Wishart, Ltd., for permission to quote from Christopher Caudwell, *Poems* (1965), and from Edgell Rickword, *Twittingpan and Some Others* (1931).

The Executors of the Estate of C. Day Lewis, Jonathan Cape Ltd. and The Hogarth Press, for permission to quote from C. Day Lewis, *Collected Poems* (1954) Copyright 1954 by C. Day Lewis, Reprinted by permission of Harold Matson Co., Inc. and Jonathan Cape Ltd.

Library of Congress, for permission to quote from Stephen Spender, *Imagination in the Modern World* (1962) and *Chaos and Control in Poetry* (1966).

Macmillan, London and Basingstoke, for permission to quote from Christopher Caudwell, *Illusion and Reality* (1937).

Harold Matson Company Inc., for permission to quote from Stephen Spender, *World Within World*, Reprinted by permission of Harold Matson Co., Inc.; and from C. Day Lewis, *Collected Poems,* Copyright 1954 by C. Day Lewis, Reprinted by permission of Harold Matson Co., Inc.

Methuen and Co., Ltd and the author, for permission to quote from Randall Swingler, *Difficult Morning* (1933).

*Michigan Quarterly Review,* for permission to quote my article "British Leftist Poetry," *The Michigan Quarterly Review 10*, no. 1 (Winter 1971): 12–22. Copyright © 1971 The University of Michigan.

The Oxford University Press for permission to quote from *The Collected Poems of Louis MacNeice,* edited by E. R. Dodds. Copyright © The Estate of Louis MacNeice 1966. Reprinted by permission of Oxford University Press, Inc.

Penguin Books Ltd., for permission to quote from Robin Skelton, ed., *Poetry of the Thirties* (1967) © Robin Skelton, 1964:

Reprinted by permission of Penguin Books Ltd; and from Claud Cockburn, *I, Claud* (1967) © Claude Cockburn, 1967: Reprinted by permission of Penguin Books Ltd.

A. D. Peters for permission to quote from Stephen Spender, *Edge of Being, The Making of a Poem* (1955), "Notes from a Diary" in *Encounter* magazine (1959). Reprinted by permission of A. D. Peters and Company; Stephen Spender, *World Within World* (1951). Reprinted by permission of A. D. Peters and Co.; excerpts from Stephen Spender, "Auden Aetat XX, LX" and "Pronouns of This Time," in *Shenandoah*, Copyright 1964 and 1967 by *Shenandoah*; and from C. Day Lewis, *The Buried Day*. Reprinted by permission of A. D. Peters and Company.

Random House, Inc., for permission to quote from Stephen Spender, *The Burning Cactus* (1936), *Collected Poems: 1928–1953* (1955), *Poems* (1933), *Poems* (1934), *Poems of Dedication* (1947), *Ruins and Visions 1934–1942* (1942), *The Still Centre* (1939), *Trial of a Judge* (1938), *Vienna* (1934); and from W. H. Auden, *On This Island* Random House, Inc, © 1937, and W. H. Auden, *The Orators,* Random House Inc., © 1966.

The Author, Edgell Rickword, for permission to quote from *The Collected Poems of Edgell Rickword,* published by The Bodley Head, Ltd. (1947).

Alan Ross, Ltd., for permission to quote from Bernard Spencer. *Collected Poems.*

*Shenandoah,* The Washington and Lee University Review, for permission to quote excerpts from Stephen Spender, "Auden Aetat XX, LX" and "Prounouns of This Time," in *Shenandoah,* Copyright 1964 and 1967 by *Shenandoah,* reprinted from *Shenandoah:* The Washington and Lee University Review with the permission of the Editor.

Stephen Spender, for permission to quote from Stephen Spender, *Edge of Being* (1949) and excerpts from "Auden Aetat XX, LX" and "Pronouns of This Time," in *Shenandoah,* 1964 and 1967. Reprinted by permission of A. D. Peters and Company.

Ruthven Todd, for permission to quote from *Until Now* (1942).

The University of Wisconsin Press, for permission to quote from my article "Stephen Spender: Lyric Impulse and Will," *Contemporary Literature* 12, no. 4 (© 1971 by the Regents of the University of Wisconsin): 451–65.

## Acknowledgements

I also gratefully acknowledge the receipt of a Grant-in-Aid from the American Council of Learned Societies, which helped me in the writing of this book. I am grateful to the librarian of the University of Sussex, and to the Trustees of the British Museum for the use of their library premises and materials. I thank Robert McCollough, Pat McDaniels, Nina Casto, and Richard Heinzkill for bibliographical and miscellaneous assistance in the University of Oregon Library. I thank my colleagues Gloria Johnson, Christof Wegelin, and William Strange for reading parts of the manuscript and commenting. For clerical assistance I thank Susan Fagan and Sharon Brunsman, and Leslie R. Weatherhead, who for 70¢ an hour suspended his sense of irony and checked the proofs. I thank my wife, Ingrid, for much help.

A. K. W.
Eugene, Oregon

# 1

# Spender's Two Worlds

In most readers the name of Stephen Spender probably evokes
memories of the poems he wrote in the thirties in which the lyrical
sensibility clashes manifestly with political statement—poems like
"The Landscape near an Aerodrome," "The Funeral," and "Not
palaces, an era's crown." Eighteen years ago, reprinting them in
his *Collected Poems*, the poet looked back to certain of the poems
with some embarrassment: he feels an obligation to "own up" to
them, he says. But they are still published in anthologies as representing his work and properly so; for though Spender has written other
poems of other kinds, very often there may be remarked, on the
surface or not far beneath it, the conflict a man faces between the
life he leads with his private sensibility, the inward life, and the
one he lives in the broad world in which he must do his duty. Spender's poems feature the self and the world, or their respective agents
or notifications: the self, pure and alienated, in a gauche encounter

with a world that remains finally unattainable, the separating gulf not substantially bridged. The poem is a social thing, however; and for all his natural reticence and all his doubt as to the reality of the outside world, the poet must make the effort to come through to it. And so we find certain poems taking on a worldliness essentially foreign to them: we see something light and ethereal ballasted with clay, a light winged dryad of the trees in Pay-Day overalls. And if the success of a poem depends on unity in its pitch and its parts, many of Spender's must be said to fail. In one that fails least, the elements of self and world have been refined into rarefied metaphors in terms of which a union of sorts is effected: it is, at any rate, announced. This is "Darkness and Light," which is the poem used as epigraph for the autobiography, *World Within World*.

Since, according to Spender himself, everything he writes is a fragment of autobiography, it is not surprising that elements of the conflict discernible in the poems should be present in the short stories. These are, in fact, not far removed in style and structure from the poems, using some of the same techniques and showing similar features. Often they center about a character who is sick; he may be physically weak, or psychologically sick, suffering from narcissism or, if nothing worse, as gravely misunderstood by society as only a brooding adolescent can be. Sometimes he is to be seen on a terraced road that traverses a mountainside: in such situations he is extroverted, making contact with the world. On the other hand, we are regularly made conscious of the room or rooms he inhabits, the places, presumably, where his sensibilities feed his inner life.

The autobiography itself, like the poetry and the fictional characters that venture forth to be social, is an act on the part of a writer naturally reticent to make contact with the alien world. It is, surely, only *a* portrait of the artist; but it portrays the life of a man of sensibility shyly encountering the outside world in many various situations, without resounding success. We do not read far in *World Within World* before there begins to appear a series of descriptions of frustrated engagements between the hero and his society: he revolts against his family—though that is hardly an original move. He is awkward at Oxford, provoking the athletic, better-adapted fauna to raid his rooms, though again this is no "first" for Stephen. In his brother and other acquaintances he has an entrée to the company of Auden; but these, as he says, "were all roads that led [him] to, and blocked [him] from Auden." He has a frustrating crush on a male friend. He is obstructed again in flirtations that looked promising, first with a nurse and second with a charmer called Polly, who seems to have been Oxford's latter-day Zuleika Dobson. He goes to Germany and mixes with German youth but fails to engage them: "There was something about my appearance at this time, so inhibited, preoccupied, and physically nervous, that it prevented these young Germans from being drawn to me as they were to one another. They looked at me and said: *'Nicht schön, sondern interessant,'* or *'unschuldig.'*"[1] It is not an exclusive pattern; but again and again throughout the book we find a mortified Stephen Spender who has failed to negotiate the icy curves of human relationships: he is awkward with friends like Christopher Isherwood and "Jimmy Younger"; he is awkward in society at Lady Morrell's; he is awkward as a lover. Repeatedly there is the breakdown or the quiet failure in his engagement with others. "All [his] friends," wrote Isherwood, referring indirectly to Spender, "betrayed him, in some minor degree, sooner or later. He asked too much of them; he trusted them absolutely—so that the blow, when it fell, was doubled in force."[2] With a comment of his own, Spender obliquely links the general awkwardness with the major conflict of the poetry: he speaks of the predicament of the idealist: "the idealist expects too much from himself and from others. He is like an artist who cannot relate inspiration to form. . . ."[3] There is the nub of the matter.

A passage in a late poem may suggest one reason why he should have been the idealist with the tenuous hold on reality that will appear throughout these pages:

1. *World Within World: The Autobiography of Stephen Spender* (London: Hamish Hamilton, 1951), p. 108.
2. *Lions and Shadows: An Education in the Twenties* (London: Methuen, 1953), p. 282. Originally published by Hogarth Press in 1938.
3. *World Within World*, p. 31

> . . . in the North, my brother Michael
> . . . . . . . . . . . . .
> . . . wills a future where he is It
> A box of instruments set down
> For measuring objectively
> Weights, temperature, distances. . . .
> There's nothing in the world but fact
> And error. Truth is what says It,
> Error forever bellows "I."[4]

Like others before and after him (the Prodigal Son and Ian Fleming, for examples), Stephen's place as a younger son in the family constellation may have accounted for the closing off of conventional avenues of success in the real objective world and determined his need to set off on his own and make a livelihood in territory which his elder brother had not pre-empted.

The desultory anthology reader who thinks of Spender as the guy in the thirties whose poems break down under the pressure of their political comments is not necessarily wide of the mark in such a limited characterization of the canon. Nor in tagging him as a a poet of the thirties is he wrong, not anyway impressionistically wrong. Since that decade Spender has written much in verse and prose; and he is not necessarily a man for one season only, a rigid period author who withers with the inexorable changes in ecology— a character that has been attributed, for example, to W. H. Auden, rightly or wrongly.[5] We may nevertheless quite properly and fruit-fully consider Spender, who gained his majority at the beginning of the decade, as a man of the thirties. In one way and another he suggests that he sees himself so. Looking back from the fifties, he tells himself, "Your era is prehistoric,"[6] as if *his* "era" were a closed book, to say the least. His autobiography was published when he was 42, and the latest episode referred to is a fire during the blitz at

4. Stephen Spender, "Draft of the First Five Sections of Part One," *Pronouns of This Time, Shenandoah* 16 (Autumn 1964): 11.

5. By Philip Larkin, "What's Become of Wystan?", *Spectator* 205 (July 15, 1960): 104–5.

6. "Letter to a Young Writer," *Encounter* 3, no. 3 (March 1954): 4–5.

the end of the decade. The book closes with the remark, albeit quoted from somebody else, " 'Tell them I have had a very happy life.' "

Spender is a man of the thirties in another sense: he was in touch with many of the people and the movements that have come to make up our image of the decade. In his autobiography there are necessarily a host of details that are personal. But we need only compare it in this respect with Leonard Woolf's autobiography—the dull housekeeping accounts, for example—or with the published letters of C. S. Lewis, or with the autobiographies of other poets, for that matter, Roy Campbell or C. Day Lewis, to recognize to what a great extent the personal details in Spender's book coincide with matters of public importance and historical interest.

One of his favorite words is "intellectual," often preceded by "young." And it seems that he himself in his twenties was in touch with the intellectual life of the times. They were times, of course, when to be in touch was tantamount to declaring allegiance to a political party, or at least a general political attitude. These times, as a Cambridge undergraduate told C. Day Lewis after the second war, were "the last time that anyone believed in anything." Like many intellectuals Spender attempted to adopt a political position left of Liberalism, and he recorded his convictions and his uncertainties in a book, *Forward From Liberalism.*[7] Like Auden, Isherwood, and Naomi Mitchison,[8] he saw fascism in operation in Germany and Austria. Like Day Lewis, Edward Upward, and others, he joined the Communist Party of Great Britain. Like Auden and others he went to the Spanish Civil War; unlike some he returned. He knew Auden, MacNeice, Isherwood, Eliot, and Yeats.

He saw more than his closest colleagues: having three hundred pounds per annum he was more able than they to keep physically in touch with the historic events of the decade. For some years he lived half the time in Germany and half in England. Auden, on the other hand, was geographically out of things: after his year in Germany, 1928–29, he withdrew to Scotland, where through the

7. (London: Gollancz, 1937).

8. Neal Wood, *Communism and British Intellectuals* (New York: Columbia University Press, 1959), p. 39.

offices of Gabbitas and Thring, a school employment agency for geniuses and others, he had secured a post as schoolmaster:

> To many an unknown genius postmen bring
> Typed notices from Rabbitarse and String.

C. Day Lewis was engaged much of the decade at a school near Oxford—a world, no doubt, like Auden's but far from that of Stephen Spender:

> of bells and tattered books and football boots and crazes and blackboards and piercing screams; of ink smells, chalk-duster smells, smells of mud and mown grass, and the mousey smell of little boys; of draughts, radiators, chilblains, stringy meat, steamed puddings; of dismal walks in the rain.[9]

Louis MacNeice, meanwhile, lectured on classics at the University of Birmingham and then to the women at Bedford College in London. Spender was free to circulate here and there, to have tea with Eliot, who didn't dare to take a cake, or with the aging, shaggy, big-bellied Yeats at Ottoline Morrell's. Indeed he was too free; he found it hard to say no to social invitations, having no regular employment for alibi.

He was able also to move around Europe as he wished. He attended the Writers' Congress in Madrid in 1937 and was momentarily in the firing line, stooping in the trenches for his unusual height. He encountered frustrated young Germans in Germany and recorded their awakening to their own strength. He was in and out of Vienna at the time of the uprising in February 1934 of the Austrian Socialists and the murder of Dolfuss in the following July.

These are matters of history. Forty years later, Spender is still the same detached observer of the passing show. Louis MacNeice died early; C. Day Lewis became laureate; Wystan Auden became orthodox and could preach from a cathedral pulpit; Spender looked on. He recently surveyed a new revolutionary movement with the same sympathetic, sceptical gaze that he cast upon that of his own youth. True, neither for the liberals of his own day nor for

---

9. C. Day Lewis, *The Buried Day* (London: Chatto and Windus, 1960), p. 187.

the young free beards and bosoms of yesterday's upheavals was he revolutionary enough to satisfy: ". . . his daring left wingery [in the thirties] was often affected to charm (his own word) the upper crust set. And now he makes a fast buck writing up US—the new radicals dimly seen by him through jaded uncomprehending eyes."[10] With them (perhaps more than they realize), not of them, Spender studies the scene.

The events of the thirties he scrutinized for whatever they might supply to symbolize the elements of his own inward life, which he bore with him as a fragment of the only secure reality. So in his latest poetry he protracts this old conflict between the known, the inward, the authentic, and the shadowy outside world of phenomena, between the buried self and the will.

10. Flier passed round during Spender's inaugural lecture at University College, London: ". . . brought to you by the U. C. Anarchist Horde."

2

# Politics in the Literary Scene

During the nineteen thirties a number of writers from liberal or conservative families, who had been educated in public schools—those institutions for the sons of the more-than-medium wealthy—formed political affiliations with the left, though they did not necessarily all become communists or fellow travelers. In 1935 Wyndham Lewis declared that the present world of journalists and men-of-letters in England was a "leftwing" orthodoxy: "On the face of it you would expect to find two schools of thought, or more, where in practice you find only one."[1] But the proportion of leftist writers in the first part of the decade must not be exaggerated, for there were many who remained politically neutral. A poll of poets made by *New Verse* in October 1934[2] seems remarkable now for

1. "First Aid for the Unorthodox," *London Mercury* 32 (May 1935): 27.
2. "An Enquiry," *New Verse*, no. 11, pp. 2–22.

the paucity of outright declared communists or socialists, even allowing for the significant gaps in the list of those canvassed and of those who replied. The questionnaire, which touched on various matters, literary and other, asked as Question 5, "Do you take your stand with any political or economic party or creed?" Of the forty British and American poets solicited, twenty-two replied. From twelve, Question 5 elicited No or a virtual negative as answer; three recorded leftist leanings; two in addition declared themselves for communism.[3] This record certainly doesn't give an impression of the intellectual youth of an age, on either side of the Atlantic, committed to a man and up in arms.

Within two years the Spanish Civil War broke out and like a play within the play brought consciences into the open and pressed men into alignment according to their colors. "On that tableland scored by rivers, / Our fever's menacing shapes are precise and alive," wrote W. H. Auden, who, though monumentally detached in most matters, himself went to Spain and seems to have sought action. The Spanish War did appear, Claud Cockburn says, "in outlines of singular purity—it was a Western, and there came the Baddies down from the hills. The Goods rallied."[4] "The issues are very simple," a young poet told Julian Symons at a party. "This is a

3. Noes came from Laura Riding, Robert Graves, Louis MacNeice, A. J. M. Smith, Herbert Read, Conrad Aiken, Wallace Stevens, William Carlos Williams, Marianne Moore, George Barker, Archibald MacLeish, and Robinson Jeffers. Roy Campbell replied, "The Nacion Gardian of South Africa, South America, Provence and Andalusia . . .". Edwin Muir came out for Social Credit as advocated by Major Douglas; Allen Tate for Southern Agrarianism; Wyndham Lewis said he stood midway between the Bolshevist and Fascist: "the gentleman on my left I shake with my left hand, the gentleman on my right with my right hand." Dylan Thomas declared himself to stand "with any revolutionary body that asserts it to be the right of all men to share, equally and impartially, every production of man"; David Gascoyne replied that his political feelings were insufficiently developed to answer the question but that he had the strongest possible sympathy for left-wing revolutionary movements; Norman Cameron said that Communism was necessary and good but that he was not eager for it; E. E. Cummings quoted a passage about electrons and light years from his book, *Eimi*. Gavin Ewart and Hugh MacDiarmid came out unequivocally for communism. Among those who did not reply specifically were T. S. Eliot, John Masefield, Walter de la Mare, A. E. Housman, Edmund Blunden, Stephen Spender, Charles Madge, C. Day Lewis, and W. H. Auden.

4. "A Conversation with Claud Cockburn," *the Review*, no. 11–12, p. 52.

struggle between the forces of good in the world and the forces of evil."[5] Whether it was just as clear as that or not, the overwhelming support for the Republic demonstrated in a poll in the second half of 1937 was not provided only by active socialists and communists.[6]

Spender, for his part, had publicized his commitment to the left earlier than this in the volume *Poems,* which appeared in 1933. Then later, at the persuasion of Harry Pollitt, the secretary of the Communist Party in Great Britain, he joined the Party and went to Spain. All this he recounts in his autobiography, *World Within World.*[7] One detail not to be found there but reported elsewhere is Pollitt's suggestion that the best way Spender could help would be: "to go and get killed, comrade, we need a Byron in the movement."[8] The personal histories of other politically active poets have also been recorded.[9]

One outcome of the widespread political commitment of writers was the discussion about the engagement of literature. Amid the rolling political enthusiasm of his fellows, E. M. Forster could

5. Julian Symons, *The Thirties: A Dream Revolved* (London: Cresset Press, 1960), p. 118.

6. Louis Aragon and Others, *Authors Take Sides on the Spanish War* (*Left Review,* n. d.). Only five writers of the 148 whose replies were published (some pro-government answers were omitted to save space) supported Franco: Edmund Blunden, Arthur Machen, Geoffrey Moss, Eleanor Smith, and Evelyn Waugh. Sixteen were neutral; they included Norman Douglas, T. S. Eliot, Ezra Pound, Alec Waugh, and H. G. Wells. The rest were for the government. The poll was taken by Nancy Cunard and brought out by Randall Swingler, then editor of the *Left Review* (Hugh D. Ford, *A Poet's War: British Poets in the Spanish Civil War* [Philadelphia: Univ. of Pennsylvania Press, 1965], p. 279).

7. (London: Hamish Hamilton, 1951), pp. 210–47.

8. Hugh Thomas, *The Spanish Civil War,* rev. ed. (Harmondsworth, Middlesex: Penguin Books, 1965), p. 436.

9. By Hugh D. Ford, *A Poet's War;* Katherine Bail Hoskins, *Today the Struggle: Literature and Politics in England During the Spanish Civil War* (Austin, Texas: University of Texas Press, 1969); D. E. S. Maxwell, *Poets of the Thirties* (London: Routledge and Kegan Paul, 1969); John M. Muste, *Say that We Saw Spain Die: Literary Consequences of the Spanish Civil War* (Seattle: University of Washington Press, 1966); Peter Stansky and William Abrahams, *Journey to the Frontier. Julian Bell and John Cornford: Their Lives and the 1930s* (London: Constable, 1966); Stanley Weintraub, *The Last Great Cause: The Intellectuals and the Spanish Civil War* (London: Allen, 1968); and Neal Wood, *Communism and British Intellectuals* (New York: Columbia University Press, 1959).

remark quite blandly that, admiring the social ferment, he was content to withdraw into literature "because it is disinterested."[10] But if it was, it wasn't to be so for long—not all of it. Julian Benda, recently the champion of disinterestedness, was at some pains to declare that the recent increase in participation of intellectuals in social and political movements, so far from being an instance of *trahison*, was a return to the writer's historic role. Earlier, in the *Trahison des Clercs*, Benda had accused the *clercs* of having preached material ends rather than transcendental truths. And this was the the great betrayal, for they should have held themselves aloof from political controversy. This condemnation, however, had in turn been condemned in 1933 by R. D. Charques, who said that to encourage the *clercs* to propagate transcendental truth implied a submission to the prevailing social and economic order. Similarly, "pure literature" was "apt to represent a ruling-class attitude to culture,"[11] a sentiment that sounds curiously topical today.

The majority of poets and intellectuals who spoke to the subject at all called for the engagement of literature. George Orwell, although he concluded that "the literary history of the thirties seems to justify the opinion that a writer does well to keep out of politics,"[12] felt also that for writers in that decade whose whole scheme of values was menaced, detachment was impossible. "You cannot take a purely aesthetic interest in a disease you are dying from. . . . [A]ny thinking person had to take sides, and his feelings had to find their way not only into his writing but into his judgments on literature. Literature had to become political, because anything else would have entailed mental dishonesty. . . . What books were *about* seemed so urgently important that the way they were written seemed almost insignificant.[13]

10. Quoted in Stephen Spender, *Forward From Liberalism* (London: Gollancz, 1937), pp. 173–74.
11. R. D. Charques, *Contemporary Literature and the Social Revolution* (London: Martin Secker, n. d.), pp. 48–49 and 54.
12. "Inside the Whale," in *Inside the Whale and Other Essays* (Harmondsworth, Middlesex: Penguin Books, 1962), p. 39.
13. "The Frontiers of Art and Propaganda," *The Collected Essays, Journalism and Letters of George Orwell; Vol II: My Country Right or Left, 1940–1943*, ed. Sonia Orwell and Ian Angus (New York: Harcourt, Brace and World, 1968), p. 126.

It was thought by some that commitment to the political left would pay a dividend: Ernest Hemingway's talent, which had fallen off with *The Green Hills of Africa*, enjoyed a renaissance with *Spanish Earth*: "It is the Spanish people and the fighters of the International Brigade who have given back Hemingway to himself, to literature, and to civilisation."[14] And Michael Roberts, in a new version of Wordsworth's old fallacy, says the novelist must turn to the working class for subject matter where he will find "the clearest symbols of those passions and activities he values, for they will be less confused and muddled by the intricacies of a crumbling system."[15]

Orwell was not the only writer who exhorted his readers to take sides. They were warned by others that he who was not for the proletarian cause was against it—an attitude itself savoring of fascism.[16] In more than one polemical essay or review readers were reminded as a warning that whereas the communist minister of education had appointed Picasso director of the art museum of the Prado, the Spanish fascists had murdered Lorca. Such gentle detachment as Forster had posited is admired hardly anywhere. More typical of its day is the either-or sentiment as it appears in a verse of Rex Warner's: "Come with us, if you can, and, if not, go to hell. . . ." During the war John Lehmann was instructed, albeit by a Russian, that his "idle chatter about the 'sacred freedom of the artist' and about the right to stand apart from the fray seems the blasphemous twaddle of a self-satisfied literary philistine, passing off vice for virtue."[17] In the last number of the *Left Review* the editor could

14. Edgell Rickword, "When Writers Unite," *Left Review,* 3(March 1938): 881.
15. Preface to *New Country: Prose and Poetry by the Authors of "New Signatures,"* ed. Michael Roberts (London: Leonard and Virginia Woolf, 1933).
16. "For the Fascists there can be only two things, Fascism and anti-Fascism. If we, in taking up their challenge, are hypnotized by them into thinking that nothing matters but this dualism, then the only significant thing of our time is this struggle—Fascism pitted against its apparent opposite—then they have won the first bout; they have made us intellectually totalitarian, robbing us to that extent of our many-sidedness, our variety of opinions, the very elasticity and freedom of mind which we set out to defend" (R. A. Scott James, "Editorial Notes," *London Mercury* 35 [February 1937]: p. 355).
17. John Lehmann, *I Am My Brother* (London: Longmans, Green, 1960), p. 249.

claim that "all artistic activity has been intimately concerned with social development and the striving for freedom, peace, and sane conditions of living."[18]

Affiliation with the great political cause was also claimed by the surrealists. At the beginning of his survey[19] David Gascoyne announced that the surrealist attitude was totally in accord with the Communist philosophy of dialectical materialism. Roger Roughton, the editor of *Contemporary Poetry and Prose*, discovered fanciful grounds for classing surrealism as revolutionary, claiming that it broke down "irrational bourgeois-taught prejudices, thus preparing the mental ground for positive revolutionary thought and action."[20] Ezra Pound, in his usual magisterial tones, soon put him right about that: "When it comes to 'breaking down irrational' (or rational for that matter) 'bourgeois prejudices' . . . the simple practice of using WORDS with clear and unequivocal meaning will blast all the London Schools of economics; history or other bourgeois dribble; without any -isms being needed as hyperdermic"[21] [sic]. As he points out, surrealism was an effort to break down or at least by-pass not only the irrational but the rational; and the suggestion that traditional poetic form is "bourgeois-taught" is mere rant.[22] As a correspondent to *New Verse* pointed out, the material in the unconscious, being originally derived from the conscious, must also be bourgeois.[23] Clearly one could be a surrealist and one could also be a communist, and while some poets combined the two

18. *Left Review*, 3 (May 1938): 958.

19. David Gascoyne, *A Short Survey of Surrealism* ([London]: Cobden Sanderson, 1935).

20. *Contemporary Poetry and Prose*, nos. 4 and 5 (August–September, 1936), p. 74.

21. Ezra Pound, "The Coward Surrealists," *Contemporary Poetry and Prose*, no. 7 (November 1936).

22. Roughton's comment beautifully illustrates a dictum of Christopher Caudwell's: "This constant revolution, this constant sweeping-away of 'ancient and venerable prejudices and opinions,' this 'everlasting uncertainty and agitation,' distinguishes bourgeois art from all previous art. Any bourgeois artist who even for a generation rests upon the conventions of his time becomes 'academic' and his art lifeless" (*Illusion and Reality* [London: Lawrence and Wishart, 1966], p. 57). Caudwell's concept of surrealism as demonstrating bourgeois attitudes is quoted below.

23. J. B., "Honest Doubt," *New Verse*, no. 21 (June–July 1936), p. 16.

persuasions there was no necessary connection. Many years later when the frenzy was all over and could be looked back to in tranquillity, Spender shrewdly commented:

> Everything about the surrealists is self-contradictory. At the time, nothing seemed more absurd than their claim to be communists, since surrealism is as much *ex hypothesi* the contradiction of social realism as it is the negation of the unconscious. All the same, it is perhaps as social prophets who are also social symptoms that they will be remembered, and it may well be that the people they most interest today are the social or the politically minded.[24]

When the question arose as to what poetry might do for the revolution and how it might become proletarian, many curious demands were made upon it, often in resounding terms more impressive than lucid. One critic announces that "the time has come to measure the poet by his *usefulness to the people* rather than by aesthetic standards. It must be remembered, however, that to be really effective satirical and revolutionary poetry will naturally be good by any other standard too."[25] This critic echoes the critical code in Russia, where, according to André Gide, the accusation of formalism was leveled against any artist who was capable of attaching less importance to *content* than to *form*.[26] Generally there is little interest either in form or technique in these debates about the political obligations of poetry. It was left to the most strongly committed communist critic of the day, Christopher Caudwell, as quoted below, to point out the social function of form. Many poets and critics however, called for a simplified language; Michael Roberts suggested a curious hybrid—a style which, coming partly from the "'shirtsleeve' workers and partly from the 'intellectual,' will make the revolutionary movement more articulate."[27] Alec Brown recommends a slogan ("with apologies to rare writers like

24. "Notes from a Diary," *Encounter* 7 (October 1956): 60.
25. Colin Drapier, "Wanted! New Poets for Revolution," *Poetry and the People*, no. 19 (July 1940), p. 24.
26. *Back from the USSR*, trans. Dorothy Bussy (London: Secker and Warburg, 1937), p. 77.
27. *New Country*, p. 18.

Bunyan and Defoe and a few others"): "LITERARY ENGLISH FROM CAXTON TO US IS AN ARTIFICIAL JARGON OF THE RULING CLASS: WRITTEN ENGLISH BEGINS WITH US."[28] C. Day Lewis felt, on the other hand, that the proletarian poet "does not need, as bourgeois poets do, to learn a new tongue: he has only to make poetry of what is his native language."[29] But concerning specific poetic techniques, there is very little *explicit* discussion in the thirties.

With the matter of content, there is more concern. C. Day Lewis declared that the proletarian poet would want to bring into poetry some new things: "Indignation at the conditions under which he is compelled to live; the feeling of solidarity with his own class and the conviction that he must be a spokesman of that class; the whole range of material data, altered values, and changed emotional stresses which his environment offers him."[30] Mayakovsky was quoted to the effect that "a poet is not he who goes about with long hair and baas on typical love themes. A poet is he who in an era of sharpened class struggle, gives his pen into the arsenal of the armed proletariat, fears no job, however prosaic, and fears no theme, whether of revolution or the reconstruction of our national economy."

The question as to what workers would *wish* to read is not often raised; it was assumed, probably correctly, that they would want to see themselves and their own material environments reflected in literature. Stephen Spender reported one worker, however, as declaring that the proletariat desired to read of the love affairs of the upper classes. Of course, there being no other tradition of art, those who read like those who created were bound to use the bourgeois tradition; as Spender points out, workers who show a taste for poetry, for example, or the highbrow Russian films have developed it only because they have been educated into the middle-class tradition.[31]

28. *Left Review* 1 (December 1934): 76–77.
29. "Revolutionaries and Poetry," *Revolution in Writing* (London: Leonard and Virginia Woolf, 1935), p. 44.
30. *Ibid.*, p. 43.
31. "Poetry and Revolution," *New Country*, p. 66.

André Breton, citing Lenin, offers a corrective to narrower views about the content of proletarian poetry, both within and without the surrealist movement: in his "Misère de la Poesie," answering his hard-line critics after the Aragon affair, Breton defends the right of the militant communist poet to deal with material other than factory life and hunger marches and quotes Lenin to the effect that workers should attain knowledge of the whole field of thought.[32] C. Day Lewis had also declared that one must not expect a revolutionary poet to write about nothing but the revolution.[33]

Many writers felt and a few feared that the engagement of literature meant propaganda. In some cases it certainly did, although the propaganda comes in varying degrees of crudeness. The contributions of C. Day Lewis to the general debate about poetry are often a little simplistic in the relation of cause and effect, in the analyses of present situations, and in the predictions of future ones. He thought of the writer as a spokesman (an obligation which, as will appear, he knew to be somewhat in conflict with his lyrical impulses), and he spoke. He offers a clever justification for *tendenz*: if poetry arises from feelings, he says, and if the feeling is related to social ills and their remedy, the resulting poem is bound to be propagandist. And that, of course, is theoretically possible. As in all art, however, the nature and the depth of the feelings would determine whether the poetry were a profound human experience or a shabby sentimental one; and of the two we would designate only the latter propaganda. ("Propaganda" usually means "mere propaganda," a poem such as Louis Aragon's "Waltz," for example, which celebrates the mixing of cement by shock workers' brigades for the Tcheliabinsk tractor factory, to which what balanced mind could respond with other than weariness and gloom?) Lewis makes a similar point when he says "propaganda verse is to be condemned

32. David Gascoyne, *A Short Survey of Surrealism*, p. 199. Gascoyne describes how the protests and counterprotests, following the indictment of Louis Aragon for incitement to murder and for provoking insubordination in the army by his poem *The Red Front*, raised the question, "Is a militant communist poet justified in writing any but propaganda poems or poems bearing on the working class struggle? Yes, say the surrealists; and No, say Aragon, Sadoul, Alexandre and a few others" (p. 117).

33. "Revolutionaries and Poetry," p. 37.

when the didactic is achieved at the expense of the poetic: poetry, in fact, whatever else it may or may not be, must be poetry. . . ."[34]

Offering suggestions for a Marxist critical position, Lewis says one must be on one's guard against the sentimentality of accepting anything written from a revolutionary standpoint and rejecting the rest;[35] one must not look for direct propaganda.

Eric Gill, the sculptor, answering an attack on the Artist's International in the *Catholic Herald,* lifts the question of propaganda above the level of hungry caviling that it finds in some of the polemical contributions to the *Left Review.* He also held that art was propaganda but in a more moderate and acceptable sense: every artist he claimed, was a missionary; and all art, including the sculpture in medieval churches, spoke to a cause.[36] We would not call such art propaganda. "The greatest art," Stephen Spender asserts, "is moral even when the artist has no particular axe to grind."[37] Louis MacNeice felt that at the moment the poet would tend to be moralist rather than aesthete:

> But his morality must be honest; he must not merely retail other people's dogma. The world no doubt needs propaganda, but propaganda (unless you use the term, as many do, very, very loosely indeed) is not the poet's job. He is not the loudspeaker of society, but something much more like its still, small voice.[38]

A number of communist poets and critics were inclined to discuss the question of politics and poetry at this kind of level, not without some manifest idealism. Among the shrewder contributions to the general debate, however, there is not much said about content. Indeed, the point is made that what is looked for in a poem is not the description of this or that particular feature of the brave new world but the engagement of the poet. Thus among the earliest writers on the subject, in 1933 R. D. Charques declares that the poet needn't

34. *A Hope for Poetry* (Oxford: Basil Blackwell, 1934), p. 49.
35. Later Geoffrey Grigson accuses Lewis of doing just this in praising *Poems of Strife* by Julius Lipton (*New Verse,* no. 21 [June–July 1936], p. 18).
36. "Eric Gill on Art and Propaganda," *Left Review* 1 (June 1935): 341–42.
37. *The Destructive Element* (London: Cape, 1935), p. 19.
38. Louis MacNeice "A Statement," *New Verse,* 31–32 (Autumn 1938), p. 7.

sing the praises of currency reform: he should show a sense of economic reality and a desire for change. "It is not so much a matter of depicting the life of the common people," he says, "as of depicting life from the point of view of the common people, not so much a matter of choice of theme as of recognition of the class struggle."[39] He doesn't say exactly how the latter should be made manifest. Later Randall Swingler says, "It is not a question of subject and it is not a question of technique. . . . It is a question of a method of living, of the quality of experience, of the immediate social position of the poet." What he wants, he says, is "Poetry to bind many together in a deeper sense of community, to move them to action and to direct that action, to make it at one time vehement and wise."[40] We would all approve of this very strongly, and it would be some poetry indeed. The poet, as generally conceived of by the avantgarde leftists, was not to sing the praises of proletarian achievement nor necessarily mouth parts of the revolutionary doctrine; he was to "assimilate" the doctrine himself and become a proletarian poet from the inside out, so to say. The word *assimilate*, used for just this purpose, does overtime during the decade.

It is astounding now, now that the fierce enthusiasms have cooled, to observe, with hindsight admittedly, the broad and bland acceptance of communism and its Russian manifestations by the intellectuals of the decade. What awkward details they were prepared to ignore or explain away, what camels they were ready to swallow in their generous and passionate admiration for the cause, when to be on the side of history was a general alignment that was allowed to excuse much particular evil. When, for example, André Gide marshaled a number of impressions of Russia, good and bad, found divergences from initial ideals, and refused to close his eyes to the fact of dictatorship of a man and not of united workers, his instructed misgivings in *Retour de l'URSS* were dismissed as purely emotional—"the babblings of the most ill-informed tourist."[41] There was the Kharkov Manifesto with clauses unequivocally inimical to the freedom of writers; but this was attributed to the

39. Charques, pp. 163 and 191.
40. "History and the Poet," *New Writing*, n.s. 3 (Christmas 1939): 52 and 53–4.
41. Pat Sloan, "The Two André Gides," *Left Review* 3(May 1937): 244.

individual incompetence of a minor civil servant in Russia, and it was thus excused.[42] Later, there was the repudiation of George Orwell's discoveries about the purging of the P.O.U.M. in Spain. There was above all the repeated viciousness of Stalin, excused in the magic words, "transitional phase,"[43] his faults described by Palme Dutt as "mere spots on the sun."

In England, the image of Soviet Russia was blown up to glorious proportions by the passionate intensity of the faithful. Majestic details about life there were made available: cartoons of Russian workers with massive jaws and farseeing eyes and female peasants with big arms, epic accounts of the five-year plans, news of dams, generators, Stakhanovites, tractor factories, endless statistics, and broad exultation in the proliferation of concrete. The size of the reading public was claimed to be prodigious; everybody was clean and happy. There was blatant and undisguised canvassing for such a way of life in England in essays, poetry, and fiction. And all along there was the humorless ingestion of all that silly party guff embodied in all that silly party jargon, that "abstract, inflexible and hideous language."[44]

How many of those who committed themselves to the cause, one wonders, had more than a glimmering of what the product of a proletarian revolution in England would involve? What had they come forth to see? In a poem called "Delusions," III, Charles Madge envisions the pillaging of a wealthy house by the mob and the arresting of this process by the "little Lenin" of the mob who addresses it as follows:

> No doubt in time you too such silks shall wear
> When luxury shall crown the common toil
> And jewels glitter in the shop girl's hair
> And gold and silver round her wrists shall coil.[45]

42. T. H. Wintringham, "Artists in Uniform," *Left Review* 1 (February 1935): 159.

43. "Now," declares an *Encounter* editorial at the time of the death of Stalin many years later, "Now, perhaps, we shall no longer be plagued by the rhetoric of a messianic arrogance of the spirit which has blithely perpetrated so many hideous crimes against the flesh" (1 [October 1953]: 1).

44. C. Day Lewis, *The Buried Day* (London: Chatto and Windus, 1960), p. 215.

45. *The Disappearing Castle* (London: Faber and Faber, 1937), pp. 54–55.

It seems unlikely that such a primitive sense of economics was shared by any but the uneducated. But one cannot be sure. Rex Warner voices the idea that the revolution will bring some extraordinary social therapy into everybody's love life ("tart" is the English for "chippie"):

> We shall listen to our own voices and shall mind our business,
> some leaders to command, others happy to lend a hand,
> all able to enjoy women and the company of men,
> not needing tarts and beer as we needed them before
> when without work we became hard and our beds were hired.[46]

Michael Roberts's notion of communism was that it would involve something like good clean fun in the fresh air with the sons of the upper middle class or the gentry—young men who had team spirit. He anticipated an "extension of personality and consciousness" such as he had once experienced working for a common purpose in adverse weather conditions in the Jura with some schoolboys and some university students. He remembered not the hardships, he says, but only counting the people at the end of the day, "nine, ten, eleven, black dots against the snow, and knowing that again the party was complete, uninjured, tired and content."[47] His commitment to communism seems to lack an empirical basis. It may be remarked that among his colleagues he had had the singular honor of being expelled from the communist party for deviationism.[48] How many such romantic memories as Roberts's, one wonders, were labeled dialectical materialism?

And what of the nastiness of the revolution itself, the blood letting, the "necessary murder"? In the essay in which he describes his cooperative work with the young people, Roberts speaks also of the horrors of war. But in the same paragraph he proceeds to remark, "It is time that those who would conserve something which

46. "Chorus" IV, *Poems* (London: Boriswood, 1937), pp. 60–61.

47. "Preface," *New Country,* p. 21.

48. Janet Roberts, "Introductory Memoir," *The Collected Poems of Michael Roberts* (London: Faber and Faber, 1958).

is still valuable in England began to see that only a revolution can save their standards."[49]

Julian Bell showed some horse-sense in this matter. Writing in the spirited style of a Bernard Shaw preface, he criticized C. Day Lewis for the "stupidity" in the use of the "blessed word Revolution."

> "After the Revolution" we shall all live happily. "After the Revolution" we shall get our own back on the bourgeoisie, liquidate them and so on. "After the Revolution" we shall all have jobs and the arts and sciences will flourish. And "the Revolution" will consist of "the workers taking the factories to run them themselves" and so on.

Revolution, Bell pointed out, meant civil war. "It seems to me rather doubtful policy to deceive your followers with a rosy Utopia when you are getting them involved in such a murderous business."[50]

Various reasons were adduced at the time and have been adduced since to account for the turn to the left on the part of the intellectuals of England. There was, primarily, the ubiquitous prospect of economic distress, which could only too easily be blamed on the failures or, the more wholesale charge, the *failure* of capitalism and, by extension, on the emptiness of the values of the middle class and its general corruption. No honest young man, whatever hand had fed him, could ignore the widespread unemployment, the abusive treatment of the employed, the shocking disparity between the conditions of life of the rich and the poor, the deprivation—indeed, the sheer hunger, and the impotence of mass indignation at these; no man of sensibility could himself be immune from the contagion of such suffering. It is interesting how often in this decade poets and essayists quoted the lines from Keats's *Hyperion* which declared that no man could usurp the heights of art except "those to whom the miseries of this world/Are misery, and will not let them rest."

There were causes for the leftward swing other than the cool

---

49. *New Country*, p. 11.

50. "The Proletariat and Poetry: An Open Letter to C. Day Lewis," *Julian Bell: Essays, Poems and Letters*, ed. Quentin Bell (London: Hogarth Press, 1958), p. 312.

political assessment, however. Wyndham Lewis, in his *London Mercury* article cited above, says, in an unfortunate piece of syntax,

> And how it comes about that the luxuries of liberalist thought can still be so blandly indulged in by the great body of educated or relatively fortunately-placed Englishmen, is because England has suffered less than other countries—is isolated still—and so "broadmindedness" of the most fantastic order is rendered possible. That is how it is that we meet with the *salon* communism that looks so hypocritical to the outsider, but is really only the self-indulgence of those who feel unassailably secure.[51]

The relationship between security and such indulgence is like the relationship proposed some years later by E. M. W. Tillyard, when he attributed the misinterpretation of Shakespeare that made Falstaff a sympathetic figure to the strength of the Royal Navy. George Orwell was also to ask the question, "Why should *writers* be attracted by a form of socialism that makes mental honesty impossible?" And his answer lies, briefly, in the fact that communism was "something to believe in . . . a church, an army, an orthodoxy, a discipline. . . . All the loyalties and superstitions that the intellect had seemingly banished could come rushing back under the thinnest of disguises. . . . The 'Communism' of the English intellectual is something explicable enough. It is the patriotism of the deracinated."[52] Both C. Day Lewis and Claud Cockburn attributed their communism to religious sources. Lewis says,

> Inoculated against Roman Catholicism by the religion of my youth I dimly felt the need for a faith which had the authority, the logic, the cut-and-driedness of the Roman church—a faith which would fill the void left by the leaking away of traditional religion, would make sense out of our troubled times and make real demands on me. Marxism appeared to fill the bill. It appealed too, I imagine, to that part of me which from time to time revolted against the intolerable burden of selfhood and desired the anonymity of a unit in a crowd.[53]

51. "First Aid for the Unorthodox," p. 31.
52. "Inside the Whale," *Inside the Whale and Other Essays,* pp. 35–36.
53. *The Buried Day* (London: Chatto and Windus, 1960), p. 209.

Cockburn says,

> The Greek dramatists and both the Testaments smoulder with passages which, at any rate to a young man, are incitements to revolt against orthodox society, to throw in his lot with the "have nots" against the "haves." And if you ask me what first . . . "conditioned" me to be susceptible to the appeal of Communism, I should have to say that it was, for example, the Magnificat I listened to every Sunday at evensong in the village church, and Antigone's defiance of Creon in Sophocles' play.[54]

No wonder the Bible is outlawed in American schools!

As in any political affiliation, there was in this one a fair admixture of irrational causes, which were no less effective for their irrationality. Virginia Woolf attributed the young intellectuals' rejection of middle-class values to guilt, and designated the more prominent rebel writers the "Leaning Tower" group, the tower symbolizing the education and security that capitalist society had brought them. They had profited, and they now expressed their guilt by abusing parts of the profitable society—the retired admiral, the spinster, the armament manufacturer.[55] There was no doubt also a degree of simple hostility toward the "old men" of the 1914–18 war. George Orwell, who was six years Spender's senior, says, "We all thought of ourselves as enlightened creatures of a new age, casting off the orthodoxy that had been forced upon us by those detested 'old men.'" And when the English master asked a class of sixteen boys to list the ten greatest men then living, fifteen of them included Lenin. "This was at a snobbish expensive public school, and the date was 1920, when the horrors of the Russian Revolution were still fresh in everyone's mind."[56]

As Christopher Caudwell realized, the anticipation of a proletarian revolution provided a useful opportunity for men and women to objectify their subjective troubles and conflicts. When Bertrand

54. *I, Claud: The Autobiography of Claud Cockburn* (Harmondsworth, Middlesex: Penguin Books, 1967), p. 212.

55. "The Leaning Tower," *Folios of New Writing* 2 (Autumn 1940).

56. *The Road to Wigan Pier,* (Harmondsworth, Middlesex: Penguin Books, 1967), pp. 121–22.

Russell, an aristocrat nourishing leftist ideals, met John Strachey, a communist out of Eton and Magdalen College, Oxford, he asked bluntly, "What's the matter with you? I had a neglected childhood." And it became Strachey's habit to attribute his political apostasy to "chagrin at not getting into the Eton cricket eleven." Claud Cockburn relates a sensational instance of a nonrational turn to the left on the part of a young woman who played a considerable role in the revolutionary youth movement of Vienna between 1917 and 1919, having initially begun to study communism as a means of "general liberation," feeling that no personal escape could soothe her agony of mind after her husband had shot her lover.[57]

Accordingly we may ask in the case of Stephen Spender, as he himself and others did, what personal factor, failure or other, dipped him in disaffection with his proper social background, its way of life, its values, and its political acceptances? At one point he asks himself, for example, whether he had turned to revolution in order to be among the elect of history or whether his politics are accountable to sexual maladjustment. In his political position there was, no doubt, an element of generational conflict, for one thing. In his autobiography, he describes his father as dominating him (and, indeed, his view of life) with a strong rhetoric that transmogrified the whole world about him into abstraction: "A game of football ceased to be just the kicking about of a leather ball by bare-kneed boys. It has become confused with the Battle of Life. Honour, Integrity, Discipline, Toughness, and a dozen other qualities haunted the field like ghostly footballers."[58] Spender suspected the presence of generational conflict in John Stuart Mill and others, and, in turn, we may suspect some subjectivity in his comment about Mill: ". . . the son exorcized the father's intellectual will with intellectual agony. I emphasize this, because such suffering is typical not only of Mill but of Clough and Matthew Arnold and perhaps many more of their contemporaries (How many of the idealistic radicals of the nineteenth century suffered in youth from the dominating will of

57. Claud Cockburn, *In Time of Trouble: An Autobiography* (London: Rupert Hart Davis, 1956), pp. 117–18.
58. *World Within World*, pp. 7–8.

the Victorian father!)"[59] Spender then quotes from Matthew
Arnold some lines that we shall have occasion to recall later in a
different connection:

> I too have felt the load I bore
> In a too strong emotion's sway;
> I too have wished, no woman more,
> This starting, feverish heart away
>
> I too have long'd for trenchant force,
> And will like a dividing spear;
> Have praised the keen, unscrupulous course,
> Which knows no doubt, which feels no fear.

In his own poetry there are strong hints that the father had crushed
the son's ability to act: In *Vienna,* the poet seems to lay upon the
father the blame for his own sexual failure:

> It surely was my father
> His dry love his dry falling
> Through dust and death to stamp my feature
> That made me ever fear that fortunate posture.[60]

Later, in "The Human Situation," he lists certain men of will,
including the "Law-giving, white bearded father," and adds, "It
is impossible for me to enter/The unattainable ease/Of him who is
always right and my opponent. . . ."[61] In "The Ambitious Son,"
the poet reveals what burden had been laid upon him by his father:

> Deep in my heart I learned this lesson
> As well have never been born at all
> As live through life and fail to impress on
> Time, our family name, inch-tall.

We are made to feel that part of his nature approves this ambition.
But there is another part that loves the contrary—". . . the glance

59. *Forward from Liberalism,* pp. 96–97.
60. *Vienna* (New York: Random House, 1935), p. 34.
61. *The Still Centre* (London: Faber and Faber, 1939), p. 81.

of failure tilted up/With swimming eyes and waiting lips, to swallow/ The sunset from the sky as from a cup."[62]

Whatever his personal subjective grounds may have been in his repudiation of his bourgeois upbringing and his acceptance of the communist vogue, he was probably hoodwinked less than many of his fellow intellectuals and certainly less willingly, on account of his disinclination to accept without enquiry what they were accepting on faith. Looking back later he describes how it was possible to be duped: there was always the uncertainty that shrouded facts about the USSR and cushioned their impact, and there was always the counter-charge, "What about you? You are just as bad."[63] Or again, by way of answer to Orwell, he says the reason that young writers could accept a philosophy "which so obviously dealt in lies" may have been that "the lies they suspected in their own hearts"— their sense of guilt, that is, at their own privilege—"were nearer to them than the lies told by the communists. The debate was puerile," but "the young writers argued with their eyes stared into by the eyes of the unemployed."[64] As C. Day Lewis pointed out, it was a generous response; none of them of the upper middle class had anything material to gain from communism.

It may also be remarked in connection with Spender, that, as will appear in discussions of his poetry, it is a fact about his personality that he never responded simply to the impact of simple blunt fact; he was always looking for something behind or beyond facts, or he was looking only for the particular facts that would reflect the light from his own mind. All the same, his commitment to communism seems to have required him to put embarrassing questions to it rather than to have precluded him from doing so. "No system is

62. *Ruins and Visions: Poems 1934–1942* (New York: Random House, 1942), pp. 109 and 111.

63. "Notes from a Diary," *Encounter* 7 (September 1956): 52–53. Auden remarked many years later that his contemporaries felt the Russians "weren't white folks" and should not therefore be too harshly judged (quoted by Francis Hope, "Then and Now," *the Review,* nos. 11–12, p. 7).

64. *The Creative Element* (London: Hamish Hamilton, 1953), p. 144. Cleanth Brooks ("Poetry and Political Faith," *Poetry* 50 [August 1937]: 280) saw Spender's commitment to communism as sentimental, observing that Spender failed to recognize it as a kind of religious faith.

complete in itself as a solution of the bad system which it supersedes," he wrote. "If there is to be any sort of freedom or improvement, one has got to push and even sometimes fight the systems one most approves of."[65] A correspondent to *New Verse* says a little bitterly, "It is a notable fact . . . that whenever Mr. Spender finds himself in agreement with someone, it is—albeit reluctantly—with some near-Fascist spokesman; and whenever he finds himself obliged to criticize and condemn, it is—albeit regretfully—invariably some Left-Wing work or writer."[66] In *The Creative Element* Spender remarked that the poetic development of Auden, Day Lewis, MacNeice and himself "was largely a matter of struggling with the views of the side they were supporting."[67]

Spender has recently pointed out that the Auden group were not political poets. They admired, for example, Eliot and Yeats, who tended toward the political right. And there was a greater gap between the Auden group and the younger left-wing writers than between the former and Eliot and Yeats.[68] What Spender says now harmonizes with his pronouncements in the thirties. Then he responded to the call for engagement with the reply that the poet "is not dealing with absolute truth or a dialectic, he is dealing with reality and establishing a significance of his emotional reactions to reality."[69] Furthermore, he insisted that the poem was complete in itself: "if its content spills over into our world of confused emotions, then it is a bad poem. . . . This is what people mean when they say that it is impossible to write propagandist poetry. A work of art cannot reach out into everyday life and tell us whom to vote for and what kind of factories to build, because injunctions how to act in a world that has nothing to do with the poem destroy the poem's unity."[70]

65. *The Destructive Element*, p. 235. Compare André Gide: "My mind is so constructed that its severest criticisms are addressed to those whom I should like always to be able to approve" (*Back from the USSR*, p. 14).

66. Yvonne Cloud, *New Verse* 1, n.s. (January 1939): 29–30.

67. *Creative Element*, p. 153.

68. "Writers and Revolutionaries: The Spanish War," *New York Review of Books*, September 25, 1969, p. 3.

69. "Poetry," *Fact*, no. 4 (July 1937), p. 25.

70. "Poetry and Revolution," *New Country*, p. 62.

The work of Spender and that of a number of his contemporaries, including Auden, Madge, and Day Lewis, drew from the young John Cornford the accusation that they were attempting to make a "literary fashion of 'revolution' among bourgeois intellectuals whilst denying the possibility of the growth of a genuinely revolutionary literature with a new class basis."[71] Cornford criticizes Spender's poetry: he quotes two stanzas (surely the worst two) of Auden's "A Communist to Others," a poem Auden later considered to be rubbish,[72] and compares it favorably, as being "a far more virile and directly revolutionary form," with the central stanza of Spender's "The Funeral." Auden's lines exhibit virility in the curses invoked upon the capitalist bosses: it is the old Adam in the young Auden, ebullient, unregenerate; one of the stanzas is as follows:

> Let fever sweat them till they tremble
> Cramp rack their limbs till they resemble
> Cartoons by Goya:
> Their daughters sterile be in rut,
> May cancer rot their herring gut,
> The circular madness on them shut,
> Or paranoia.[73]

Spender, on the other hand, envisaging the post-revolutionary Utopia, lacks such violence:

71. "Left?" *Cambridge Left* 1 (Winter 1933–34): 25.
72. Monroe Spears, *The Poetry of W. H. Auden: The Disenchanted Island* (New York: Oxford University Press, 1963), p. 154. Robin Skelton reports that this poem and four others Auden considered to be "trash which he is ashamed to have written," *Poetry of the Thirties* (Harmondsworth, Middlesex: Penguin Books, 1964), p. 40. The poems of his that a poet recalls with torment and shame, said Auden, are "those which he knows to be clever forgeries, expressing feelings or attitudes which were not really his, but which vanity, a wish to please an audience, or the wrong kind of conscience, deluded him into fancying were genuine" (*Louis MacNeice: A Memorial Address* [London: Faber and Faber, 1963], p. 11). The feelings in this poem, however, he may never have fancied as wholly genuine. Justin Replogle says of it that "the Poet . . . collapses before half a dozen lines have passed, overpowered by an Antipoet who finds this pretended brotherhood preposterous. . . ." (*Auden's Poetry* [Seattle: University of Washington Press, 1969], p. 119).
73. *Look, Stranger!* (London: Faber and Faber, 1936), p. 37.

They walk home remembering the straining red flags,
And with pennons of song still fluttering through their blood
They speak of the world state
With its towns like brain-centres and its pulsing arteries.[74]

Cornford approvingly quotes Charles Madge's observation: "They get relief from speaking of the horrors they have seen and from pictures fulfilling their wish for a better world." Cornford is probably responding to Michael Roberts's favorable (if inexplicable) comment about this poem when it appeared in *New Signatures:* "Poetry is here turned to propaganda, but it is propaganda for a theory of life which may release the poet's energies for the writing of pure poetry. . . ."[75] Cornford then quotes Spender's superb lines.

> . . . architectural gold-leaved flower
> From people ordered like a single mind,
> I build.

But he prefers these lines of Louis Aragon:

> I am a witness drunkenly to the stamping out of the bourgeoisie
> Was there ever a finer chase than the chase we give
> to that vermin which flattens itself in every nook of the cities
> I sing the violent domination of the bourgeoisie by the proletariat
> for the annihilation of that bourgeoisie
> for the total annihilation of that bourgeoisie.

Part of the charm of this is perhaps lost in translation. Cornford says that "the future is with the revolutionary participator and not the 'impartial' observer, nor the romantic-utopian idealist."[76]

In making these comparisons and duly preferring the inferior in each case, Cornford is not actually assessing the poetry as such. He apparently thinks of poetry as action (though action is absent from his own best verses). It is probably the contemplative vein in Spender's poems that brought Cornford to prefer Auden and

---

74. "The Funeral," *Poems* (London: Faber and Faber, 1933), p. 41.
75. Preface, *New Signatures: Poems by Several Hands* (London: Leonard and Virginia Woolf, 1932), p. 14.
76. "Left?" *Cambridge Left,* p. 29.

Aragon. Spender himself talks in a half-hearted way about action as seeming "to be a kind of poetry to those who take part in it."[77] If the converse is true, he may be thinking of Cornford's kind of poem, generously granting it a place in the pantheon, although it is signally different from his own. His own kind is thoroughly meditated; and he doesn't fit at all Virginia Woolf's characterization of the Leaning Tower poets as having no tranquillity in which they could recollect. "The inner mind was paralysed, because the surface mind was always hard at work."[78] Another communist critic, Edgell Rickword, takes exception to the idea of poetry as contemplation as he finds it in C. Day Lewis's *Noah and the Waters*:

> The theory of contemplation as the essence of poetic vision is the reflection of the squeezing out of the poet from social-political life which has been going on now for a century. But it has no universal historical validity and the creations of the major poets refute it. Of course, Day Lewis knows as well as anybody that the poet cannot stand outside the dialectical process, but his poetry is still infected with the feeling that struggle is transitory, and that "afterwards" we shall get down to work.[79]

Any number of his contemporaries were aware that Stephen Spender was unhappy or heretical or both in his communism, and they were eager to correct the homework of this backward son. Kenneth Allott, reviewing *Trial of a Judge,* finds it to be a morality play in which a verbal victory is awarded the communists over the fascists; but the good arguments and the feeling are inappropriately assigned, and the only moral he could find was "that Stephen

77. "Introduction," *Poems for Spain,* ed. Stephen Spender and John Lehmann (London: Hogarth Press, 1939), p. 8. The lust for action among men of words that took Cornford and others to the front is remarked upon by Claud Cockburn; it affected even Auden on his visit to Spain. Auden was supposed to "be whisked to the front and returned to write some pieces saying hurrah for the Republic. . . . But not at all: the bloody man went off and got a donkey, a mule really, and announced that he was going to walk through Spain with this creature" ("A Conversation with Claud Cockburn," *the Review* nos. 11-12, p. 51).
78. "The Leaning Tower," *Folios of New Writing* (Autumn 1940), p. 28.
79. Edgell Rickword, "Who is This Noah?", *Left Review* 2 (April 1936): 339–40.

Spender ought not to be a Communist."[80] T. H. Wintringham found in *Vienna* a "remoteness" and a "coldness of image," which weakened both the texture of the verse and the whole structure of the poem and was due to Spender's inability "to associate himself with the living stuff of the revolution." The roots of the inability lay, Wintringham thought, in "a difficulty as to the relation between art and propaganda: the revolution seems to threaten a loss of liberty."[81] Again, the reviews of *Forward from Liberalism* dwell on the author's discomfort, which in the middle section of questions and answers is frankly revealed. The *New Verse* reviewer is embarrassed at the "naked appearance of this author arguing with his past";[82] in the *Left Review,* Randall Swingler complains that the book reveals its author valuing freedom "as an emotion." "Spender," he says, "has not come near to understanding that most concise of Marxist aphorisms, 'Freedom is knowledge of necessity.'"[83]

This comes close to the fundamental flaw in Spender's communism: the rich young liberal was prepared to sell much of his heritage, but not his belief in individual freedom. This, the last bourgeois illusion, so-called, he planned to hang onto; and the belief underlies many of his various pronouncements about poetry and poet. Again and again, for example, Spender supports the right of the poet to take his stance where he is and to write whatever he wants; he is concerned about the opposite process—when poets "deliberately cut themselves off from the roots of their own sensibility which derive from a life they have come to despise." Of this kind of self exile, Spender finds that Randall Swingler happens to be an instance: he was educated at Winchester and New College, Oxford; he was "sensitive, perhaps deeply impressed at a decisive

---

80. "Play for Puritans," *New Verse,* no. 30 (Summer 1938), p. 20. Richard Hoggart, on the other hand, finds *Trial of a Judge* the only place where Spender the political poet was successful (*Auden: An Introductory Essay* [London: Chatto and Windus, 1951], p. 116).

81. "Artists in Uniform," *Left Review* 1 (February 1935): 158n.

82. Unsigned, "Books Lately Published," *New Verse,* no. 24 (Feb.–March, 1937), p. 22.

83. "Spender's Approach to Communism," *Left Review* 3 (March 1937): 111–12.

stage in his development by some such aesthetic experience as reading the *Testament of Beauty*. . . ." But now he writes "poems which in delicate tracework show all these influences, except for their grimly class-conscious subject matter: the effect is of an agricultural instrument wrapped up in lace."[84] Again: writers who have attempted to throw off their bourgeois environment to enter a revolutionary one, he says, have only succeeded in uprooting themselves, in getting killed, or in ceasing to be writers and becoming politicians. Ashamed of the environment to which they are accustomed, they have not been able to acquire a convincing knowledge of any other.[85] Spender praises Auden's detachment in the poem "Spain", on the other hand, finding it to be creative, realistic, and valid; while another, doctrinaire critic of the same poem, Edgell Rickword, upbraids Auden for referring in that poem, to the party gathering as "the boring meeting," labeling such phrases "emotionally irresponsible statements."[86] Spender repeatedly repudiates the idea that a communist's poetry ought to be propaganda: "if one is on the side of the greatest possible degree of freedom, if one insists that one should write as one chooses and about what one wishes, one is not a traitor to the cause of world socialism."[87] He felt also, in one further interesting comment, that poetry was "certainly 'counter-revolutionary'" in the sense that it contained "an element of pity."[88]

He was aware, however, that his belief in his own individuality and its freedom divided him from the revolution. The subject of Auden's poetry, he says, is the struggle seen by someone outside it, and the "ultimate" criticism of himself and Auden and those

84. "The Left Wing Orthodoxy," *New Verse*, nos. 31 and 32 (double number) (Autumn 1938), pp. 13–14.

85. *The New Realism: A Discussion* (London: Hogarth, 1939), p. 19.

86. "Auden and Politics," *New Verse*, nos. 26 and 27 (November 1937), p. 22. Rickword is more than somewhat doctrinaire: "Auden expresses, more poetically than any of his contemporaries, the feeling of insecurity that afflicts a section of the middle-classes as the ceaseless concentration of capital into fewer hands undermines their comparatively privileged position."

87. "Writers and Manifestoes," *Left Review* 1 (February 1935): 150.

88. "Poetry and Revolution," *New Country*, p. 69.

associated with them is that "we haven't deliberately and consciously transferred ourselves to the working class." Such a translation is easier said than done, however. And the experience would in fact have been grueling for Spender or anyone else from the middle class with like sensibility, as George Orwell learned and reported in *The Road to Wigan Pier;* furthermore, to be perfectly practical about it, as C. Day Lewis observed, if one became a worker one wouldn't have any time left for writing.[89] But Spender felt the profound social claims upon him and his art, especially the claims of suffering people—a problem that still preoccupies him.[90] And he refers his readers to the last chapter of Christopher Caudwell's *Illusion and Reality,*[91] where the argument for joining the workers is forcibly put.

Under the pseudonym of Christopher Caudwell, Christopher St. John Sprigge, born in 1907 and killed in action in the International Brigade in 1937, produced during the few years of his life a surprising variety of work: textbooks on aeronautics, poems, short stories, detective and other novels, literary criticism, and essays and fragments in social studies and the philosophy of science.[92] His criticism of Spender, Auden, C. Day Lewis, and others in *Illusion and Reality* is part of a large conception of the nature of poetry and is thus immediately distinguished from the relatively *ad hoc* comments of the critics who have been quoted above. At the present moment in history, Caudwell declared, the bourgeois artist had three possible roles in relation to the proletariat: opposition, alliance, or assimilation. Opposition involved a reactionary regression "to almost mythological themes, to interpret the world in terms of the blood and the unconsciousness."[93] Such was the role of D. H. Lawrence, who tried to return us from consciousness to instinctive living.

89. "Writers and Morals," *Revolution in Writing,* p. 22.

90. See his comment to John Press in *The Poet Speaks: Interviews with Contemporary Poets Conducted by Hilary Morrish, Peter Orr, John Press and Ian Scott-Kilvert,* ed. Peter Orr (New York: Barnes and Noble, 1966), p. 240.

91. "The Future of Poetry," pp. 270–98.

92. More details about Caudwell and his various writings appear in D. E. S. Maxwell, *Poetry of the Thirties,* pp. 38–40 and 63–82.

93. *Illusion and Reality,* p. 282.

It was the road of alliance, of course, that most bourgeois artists were at that time treading, including Gide in France, Day Lewis, Auden, and Spender in England. "They often glorify the revolution as a kind of giant explosion which will blow up everything they feel to be hampering them. But they have no constructive theory . . . as artists they cannot see the new forms and contents of an art which will replace bourgeois art." These poets are preoccupied with personal freedom from social restraints; even when they join the communist party they announce themselves as prepared to merge with the proletariat, to accept its theory and its organization, in every field of concrete living except that of art.[94] There ensues then a separation of art and life: the "proletarian living" of the artist "bursts into his art in the form of crude and grotesque scraps of Marxist phraseology and the mechanical application of the proletarian theory—this is very clearly seen in the three English poets most closely associated with the revolutionary movement."[95]

The conscious proletariat would tell the bourgeois revolutionary that his concept of freedom is wrong: "You imagine your consciousness to be free and not determined by your experience and history. This illusion you exhibit so proudly is the badge of your slavery to yesterday, for if you could see those causes which determine your thought, you would be like us, on the road to freedom. The recognition of necessity in society is the only passage to social freedom" (p. 287). He would insist that thought is inseparable from concrete living; and whereas the bourgeois hoped, by segregating thought from life, to preserve a part of man's freedom, "freedom is not a substance to be preserved and isolated but a force generated in an active struggle with the concrete problems of living" (p. 288).

Our demand—that your art should be proletarian—is *not* a demand that you apply dogmatic categories and Marxist phrases to art. To do so would be bourgeois. We ask that you should *really* live in the new world and not leave your soul behind in

94. C. Day Lewis said that the heart of the ineffectiveness of contemporary poetry was summed up by Christopher Caudwell in these words ("A Reply," *Julian Bell: Essays, Poems and Letters*, p. 322).

95. *Illusion and Reality*, p. 285.

the past. It is your artist's soul for which we value you; and how can your soul be in the new world if your art is bourgeois? We shall know that this transition has taken place when your art has become *living*; then it will be proletarian. Then we shall cease to criticise it for its deadness. (pp. 288–89)

Meanwhile bourgeois poetry had in fact developed along lines directed by the bourgeois illusion, that freedom existed not through but in spite of social relations: ceasing to be conceived of as a social fact, a relation between men, artist and audience, it had begun to ignore the social values inherent in it, "such as syntax, tradition, rules, technique, form, accepted tonal scale," and more and more had come to exist for the individual artist alone. Thus *surrealisme*, representing the anarchy of "the final bourgeois position," is the logical outcome of a development that minimizes the social and maximizes the individual significances of art; and, in exploiting free association and hoping thus to realize spontaneous artistic production, it "only displays the classic bourgeois illusion that freedom is the ignorance of necessity."

It is interesting to observe Christopher Caudwell almost alone in this general debate, bringing in matters of form, which, as noted above, were infrequently discussed and in the official Russian attitude toward literary criticism, were considered a heretical red herring. Caudwell seems to have believed that the formal elements of art were an index of its social relatedness—rhythm, for instance, is "the impress of the social mould in which poetry is generated" (p. 123). But form is a necessary component of expression: it is, again, a bourgeois illusion to suppose that the artist adulterates his pure, individual self-expression, formalizing it in order to make it socially acceptable: on the contrary, "he finds free self-expression only in the social relations embodied in art. . . . [I]n pressing his inner self into the mould of social relations, he not only creates a new mould, a socially valuable product, but he also moulds and creates his own self."[96] In the "final anarchic" phase of bourgeois art, on the other hand, the artist works in the void of free verse, which reflects his attempt "to abandon all social relations in a

96. *Concept of Freedom* (London: Lawrence and Wishart, 1965), p. 17.

blind negation of them, because man has completely lost control of his social relationships."[97]

Answering Caudwell, Spender points out that if it is in fact absolutely essential for the artist to go over to the working class, then the work of great contemporary artists who have not done so is, accordingly, valueless. In Caudwell's *Studies in a Dying Culture*, he says, Caudwell finds Wells, Lawrence, Proust, Huxley, Russell, Forster, Wasserman, Hemingway, and Galsworthy pathetic. The fundamental weakness of his position, however, is the assumption that "the writer who is in a divided position is not in a position to portray historic truth. . . ." It would be absurd, surely, says Spender, to wish that Chekhov had joined the working-class movement; for if he had, his work as we know it would not have materialized. Spender feels that even conservative and traditional men like Rilke, Yeats, Eliot, Maritain, and Bergamin "have made the most profound analysis of contemporary society, much of which is certainly incorporated in Left Wing writing."[98]

Spender believed that the poet could "only write about what is true to his own experience, not about what he would like to be true to his experience." Although the poet might side with the political left, since Socialism had "a far profounder grasp of the political and economic problems of our time" and since he is of all men vulnerable to tyranny, the poet "is not dealing with absolute truth or a dialectic, he is dealing with reality and establishing the significance of his emotional reactions to reality . . ."[99] He recognized the contemporary disadvantages for the bourgeois writer who was condemned to individualism,[100] and he believed with the communists that the future of individualism lay with the classless society.[101] But at the same time he could not envisage as a good society that which totally submerged individual personality and discovered freedom for it only in its own terms. There was, he held, a residual state of being that was independent of all the claims of

97. *Illusion and Reality*, p. 124.
98. *The New Realism*, pp. 21–22.
99. "Poetry," *Fact*, no. 4 (July 1937), p. 10.
100. *New Country*, p. 71.
101. *Forward From Liberalism*, p. 64.

environmental conditioning—a margin of freedom that no system could deny where there was room always for "pure states of being,"[102] a concept that was, of course, simply bourgeois illusion to the orthodox Marxist.

A number of poets of the thirties, Auden, Madge, and others, conveyed political and social messages in prose allegories about newly discovered territories. So, in a similar geographical idiom, we may consider Spender as having gone to a new country, having studied the local flora and fauna with extreme interest and care, and having sympathetically adopted the local clothes, customs, and beliefs and learned a little of the language, but remaining as rigidly determined as any Englishman anywhere on the Continent not to touch the water.

102. *Life and the Poet* (London: Secker and Warburg, 1942), p. 35.

3

# Political Poetry

Much of the debate about poetry and politics and some of the
political poetry appeared in the *Left Review,* a monthly political
journal which contained poems, articles, short fiction, cartoons, and
reviews. It was started in October, 1934, under the joint editorship
of T.H. Wintringham, Amabel Williams Ellis, and Montagu Slater.
In January, 1936 Edgell Rickword became editor and in July,
1937, Randall Swingler, who remained in the chair until the review
was discontinued after the May issue in 1938. The editorial of the
last issue summarizes the review's achievements. It was started,
the editor says, "at a time when the horrors of Hitler's seizure of
power in Berlin had brought appallingly near to us the reality of
Fascism, and in particular the barbarity of its offensive upon all
valid culture."[1] The first year's work of the review, the editor goes

1. "Left Review," *Left Review* 3 (May 1938) : 957.

on, was the effort to establish "the core of a true social culture," in the belief that in order to protect itself from fascism a culture must be firmly rooted in the life of the people. The second year the review turned increasingly political in its effort to "get down to the real job," which was "to oust the National Government and call a check to the advance of Fascist barbarity." In the editorial of the December 1936 issue, the editor recalls, "it was stated that 'it is not in the ivory tower, but in active participation in the urgent issues of the day that a writer develops his gifts.' And it is this uncompromising principle," he says, "which, underlying all the work done by and through LEFT REVIEW, has distinguished it from any other review in England." In the third year the review increased its scope: there were critical essays on literary figures of the past, such as Shakespeare, Blake, Swift, Dickens, Spenser, Hopkins, and Ibsen; and painting, cinema, music, and theater were brought to critical consideration.

Of the writers whose names have survived the thirties, C. Day Lewis was the most frequent contributor to *Left Review*; Spender and John Lehmann contributed often; Auden, once. Other miscellaneous names occasionally embellishing various issues included Bert Brecht, André Malraux, Romain Rolland, Sidney Webb, and Bernard Shaw. Wintringham, Rickword, and Swingler regularly contributed. Many of the well-known and less well-known poets of the period contributed. It was not the place, however, for Roy Campbell, from whom there is nothing. He has a poem amid translations of Charles Maurras in *The Right Review*, an organ whose aims were to make a counter-attack against the propaganda of the communists, to harbor poets and men of real genius, and "to voice the opinions and the works of the editor,"[2] Count Potocki of Montalk, who in 1939, assessing the depletion of the nobility of his country, assumed the title of King of Poland.

The three volumes of *Left Review* contain a wide variety of social criticism in the form of fiction, verse, and straight exposition. Some of it is raucous and puerile, some well weighed. Of the verse,

2. *The Right Review*, no. 7 (October 1936). No page numbers. Two or three issues appeared sporadically after this.

there is virtually nothing that, for its intrinsic merit, aftertimes ought not willingly to let die. One regular feature of the political poetry of the decade in description of the good life as it was thought to obtain in Soviet Russia. Left Wing idealists in those days nourished a specific plan: they had a blue print, a model of the Utopia they wanted to create among the dark Satanic mills of England, as our own recent discontented did not. Before the unmasking of the Machiavellian Russian role in Spain, before André Gide's celebrated return from the U.S.S.R., the Molotov-Ribbentrop pact and all the curious realignments it occasioned, the English radicals could point to an actual country over the eastern horizon where an apparently better way of life under an alternative economic system was no mere chimera of pastoralists or armchair politicians but a reality. As Randall Swingler put in in a poem, "There all we fight for, is already growing."

Here and there the poetry of the period is informed by this positive vision. *The Magnetic Mountain*, for instance, by C. Day Lewis, consists largely of complaint against the current situation, the culture, and its villains; but the few glimpses of the supposedly desirable future come in images derived from the story of Russia: there are "tools, dynamos, bridges, towers,/Your tractors and your travelling-cranes"; "Young men proud of their output" (Stakhanovites, perhaps), and people singing their own songs.[3] A detail from Rex Warner's poem, "Future," derived from reports of real life in Russia, instructs us that "Women work with men and love is voluntary."[4] And in the poem by Swingler already quoted, the comrades are exhorted to encounter the temptation to despair by remembering that

> . . . already the lands live, where men
> Spread forth their life like an ordered and opening flower
>
> Where the factories and the growing machines
> Compact as coral, no longer devour their flesh and time . . .
>
> There all we fight for, is already growing.[5]

3. *Collected Poems of C. Day Lewis* (London: Cape and Hogarth, 1954) pp. 111 and 119.

4. *Poems* (London: Boriswood, 1937), p. 62.

5. "Poem," *Left Review* 2 (July 1936): 514.

Taking some of his images from the funeral of Vassily in Dovzhenko's film, *Earth*, which gains its plot from collective farming in Russia, Stephen Spender can offer in his poem, "The Funeral," a vignette of the good life the intellectuals looked to:

They walk home remembering the straining red flags,
And with pennons of song still fluttering through their blood
They speak of the World State
With its towns like brain centres and its pulsing arteries.

They think how life hums, revolves and toils,
One cog in a golden singing hive:
Like spark from fire, its task happily achieved,
It falls away quietly.[6]

When poets refocused on the local scene they found much less to inspire their song. An appreciable quantity of the political poetry of the thirties, as no doubt of any other decade, is cursed by the feverishness of its commitment to the leftist cause, an uncontrolled sense of outrage at the conditions obtaining for working-class men and women, or anger at this or that or the other prevailing moral evil. In the short poem "In this Midwinter," for one example, Sylvia Townsend Warner plays her strong cards early on in the trick. It begins:

In this midwinter, shepherds, not a lamb possibly.
No green thing, green not even on wintercoat church yard yews.
Air-borne, a poison-gas bomb let fall accidentally
On our uplands has blasted the penned pregnant ewes—[7]

a curious anticipation of an incident thirty-five years later in Colorado. This poet is out to shock us, one way or another. Her "Red Front" is similarly sensational:

Comrade, are you cold enough,
Lean enough, bold enough . . .
. . . . . . . . . . . .
Can your cunning foot the swamp
Where you tread on the dead?—
Red! Red![8]

6. *Collected Poems* (London: Faber and Faber, 1955), p. 53.
7. *Left Review* 1 (January 1935): 101.
8. *Left Review* 1 (April 1935): 255.

A number of passionate, politically minded men and women in the thirties purchased intensity for their poems in such coinage as this: "Red Front" proceeds heavily through an extended metaphor of blood and wine: the blood of friends tastes thin; the vineyard was "too heavily dunged" with "too much blood" and "too many brains spattered." A poem of John Lehmann's published in *Left Review* has a conclusion with tones as shrill as those in Sylvia Townsend Warner. He is reflecting upon the oppressions in Vienna—the prisoners, "the insolent prowling of police," and other horrid stage properties of the totalitarian regime; and he asks finally, Who will not be seized with rage, "and crying—/'Hypocrites! Parasites! Oppressors!/I too will swear your end!'—declare for freedom." This kind of outburst is not uncommon in the verse of the day.

There is also some nonhysterical, good-natured rant in Auden, of which we have already seen an example in the previous chapter, and in C. Day Lewis, imitating him, in *The Magnetic Mountain*. Auden wrote little if any unequivocal communist poetry; but there is an appreciable amount of social discontent in his poems of the thirties, much of it aired in the swashbuckling tone used in the following assault on Lords Beaverbrook and Rothermere, the newspaper kings:

> Beethameer, Beethameer, bully of Britain,
> With your face as fat as a farmer's bum . . .
> In kitchen, in cupboard, in club-room, in mews
> In palace, in privy, your paper we meet. . . .

This appeared in *The Orators* as part of the "Journal of an Airman" in 1932.[9] In *The Magnetic Mountain*, which is dedicated to Auden and heavily indebted to him in style, C. Day Lewis has his smack at Beaverbrook:

> Isn't it grand
> Where the offal of action, the rinsings of thought
> From a stunted peer for a penny can be bought?
> It seems a bargain, but in the long run
> Will cost you your honour, your crops and your son.[10]

9. (London: Faber and Faber, 1932), p. 65. The passage was not later reprinted.
10. *Collected Poems*, p. 101.

Even Ronald Bottrall, whose criticism of his age is more often a non-specific complaint in the style of Pound and Eliot, directed at "we" rather than "they"—even Bottrall has a sarcastic word for Beaverbrook, associating him with the fascist emblems:

> . . . our truth will stand
> and prevail, transported canned
> By a Canadian peer, his emblems an economic axe
> To clear the road and withes to twist
> The limbs of empire fast. . . .[11]

Auden's influence was pervasive during the thirties and its effect upon many poets of the day will be duly noted. One close imitator is Gavin Ewart. In a parody of Auden, he picks up the "Locksley Hall" rhythms of Auden's poem that begins, "Get there if you can," from *Poems* (1930), [12] and the military fun and games that the early work constantly features, including the figure of Captain Ferguson, who mysteriously appears and disappears in "Taller today we remember similar evenings."[13] The following lines are from Ewart's "Audenesque for an Initiation":

Every minute scouts give signals, come reporting what they've seen,
"Captain Ferguson is putting." "Undermine the 18th green."[14]

Ewart incurs a similar debt when he is writing seriously, or at least more seriously, as in the image of the nurse, in "Political Poem":

> O Communists
>
> . . . . . . . . . . . . . . . . .
> We believe that you are our enormous nurse
> Helping us not to cry in the dark, not to steal sweets,
> Kindly to many, a savior of rearrangement.[15]

11. "Salute to Them That Know," *Selected Poems* (London: Editions Poetry London, 1946), p. 13.
12. (London: Faber and Faber).
13. *Poems*, p. 82. (Rex Warner goes one up with a Colonel Humphries, equally mysterious, in "Chorus," *Poems* [London: Boriswood, 1937] p. 57.)
14. *Poems and Songs* (London: Fortune Press, [1939]), p. 12.
15. *Ibid.*, p. 31.

The last line quoted echoes the rhythms at the end of Auden's "Petition."

Lewis's *Magnetic Mountain* contains some vindictive lines against those with an "assured income," against "fine ladies" who are "Weedy, greedy, unsatisfied, unsexed," and against "Nasties, nudists, bedlamites, buddhists," who, "Too feeble to follow, unable to guide,/ It's time we asked . . . to step aside." Rex Warner is also anxious to pull down the middle classes from their seats, and writes in somewhat the same vein:

> Come away then,
> you fat men!
> You don't want your watch-chain.
> But don't interfere with us, because we know you too well.
> If you do that you will lose your top hat
> and be knocked on the head until you are dead.[16]

The Spanish Civil War inspired the best political poem of the period, Auden's "Spain," and stimulated the production of many other pieces of varying merit. Some of these were collected by Stephen Spender and John Lehmann in an anthology, *Poems for Spain*.[17] Spender observes in his introduction that although Auden had actually been in Spain, the fact is irrelevant to the poem

> in a way in which it is not irrelevant to the poems of Cornford and Wintringham.
> For the essential quality of other poems here is that they are written from *inside* Spain; they have the merits and defects of being extremely close to experience. Of the fighters here, John Cornford was killed, the day after his 21st birthday. Charles Donnelly was also killed; Tom Wintringham, who was Political Commissar in the [International] Brigade, was wounded at Jarama.[18]

The merits, presumably, are the genuine raw details of the war scene; the defects are the raw emotions which the poets had neither the

16. "Hymn," *Poems* (London: Boriswood, 1937), p. 39.
17. (London: Hogarth Press, 1939).
18. *Poems for Spain*, p. 11.

time nor the place to recollect in tranquillity, even if they had wanted
to. In John Cornford's "Full Moon at Tierz," the reader is embarrassed by an outcropping of passionate canvassing:

> Our fight's not won till the workers of all the world
> Stand by our guard on Huesca's plain,
> Swear that our dead fought not in vain.
> Raise the red flag triumphantly
> For Communism and for liberty.[19]

Spender is quoted as saying that Cornford was not a poet, and the
lines quoted may confirm that judgment. But Cornford could write
otherwise on occasion and show talent:

> And if bad luck should lay my strength
> Into the shallow grave,
> Remember all the good you can;
> Don't forget my love.[20]

"Full Moon at Tierz" has few details from the Spanish War. Details
of the war available to poets who were fighting it are not, in fact,
put to great advantage in the poems in the Spain anthology. Much
of what was written on or near the field might have been improved
with some later scrutiny. A great deal of it, however, was written by
men who were not poets, either in their own or anybody else's eyes,
but had broken into this unfamiliar mode of expression for this occasion. Sometimes, by luck, perhaps, the details are evocative; the
poems of T. H. Wintringham make use of this poet's own situation
in the catastrophe, though they don't necessarily come out of the
actual fighting. Some lines of David R. Marshall succeed somewhat
in getting facts to speak:

> . . . Shattering, rumbling racket
> Glass smashing and one thin endless scream
> Then a dullness in the head,
> We stand over the table,

19. "Full Moon at Tierz: Before the Storming of Huesca," *Left Review* 3 (March
1937): 70.
20. "To Margot Heinemann," *Poems for Spain*, p. 27.

> A glass falls, ring,
> The air tastes of the Metro.
> The cigarettes are all out.[21]

Sometimes the writer has less luck; here is a fragment from T.A.R. Hyndman, Spender's protegé, who appears in the autobiography as Jimmy Younger; it is filled with his own private sense of horror, no doubt, but communicating little of it:

> I hardly knew
> I tore his coat
> It was easy—
> Shrapnel had helped.[22]

Many of the poems in *Poems for Spain* express crude and insubordinate emotion, whether composed at the front or in England. "Looking at a Map of Spain on the Devon Coast," by Jack Lindsay was composed in England. It concludes:

> I stand at the atlantic edge and look
> southwards and raise my hand to Spain. Salute.[23]

It is understandable that the volume should show a great deal of strong sentiment at the prospect of what all then considered the most public, unambiguous, and injurious outrage that fascism had inflicted upon humanity. There was not a great deal of talent, however.

Another poem of Lindsay's, not included in *Poems for Spain* but appearing in the same issue of *Left Review* as Cornford's "Full Moon at Tierz," was "On Guard for Spain,"[24] which runs to nearly 400 lines of highly impassioned rhetoric, against which the rallying cry in Cornford's poem seems relatively mild. It was designed for mass declamation and was performed all over England in order to

21. "Retrospect," *Poems for Spain*, p. 32.
22. "Jarama Front," *ibid.*, p. 40.
23. *Poems for Spain*, p. 64.
24. *Left Review* 3 (March 1937) : 79–86.

engender public feelings favorable to the Spanish Republic. It could have "come off," Edgell Rickword later said, "only in a time of exceptional emotional intensity."[25] Its metrical kinship with *Howl* will be observed in the following line:

> they shot the workers at Badajoz
> gouged and scourged and maimed and lamed and murdered,
> blew up with grenades the wounded in hospital wards,
> mangled and hanged and flogged and smashed and ravished,
> a fist of force slogging at every heartbeat. . . .

Harry Pollitt praised the poem highly.[26]

Finally, one exceptional, long poem about Spain is "The Nabara," by C. Day Lewis, not included in *Poems for Spain* but appearing in 1938 in *Overtures to Death*.[27] The poem describes a sea engagement between Spanish trawlers, notably *Nabara*, and a rebel cruiser; and it is excellent for the clarity with which the action is described, particularly the movements of the seven ships involved, which is not easily achieved even in prose. The poem appeals on account of the conventional heroism of the men in the smaller, legitimate, outgunned vessel; and in telling the story Lewis does not often attempt to augment the proper effects of such heroism by rhetorical additions. His introduction and conclusion, however, are not restrained by the decency that operates in the body of the poem. He begins with, "Freedom is more than a word, more than the base coinage/Of statesmen," a corny declaration that might appropriately open a poem far inferior to "The Nabara." Still on the subject of freedom (a word so bound up with rant that it can scarcely be used seriously in a modern poem), he shortly announces, "Mortal she is, yet rising always refreshed from her ashes," which is probably a sentiment that came to the poet after he had been reading Byron, who is given credit for a borrowing in a footnote later on. In neither

25. "A Conversation with Edgell Rickword," *the Review*, no. 11–12, p. 19. The facts about Lindsay's poem are taken from Stanley Weintraub, *The Last Great Cause* (London: Allen, 1968), p. 78.
26. Weintraub, p. 78.
27. *Collected* Poems, pp. 191–200.

of its meanings has the proposition been frequently borne out by history.

How alien to and beyond such heroics are the mind and hence the poetry of Spender. His dead soldier is presented not as hero but as a "better target for a kiss"; he reports in the *New Statesman and Nation* that the "dead in wars are not heroes: they are freezing or rotting lumps of isolated insanity" and says that the "propaganda which turns men into heroes" is not the least of the war's crimes.[28] He looks beyond pomps of traditional glory and the panoplies of death to enquire what has happened to divide the "palpable love of man for man."

Political poems in the *Left Review* and elsewhere are not all composed of such tropical passions as inhabit Lindsay's oration or such Baden-Powelling instincts as inform Cornford's rallying cry. Here and elsewhere in the decade, more measured voices might be heard commenting with controlled bitterness upon the social scene and the credibility gap in politics. There are many various forms. There is, for example, the short sentimental narrative as spoken by a victim of the system, with echoes, vague enough, of Blake and Hood:

> I had a job in a laundry
> I had a job in a shop
> My hands were caught in a factory
> Till I thought that I should drop.[29]

In nondramatic poems, parody is quite often used as a cutting edge for descriptions of the conditions of the poor, the insouciance of the rich, and the general evils of the times, implicitly contrasting the present bitter subject with the echo of some innocent theme from sweeter and sunnier days. W. R. Nettlefold's "Remembrance Day," for example, responds to Poppy Day with the anticipation of another war and grotesquely recalls Herrick:

28. "Heroes in Spain," *New Statesman* 13, 323 n.s. (May 1, 1937): 715, quoted from Katharine Bail Hoskins, *Today the Struggle: Literature and Politics in England During the Spanish Civil War* (Austin, Texas: University of Texas Press, 1969), p. 224.

29. Maurice Carpenter, "A Welsh Girl," *Left Review* 3 (July 1937): 340. See also his "We Ask for Life," *Left Review* 3 (February 1937): 30.

> Purchase the poppies while you may,
> Symbols for someone else today

and

> Gather the poppies while you may:
> Fingers are easily blown away.[30]

With the same foreboding, Nettlefold croons his unusual lullaby:

> Sleep deeply my baby, 'tis I who should cry
> The Masters are planning the way you shall die.[31]

Similarly, Julian Bell has his own tendentious song of sixpence, which closes,

> The banker turns his gold about
> But that won't sell the rye.
> Starve and grow cold without,
> And ask the reason why
> The guns are in the garden,
> And battle's in the sky.[32]

C. Day Lewis, a master of poetic imitation, parodies "Away in a Manger," the children's Christmas carol:

> The hooters are blowing,
> No heed let him take;
> When baby is hungry
> 'Tis best not to wake.
> Thy mother is crying,
> Thy dad's on the dole:
> Two shillings a week is
> The price of a soul.[33]

There were few poets whose work in this decade did not some-where include political statement, allusion, or reference. General and vague dreams for a better world, such as poets have always been

---

30. *Left Review* 3 (December 1937): 661.
31. "A Lullaby for a Baby Born in 1937," *Left Review* 3 (December 1937): 662.
32. "Nonsense," *Poetry of the Thirties*, ed. Robin Skelton (Harmondsworth, Middlesex: Penguin Books, 1967), p. 62.
33. *Collected Poems*, p. 140.

heir to, might be construed as political commitments.[34] A poem by Richard Goodman, "It is Too Late," which has the most remarkable affinity to Spender's "I think continually of those who were truly great," concludes with what may quite easily be taken as left political sentiment, though in fact it need not be:

> On the hills in the sun where the clouds are banners
> I see them march and curve their lips in song:
> they tell of the day when the sons of their sons' sons
> shall attain the goal which beckons through their dreams.[35]

We have not been instructed as to who "they" are; just that they were "born of the central flame" and "affirmed with laughter and blossoming of the Spirit,/ like brilliant April, what those denied." Stephen Spender's "The Express," with its "powerful plain manifesto," has been taken as political; but it has also been read as a description of a girl's first orgasm.[36] Spring came to the poets of the thirties as it has come to those of all other decades, and it need not be an oblique expression of a particular new political dispensation. But it very often is; for Rex Warner and Randall Swingler, for two examples, it hardly ever comes simply as a season.

One cannot cite all the kinds of poems in the decade that show political commitment or, at the other end of the spectrum, merely hint that their authors wish the social or political situations were otherwise. Here and there, in later parts of this chapter, a few more examples will appear. One special case of commitment is worth mentioning: David Gascoyne, who had previously realized that surrealism was no method for an English poet with political convictions,[37] prefaces his volume of surrealist poems, *Man's Life is*

---

34. D. E. S. Maxwell gives some interesting examples (*Poets of the Thirties* [London: Routledge and Kegan Paul, 1969], pp. 48–49).

35. *New Country Prose and Poetry by the Authors of* New Signatures, ed. Michael Roberts (London: Leonard and Virginia Woolf, 1933), p. 219.

36. Richard C. Blakeslee, "Three Ways Past Edinburgh: Stephen Spender's 'The Express,' " *College English* 26 (April 1965): 556–58.

37. "The Surrealists themselves have a definite justification for writing in this way, but for an English poet with continually growing political convictions it must soon become impossible" (*New Verse*, no. 11 [October 1934]). Quoted by Robin Skelton in his introduction to David Gascoyne's *Collected Poems*, ed. Robin Skelton (London: Oxford University Press, 1965), p. xii.

*This Meat*,[38] with "Critique of Poetry," a poem of Paul Eluard's in translation, so that his radical sentiments might not go entirely unvoiced. Eluard's poem is only a few lines; it makes its point at once, beginning, "Of course I hate the reign of the bourgeois/ The reign of cops and priests. . . ."

One of the more interesting problems faced by politically committed poets was the embodiment of their political sentiments in lyrical poetry; and in politically colored lyrical poetry there is often a bad joint, a rough transition between the dogma and the singing tones. The work of George Barker will illustrate some aspects of the matter. The Spanish war awakened in Barker a strong passion that had not previously been aroused by political matters. His long poem, *Calamiterror*,[39] concerns itself among other things with some of the details of the war, making repeated mention of the women weeping in Irun's ruins. It is an overwrought poem, bejeweled, and curiously distorted with extraneous images and gaudy rhetorical techniques, which are considered in a later section below. Stephen Spender, however, reviewing it in *Left Review*, although he recognized its weaknesses, designating it a "firework" rather than an "organism," finally grants Barker a stature that he denies Rex Warner, whose work he is reviewing alongside. Barker's poems "give . . . a far deeper sense of the confusion and frustration of European civilisation" than do those of Warner and of some others. Why is this so? "George Barker's world"—Spender's way of saying "George Barker"—"is obsessed, over-sensitive, hysterical, and perhaps . . . too passive towards experience." But he has a personality which, unlike the "determined 'character'" of Rex Warner, will permit engagement with the imaginative experience. Warner is at fault for exerting his will in his poetry; Barker, on the other hand, is successful, it seems, inasmuch as he has failed to exert control

38. (London: Parton Press [1936]).
39. (London: Faber and Faber, 1937). Spender said the poem concerned the death of the poet's child, but Barker says it was occasioned "when a sporting accident happened and I blinded my brother in one of his eyes." He mentions associated incidents and adds, "All these images got together at the same time, and they're all to do with the act of observing the objective world" ("An Interview with George Barker," *Contemporary Literature* 12 [Autumn 1971]: 389).

over the expression. His will, we may say, anticipating a later discussion, has bowed before his sensibility. The passivity is recorded in another critic's comment: "Barker has never addressed the world," says David Daiches, "but he has preferred to make himself a symbol of it." Daiches remarks also that the danger of this kind of poetry is that the poet, speaking from the inside of his subject "never talking to it or about it, but embodying . . . is not always able to impose a unity that is clearly apparent to the observer."[40]

*Calamiterror* makes repeated mention of women weeping in Irun's ruins. "'Irun's ruins,'" says Spender, "would speak to Warner with the voice of conscience demanding the voice of protest: they become part of Barker's spiritual habitation, and therefore Barker is capable of development, because he is capable of imaginative experience to the degree to which it is only possible to the true poet, the degree by which an imagined experience modifies the poet's whole being."[41]

We shall have occasion to refer back again to the distinction Spender makes between Warner and Barker, in particular to remark Warner's obtrusive act of will. Meanwhile the review introduces the matter of a poet's ability to absorb political material into his "spiritual habitation," which Warner apparently lacked but Barker possessed. The modification of the whole being was the consummation desiderated by the communist critics mentioned above whose watchword was "assimilation." And it was felt that the contemporary poets fell short in the extent to which they permitted the communist ideology to so affect their personalities; thus their poems contained or, if not contained, bore communist slogans and sentiments as excrescences. There was a fission between the poetry and the politics: so Christopher Caudwell charges Auden, C. Day Lewis, and Spender; so Spender charges Rex Warner; Randall Swingler charges Spender; Spender charges Swingler; and Spender, Spender.

It is true of an appreciable amount of lyrical poetry in the decade that the involvement of political matters resulted in incongruity

---

40. "The Lyricism of George Barker," *Poetry* 69 (March 1947): 336 and 340.
41. "New Poetry," *Left Review* 3 (July 1937): 360.

that was sometimes grotesque. It is by no means certain, however, that this is an index of political half-heartedness on the part of the poet or his failure to assimilate communism. It might be the result of a less radical failure, one in technique, perhaps, or simply a matter of poor taste. John Cornford's communism was not, surely, to be faulted; but his taste, in the "Full Moon at Tierz" poem, certainly was. You cannot say he was a good poet because he was a good communist any more than you can say Charles Wesley was a good poet because he was a great Wesleyan.[42] The passage of Cornford's quoted above is bad (in spite of poetic ability manifest elsewhere) because, for one thing, slogans are not the means by which feelings are expressed in poetry; and they are savored as gratefully as London water, which has all been drunk before. "Our fight's not won till the workers of all the world" etcetera is a crude means of magic, which taste and decency eschew, incongruous not because the poet had not assimilated the dogma, but because it is not poetic. In poetry feelings do not come raw and single; they are complicated and related; they are rendered in personal utterance, not slogans; and they are controlled. Marianne Moore considers her piece, "In Distrust of Merits," not to be a poem, widely anthologized though it is; and what she says could be applied to Cornford's piece, *mutatis mutandis*: "It is just a protest—disjointed, exclamatory. Emotion overpowered me. First this thought then that."[43]

C. Day Lewis claims to have written only two political poems of any value,[44] "The Conflict" and "In Me Two Worlds." In both the advancement of communism is adumbrated; but each poem has its own life, so to say, that controls what is contained in it. The political feeling is the poet's own and it comes in his own words, integrated

42. Of Cornford's poems, John Lehmann has recently written, ". . . they *are* poetry, not merely because Cornford was obviously a very strong poetic personality, but chiefly, I think, because the Communist creed had become so deeply embedded in his nature that he didn't have to protest about it, nor feel that he had to suppress natural human reactions of dread and nostalgia as he faced the bullets" (Review of Hugh D. Ford, *A Poet's War: British Poets and the Spanish Civil War*, *London Magazine* 5 n.s. [November 1965]: 85).
43. *A Marianne Moore Reader* (New York: Viking, 1965), p. 261.
44. Maxwell, pp. 117–18. The poems appear on pages 128 and 130 respectively of Lewis's *Collected Poems*.

with other feelings and controlled. In the former poem, the lines "The red advance of life/Contracts pride, calls out the common blood,/Beats song into a single blade," are speaking to the union of the workers of the world; but they are poetic: the words "common blood" and the image of beating into a single blade open them to complication and enrichment by auxiliary feelings (swords were *beat* into ploughshares; here songs are *beat* into a sword). In the latter poem, "In Me Two Worlds," the allegorical arrangement is bothersome because the two worlds warring within the poet's body seem occasionally to be confined there and to be using its inventory of the blood and bones, but then again they seem occasionally to have got outside and be operating elsewhere. Once more, however, the richness of individual feelings makes its impact upon us:

> The insolence of the dead
> Breaks on their solid front:
> They tap my nerves for power, my veins
> To stain their banners red.

A world of difference distinguishes this from the flat invective in the lines about Beaverbrook in *The Magnetic Mountain*, or the shouting in Cornford.

Neither of Lewis's poems suffers a fracture in pitch or tone on account of the presence of the ideological element, even though Lewis is here dealing with the struggle itself, not the glorious Utopian aftermath, which lent itself much more easily to the lyric pitch. The success is in part due simply to terminology: whereas "workers of the world" is a technical term with a narrow range of meaning, "blood red dawn" and other such terms as Lewis uses have less confined meanings, can let in a range of suggestion that the slogan denies. Similarly, when elsewhere he is introducing industrial imagery, Lewis is more successful with his "flange," "shafting," and "signal," the images in the opening poem of *Feathers to Iron*, praised by Michael Roberts in the preface to *New Signatures*, than Stephen Spender with his "driving belts," largely because of the imprecision and vagueness.

Often in poems of this period the fracture in the tone and pitch is very evident: poems try, as it were, to be lyrical; then, since there

seems no way of singing the politics, they give up the unequal struggle
in favor of an outburst of party dogma, or other raw, unmodulated
data, or a sentiment as alien to its context as the farm implement
wrapped up in lace, which was Spender's simile for the poetry of
Randall Swingler.

Swingler provides an interesting study in the ways in which
political feeling can be incorporated into or stuck on to lyrical poems.
His poetry as a whole uses repeatedly the natural imagery of the
seasons and of growth: winter approaches, but deep in the earth
life stirs the roots; with spring, buds break, leaves uncurl, greenness
breaks through earth, shoots pierce their old confinements. "Instructions for Hermes," a poem that is the third part of a larger one
called "Preludes," tells the god to

> Find out again
> the rhythm of belief; till nothing remains
> desirable but beauty alone,
> and there's in us no wary
> motive mining the simple blood's
> geography, but our unhampered love.[45]

To some extent Swingler's poetry follows what this precept implies:
the poet finds himself able to convey social and political sentiments
in terms that are not at odds with his lyrical expression. The best
example is "The Swans," the fourth part of "Preludes," which
immediately follows upon the lines quoted above. The last two
stanzas of the three in "The Swans" describe the arrival of the birds
upon a lake and the water's subsequent return to its proper placidity,
"At the grey conclusion of flight,/The locked wings, the calmed
heart."[46] The reader may deduce that he has experienced the vision
of postrevolutionary calm, for he is informed that the vision is
vouchsafed only "to those who have climbed the dusky hill"—a kind
of eligibility that suggests an inward meaning. But no incongruity
destroys this poem, which successfully brings its political comment
within the geography of the lyric. It is, of course, as mentioned,

---

45. *Difficult Morning* (London: Methuen, 1933), p. 6
46. *Ibid.*

easier to flute wild carols about the postrevolutionary dawn than about the fight itself.

Often in Swingler the imagery of spring carries an oblique but unequivocal social message; sometimes the theme of social revolution is carried in allegory. In the following, spring is literal, in which form it "smothers with content" the wounds of society and thus inhibits the urge for social change; at the same time the familiar metaphorical value of the seasons is felt:

> I knew that green siesta must postpone
> Their [the people's] critical hour, and prayed
> for the bare frost soon
> To make tense their fields in fallow, and complete
> The circumference of the spring's incipient change.[47]

Often, however, Swingler rudely breaks out of his easy seasonal allegory into literal language, and the shift may be sudden. In Part I of "'The New World This Hour Begets,'" a poem in sections, the reader is first engaged with the seasons and the echoes of "The Burial of the Dead": "Winter withered off the past, assessing/Our data . . . . Spring absolves us . . . breaking/New days out of the pod." Then, in imagery of diver and airman, the poet declares the validity of poetic truth, truth felt in the heart rather than measured scientifically. By such means, we believe,

> that He the People the King

> Soon will reject that idol, set up in smug
> Stance in the hot envious palaces,
> Whose taloned feet are rooted profane, within
> The glacial security of the Bank. . . .

The literal entry of the bank, the old socialist *bête noir*, comes suddenly upon the poem, and almost as suddenly it is relinquished for images of the railway, flowers, trees, and bird.

Such incongruity is not unusual in this poet. "Prelude to Revolution," from his earlier volume,[48] is worth consideration for the

47. *Ibid.*, p.16.
48. *Reconstruction: Six Poems* (Oxford: Blackwell, 1933), p. 16.

problems of poetry it unwittingly reveals. It is titled "Prelude," but, again, it happily looks to the time when the dirty work has been done. It opens in a pure lyrical vein:

When it is done perhaps we shall again
Sing up through buds lighter than birds in the undying tree,
Resigned in summer's paralysis of pleasure
And thought's gentle profusion and time's suspended measure.

Shortly the poem shifts from lyrical to political statement:

Vehement in their fear we saw the middle-class withdraw
To patch up their old house, benignly disregarding
The landslip near the garage and the empty well
Discovered under the floor.

Futile they bar their doors against the beleaguring future
With signification of time's foreshortened values still,
Like where on glad sands shining bodies laugh,
The mobled shark moves near the shore.

Plunging through these unheroic ruins, bugle to lip,
Coarser we seem than once, uprooting the dunghill,
Until by barest poverty unthinking we arrive
At true delight of the sun, the elemental touch.

(Moble: to muffle one's head or face.)

Many qualities of the decade's poetry and some of the difficulties of its political poetry are represented here. There is, for example, in the second line, an echo of Wilfred Owen, who was admired and repeatedly imitated in the thirties; in the last stanza quoted, a primitive delight in the sun is presented, which, again, thanks perhaps to Lawrence, is repeatedly seen in the poetry of this period, especially in Spender's. Then, as in other examples of political poetry, there are uncertain lyrical touches; there is a discontinuous effort to allegorize the message, leaving undisguised such lumps as "the middle-class" lest the message should be completely obscured by its stage clothes; there are tastelessly mixed metaphors ("bugle to lip . . . uprooting the dunghill"); and there are gleams of misplaced splendor, gaining our sympathy for the images associated with what the poet is dismissing, such as the laughing and shining bodies on the sands.

Some of the political poems of Stephen Spender show symptoms of distress similar to those in Swingler. Such poems, no less than the latter, might be described as farm things wrapped in lace. They show especially, first, the improper disposition of the reader's sympathy and, second, the inclusion of incongruous political elements. It is claimed, for an example of the former phenomenon, that in "The Funeral" "Spender's language contradicts his intention." The line in question is the last one: "Mourned by scholars who dream of the ghosts of Greek boys." "The beauty of the Greek image," says Willis D. Jacobs, " —its long vowels, the sweetness and solemnity of its sounds—engenders nobility and loveliness in the past, in the very era Spender is terming inferior through the rest of the poem."[49] This may not be exactly so; but what does certainly appear in Spender's work is a deliberate practice of countering the lyrical lines that handle the conventional poetic subjects with images that are not conventionally beautiful, which the poet's conscience for communism and progress, perhaps, has prescribed for the poem in question, to be worn like a hair shirt, and which the poem's rhetoric instructs the reader to prefer to conventional beauties.

This practice is, of course, related to the other, the inclusion or the attachment of incongruous political sentiment. There are the well-known instances: the gratuitous cynicism directed against religion in "The Landscape Near an Aerodrome," the admiration for the prowess of the worker in "The Funeral," and the murderous intentions revealed at the end of "Not palaces an era's crown." These impulses are absorbed from Spender's brave new political ambience, and in each poem their appearance is sudden, awkward, and incongruous.

"The Landscape Near an Aerodrome" presents the contrast between the beautiful descending sweep of the mothlike airliner and the sordid industrial outskirts of the city with its human squalor, which, necessary to the construction of the plane, has thus contributed to the luxury of the passengers. The last line of the poem,

49. "The Moderate Poetical Success of Stephen Spender," *College English* 17 (April 1956): 376.

"Religion stands, the church blocking the sun," is an afterthought, according to Willis D. Jacobs, "a structural flaw that bespeaks an earnest and dedicated young man but also an imperfect artist";[50] more argument than Spender offers us is necessary to relate Christianity to the ugly phenomena of the city. In any case, the sun, which the church is said to be blocking, had already gone down in the first stanza.

There is another small motif of interest in the poem that might be mentioned here:

> fields
> Behind the aerodrome, where boys play all day
> Hacking dead grass: whose cries like wild birds,
> Settle upon the nearest roofs
> But soon are hid under the loud city.

This passage looks somewhat like an outcropping of the old Georgian town-country conflict. But in other poems, as will appear, Spender as a socialist is not unfaithful to the city, where the social scene is set. And it is possible that the images here have a larger but private meaning for the poet as they certainly do elsewhere. In *Trial of a Judge*, the "edges of the city/Where greenness first begins" are a metaphor for the private life as it is about to be invaded by public politics; and it seems probable that the images quoted above notify the poet's anxiety about the vulnerable privacy of the individual, the invasion of the untamed private life by inhuman agencies, and the invasion of play by work. It is not more than a hunch, but one wonders whether the poem was begun with ends in mind other than those which it achieves.

As ill-mannered as the side-swipe against Christianity in "The Landscape Near an Aerodrome" is the banal remark in "The Funeral" that, suddenly amid the poetry, claims the status of Stakhanovite for its protagonist:

> With laughter on their lips and with winds blowing round them
> They record simply
> How this one excelled all others in making driving belts.[51]

50. P. 376.
51. *Poems*, 1933, p. 41.

Factory products in their specific designation ineluctably injure the pitch of lyrical poetry, *pace* whatever defences may have been made for Hart Crane's giggling ball-bearings. "The Funeral" did not even please the comrades—not, at least, John Cornford, as we have seen. It is an unusual poem for Spender, and is not really to be judged in the manner Cornford adopts. It describes the funeral at greater length than Spender normally devotes to a situation, dramatic or static, because he has derived the setting and some of the imagery from Dovzhenko's *Earth*, which he saw in Germany in 1932, which silently relates the story of Vassily, the hero of collective farming. After the climactic moment of Russian triumph when the tractor arrives,[52] Vassily rides down the fences against the opposition of the conservative landowners, who include his own family. That night he dances in jubilation through the village; as he does so, he is shot by a property owner. After nights and days of meditation, the father requests the village council to have Vassily buried after the new way, since he had died for the new life. Thus, as they bear their hero to the grave, the young people sing songs of the new life. The scarves of the women flutter in the wind. Spender has taken the funeral for the large situation of his poem, he has taken its mood of joy, and he has incorporated some of the details, most notably "the laughter on their lips" and "the wind blowing round them."

The adverse criticism this poem attracted to itself was not so corrosive as that which was directed against "Not palaces, an era's crown." This poem is, indeed, a singular exhibit: never was there such a curious counterpointing of ugly self-consciousness, brutish "program," and pure lyrical poetry. The speaker exhorts the reader (and, no doubt, himself) to turn away from his heritage, "palaces," and so forth, from the pleasures of the senses, and from the beauty of culture in general and the arts in particular and to take energy to "will this Time's change," a change that was to bring about that "No one/Shall hunger: Man shall spend equally" and, in short, that "Man shall be man." Here is another instance where, notwith-

52. This film, which C. Day Lewis also saw, perhaps gives him the image in the 26th poem of "From Feathers to Iron": "all is recorded/. . . When the first tractor came and how we cheered it."

standing the "architectural gold-leaved flower" that the poet claims to be building, the appealing imagery in the poem is given to the life of the senses that is being dismissed, while the reader is instructed to lend his sympathy to the dark brown sociological improvement recommended. The poem concludes with a reference to the program that is to be replaced; then,

> Our programme like this, but opposite,
> Death to the killers, bringing light to life.

As we have seen, John Cornford, with the taste of the fire-eater, preferred Louis Aragon's poem to Spender's. Spender's poem, especially its last two lines, earns also some abuse from Roy Campbell in an unelevated passage in "Talking Bronco."

> A more ferocious, bloodthirsty poltroon
> Has never howled for blood beneath the moon

> Than joint MacSpaunday [Campbell's compound name for MacNeice, Spender, Auden, and C. Day Lewis], when his leash of heads

> To murder, rape, and arson roared the Reds.
> For then he 'stamped with emphasis' of tone
> For 'Energy and Energy alone' [phrases from "Not palaces"]
> But when in answer to his Fee-Fo-Fum
> As to an urgent S.O.S. I come
> With "Death to killers'—yes, he roared for that!—
> And 'Energy' enough to knock him flat. . . .[53]

But the best comment upon the murderous passage at the end of the poem is, obliquely and paradoxically, Spender's own, though it is specifically a comment upon Aragon's *The Red Front*. Of this work, in a review that appeared in *New Verse* shortly after the book publication of "Not palaces," Spender writes, "If bloodshed is a criterion of communism, Hitler is as much a communist as Messrs.

---

53. *Talking Bronco* (London: Faber and Faber, 1946), p. 81.

Aragon and Cummings [the translator of *Red Front*], and his rhetoric even more effective."[54] He argues that Aragon's poem fails because it doesn't convince us why the proletariat should kill the bourgeoisie; and such a criticism is valid also for "Not palaces," in which the killing (though so-called poetic justice, perhaps) is similarly unjustified poetically. Once again, the political elements, the naive aims, and the cramped dismal values fail to be blended into the poem.

54. *New Verse*, n.s. 3 (May 1933):·25.

# 4

# Repudiating the Georgians

Political and social concerns in the thirties exerted strong pressures on poetry which were indirectly manifested in various features in poems different from those in which the poet weeps, rallies his comrades, or condemns opponents. Stephen Spender's poem, "Not palaces, an era's crown" arises, to be sure, from a conflict which, as will appear, is very peculiarly Spender's own. But the abnegation of the enjoyment of the senses that it recommends on account of social and political responsibility is an instance of a moral demand felt widely enough in the decade.

Such abnegation extended to poetry about those simple pleasures that had given much of the content to the volumes of *Georgian poetry,* edited in the second decade by Edward Marsh. The subject matter may remain, but its treatment is altered on account of the new attitudes dictated by fear, commitment, and guilt. The poems to be considered here concern such activities and experiences, intrinsically simple and innocent, as constitute the employ of wholesome people in the earned freedom of their Saturdays— conversation, cricket, homemade bread, pots of tea, beer, sitting with a girl before the fire, and, ubiquitous in the poetry, a motif more frequent than any other, the enjoyment of the English countryside, with its lanes and footpaths, its fields of grass or waving corn, hedges, trees, farm buildings, and cottages, and, fooling around among all these, British birds, with their great charm, in the various seasons of the year.

To stereotype the native poetry before the thirties as Georgian and think of it as using its subjects as escape from crises or irksome quotidian routine, as idyllic weekend withdrawal, and, in Stephen Spender's sense, as "non-recognition,"[1] is not to be unaware of its variety.[2] The thirties poets, nevertheless, seem to have looked back to the Georgians as the purveyors of poetic tributes to the simple life: they had in mind probably the the "drenched-in-moonlight" verse,[3] the titmouse and the jenny wren in Ralph Hodgson, or the rainbows, moons, and nightingales in W. H. Davies; or Rupert Brooke longing to be back in the Grantchester vicarage in time for tea. Michael Roberts called such rural poetry "a cowardly escape into the past"[4] and the increasingly widespread repudiation of the older attitudes is, no doubt, what Charles Madge referred to when he remarked in 1933, "the separatists are definitely returning from their 'little worlds of the imagination.'"[5]

1. The Georgians, says Spender, are the classic examples of "non-recognizers." "The non-recognizer does not recognize the world of today, or the need to deal with it. He has the attitude to aesthetic enjoyment that the weekender has to the countryside. His true life, he maintains, is a world apart from the town, the office, the factory. What is 'real' for him is not all this world of material involvement but the moment when the train slides past the last house of the city of a Friday evening, and the green fields begin." "Non-Recognizers," *The Struggle of the Modern*, (Berkeley: University of California Press, 1963), p. 159.

2. ". . . not every poet published in the five volumes of *Georgian Poetry* was a glib, pseudo-pastoral lark-lover." Robert H. Ross, *The Georgian Revolt 1910–1922* (Carbondale: Southern Illinois University Press, 1965), p. ix.

3. Ross, p. 196.

4. "Preface," *New Signatures,* ed. Michael Roberts (London: Leonard and Virginia Woolf, 1932), p. 8.

5. "Poetry and Politics," *New Verse,* no. 3 (May 1933), p. 3.

Thus, although much of the poetry of the thirties may have the same subject matter as the Georgian, it is distinguished from it inasmuch as it is tense. If, for instance, it is an escape, it is so, so consciously that it may throw more emphasis on the threat or the anxiety from which it is recoiling than on the subject matter in which it has found relief; and sympathies for victims are sometimes expressed more strongly in the efforts made to resist sinister memories of social and political outrages than they would have been in direct statements of responsibility. And sometimes the poetry is tense because its subject, a landscape perhaps, is being enjoyed for the last time.

One mood that appears in the poetry very often as the decade grows darker comes in response to the anticipated or already experienced loss from violence of traditional and legitimate sources "Still I drink your health before/The gun-butt raps upon the door," says Louis MacNeice. In this mood a poet may announce the withdrawal of the pleasures, or alternatively he may dwell the more insistently upon them as they are caught in the vivid light from beneath the impending cloud. The classic statement of this mood of the thirties is MacNeice's "The Sunlight on the Garden," which appeared in *The Earth Compels* in 1938:[6]

> The sunlight on the garden
> Hardens and grows cold. . . .
> Our freedom as free lances
> Advances towards its end;
> The earth compels, upon it
> Sonnets and birds descend;
> And soon, my friend,
> We shall have no time for dances.

Auden sounds the same note, though the joys whose loss he anticipates are not the usual simple ones of nature:

> Louder today the wireless roars
> Its warnings and its lies, and it's impossible

6. (London: Faber and Faber, 1938).

> Among the well-shaped cosily to flit,
> Or longer to desire about our lives
> The beautiful loneliness of the banks . . .[7]

Soon enough thereafter the Spanish War bore out Auden's warning (and no doubt more immediately, the radio's). Julian Bell, who was to be among its victims, had anticipated the darkening of the garden in the title poem of his last volume, *Work for the Winter,* 1936. Here the summer garden is already a memory—the imagery more vivid, perhaps, for the glow of nostalgia—a memory with which the present wintry scene has already blended:

> Do you remember what dancers,
> What a laughing troop of children circled about the fountain,
> What dropping garlands of roses, what laurels now cut down?

Now it is time for winter and winter's tools, symbols of the weapons of war:

> But now take stronger tools,
> Axe, fire, plough.
> Metal sheathed in despairs, winter is fast come on us. . . .

> . . . for us only
> Iron the sky,
> The bite of wind and frost,
> Flashing bite of the axe.[8]

Geoffrey Grigson's poem, "And Forgetful of Europe," uses memory in a different fashion. It suggests, I think, a degree of responsibility and concern for Europe the magnitude of which is to be measured by the lengths to which the poem must go to forget them momentarily. The method by which oblivion is sought is the recalling of the details of a holiday in Jugoslavia. Precisely what it is the poet is bent on forgetting is not explicit: after the title come the words "Mlina 1935 to 1936"; and the poem appeared in *New Verse* (no. 30) in the summer of 1938, when anyone might wish to

7. "To a Writer on His Birthday," *New Verse,* no. 17 (October-November, 1935).
8. *Work for the Winter and Other Poems* (London: Leonard and Virginia Woolf, 1936), pp. 11-12.

forget the contemporary history that was being enacted, especially in Spain or east of the Rhine. The poet insistently marshalls his details. Like a number of other poems of Grigson's, this one begins with an imperative enlisting the sight, though it is sight-in-memory and not immediate vision that is to be called into play here: "Think now about all the things which made up/That place. . . ." Then follows the catalogue: the canoes, the market with peppers and figs, the oleanders, and old countess, and various named species of birds. These are all briefly but vividly presented in bright light; then comes a scene under the waning sun, a meal of fish, olives, and chocolate cake, bridge with the countess, and finally "forgetful of Europe" they "walked to bed/in the warm wind from the mountain." The deliberately proliferating memories are retailed with increasing excitement and pace; for the insistence on one item after another ensures the diversion of attention from memories of sights and sounds the poet is anxious to preserve his mind against. And the items are the more vivid because they are being sought as escape from horror.

Grigson has not defined any conflict in this poem, which gains some intensity from this very abstention, but the words "forgetful of Europe," in both title and body of the poem, intensify the vivid light that in thrown on all the good details. The impulse to escape is admitted; the business of the poem is transacted at a level of self-consciousness at which the Georgians did not operate: we remain aware of the subterfuge that bids us attend to the doves in the teeth of the storm and observe the swallows, with which has become associated a fear the more sinister for the intrinsic innocence and charm of the birds. Louis MacNeice provides a similarly ironic distortion of the idyllic details in the following, by the first word and by the last two lines:

> Forgetfulness: brass lamps and copper jugs
> And home-made bread and the smell of turf of flax
> And the air a glove and the water lathering easy
> And convolvulus in the hedge.
>
> Only in the dark green room beside the fire
> With the curtains drawn against the winds and waves

> There is a little box with a well-bred voice:
> What a place to talk of War.[9]

Again, Bernard Spencer in his best known poem, "Allotments: April," uses natural sights and sounds as a means of escape, consciously as Grigson does, but quite explicitly: he depicts the items of spring, asks, rather as Wordsworth does in the "Immortal Ode," "In what sense am I joining in/Such a hallooing, rousing April day," and finds that the things of April

> make a pause in
> The wireless voice repeating pacts, persecutions,
> And imprisonments and deaths and heaped violent deaths,
> Impersonal now as figures in the city news.[10]

There remain "real poverty" and "the sour doorways of the poor." April does not deny these, but the poet turns from them to relish the vitality in himself that April has brought. A recent critic remarks, "Spring is Spencer's consciousness of his own self set off against his awareness of things that call him out of himself—imprisonments and deaths' and 'real poverty'—and he sees it as part of a larger movement in the world of which he is only one inhabitant."[11] He is turning away from social and political evils, but his very art and his awareness bring them to the foreground. In another poem there is an expression of social sympathy that is the more powerful simply because Spencer says he is going to limit it. "Only for a moment," he says, in "A Cold Night," is he going to "think of those/Whom the weather leans on under the sky"; these are newsmen, whores, "the soldiery who lie/Round wounded Madrid," and other cold people; only a moment for these, because

> one needs time too to sit in peace
> Opposite one's girl . . .

9. "Cushenden," *The Collected Poems of Louis MacNeice,* ed. E. R. Dodds (New York: Oxford University Press, 1967), p. 165.

10. *Aegean Islands and Other Poems* (London: Editions Poetry London, 1946), p. 31.

11. Martin Dodsworth, "Bernard Spencer: The Poet of Addition," *the Review,* no. 11-12, p. 75.

>     ... and not be always
>     Opening one's doors on the pitiful streets
>     Of Europe. ....[12]

The human element expressed here in the less-than-heroic attitude
of the speaker persuades us of the presence of more genuine pity
and a stronger sense of responsibility than some other highly
wrought laments for the oppressed.

Ruthven Told finds refuge in the rural scene, and again it is a
perfectly conscious escape. "In September 1937," the poem that
opens the volume *Until Now,* contrasts the northern territory—
Mull or Islay—with an urban place of "thin streets" and "dull
streets." The details of the northern place are not romantically
luscious or unequivocally pleasurable: "the Atlantic's murky blue/
Swung sluggishly"; the "hills/Were brown lions, crouched to meet
the autumn gales"; there are a dead foal and rams that smashed
the fank-gate. All such disorder, however, is preferable to the
"drab newsposters" in the city, "Talking of wars, in Spain or in
the East"; he wishes he had stayed on Mull. But conflicts in Ruthven
Todd are not overwhelmingly resolved one way or the other, and
this one is not resolved in favor of the north: the conflict of place
is forgotten in matters more engrossing than either one:

>     ... we lit the fire and talked together,
>     Discussing the trivialities of a spent day
>     And what we would eat. ...
>     ....I lost my carefully-kept count
>     Of the ticks to death, and, in September, was content.[13]

The resolution and the poem's arrival at it are not dissimilar from
the equivalent things in Grigson's poem, where hard, unyielding
details of memory are amassed against, one assumes, the pressure
of bad news in the present.

In a poem about Spain, once again contrasting scenes, Todd
demonstrates the contemporary pressures of hard political and
social realities and the impulse to escape them. "It Was Easier" is

12. *Aegean Islands,* p. 30.
13. *Until Now: Poems* (London: Fortune Press, [1942], p. 7.

a poem about the map of Spain and the poet contemplating it at his ease; there are images also of the realities that exist in the territory to which the map refers. The poet loses the romantic refuge that he had created for himself and becomes imaginatively involved in the terror of the actual:

> It is easier to sail paper boats on lily-ponds,
> To plunge like a gannet in the sheltered sea,
> To go walking or to chatter with my friends
>
> Or to discuss the rare edition over tea,
> Than to travel in the mind to that place
> Where the map becomes a reality, where cracks
> Are gullies, a bullet more than half-an-inch
> Of small newsprint and the shaped grey rocks
>
> Are . . .
> . . . cover for the stoat-eyed snipers
> Whose aim is fast and seldom known to fail.
>
> (p. 22)

Escape as a subject, not the poetic creation of it, is regular in Todd: in "Poem (For C)" he sits in a "quiet spot, apart/From the turmoil of Europe" (p. 11); and he awaits the morning paper with its sorry burden. "It Was Easier" no doubt owes much to Auden's "Spain," which zeroes in on the map, without indeed ever enduring Todd's final imaginative experience: "I was quite happy dreaming and had no fear;/But now, from the map, a gun is aimed at me."

The development away from Georgianism, a development that is characteristic of the poetry of the decade, can be seen *in parvo* in the body of John Lehmann's verse. Early, his poems consist of nature description in and for itself, sometimes strongly reminiscent of the Georgians:

> Our throats were dry (all day the sun had burned),
> When, hearing feet that crunched the path, we turned,
> And there, against a forest of sweet-pea,
> Orinda came, with apricots for three.[14]

14. "Phoebe in America," *A Garden Revisited and Other Poems* (London: Hogarth, 1931), p. 50.

But before long, in his next volume in fact, *The Noise of History,*[15] images of the countryside are remembered for the now familiar remedial purpose—as antidote for the thoughts of "gathered armies, the machine guns," the noises of history, in a word, that bedeviled the consciousness of the age (p. 13). In "The Door Flies Open," on the other hand, the "comfort of busy streets, and flowers, and the flush/Of morning over belfries" are of no avail before the nightmare terrors of torture. It is an indecisive conflict in Lehmann: whether the poet's sensuous hold on the things around him or his memory of them—things either traditionally poetic or merely neutral—will suffice to hold at bay the contemporary horrors being enacted in Europe. Lehmann had learned from Edward Thomas the good effects to be derived from the presentation of rich catalogues of rural particulars in the conversational rhythms that Thomas himself had learned from Robert Frost. And what F. R. Leavis claimed for Thomas, that the exquisite particularity distinguished his work from Georgian nature poetry, could be claimed for Lehmann too in his later work. In any case, he is always conscious of the suffering in Europe: a number of his poems are apt to present first a "poetic" scene—a sunlit scene perhaps, or a series of images of the withdrawn good life; then they proceed to balance the good with sobering thoughts of violence, of social inequity, political threatening or imprisonments, and the shedding of blood. In "The Young Girl to Her Lover" the legitimate pleasures of the good life are dramatically confronted by political evil. "Do not pretend the world is in this room," says the girl, for she knows there are other commitments:

> I know your eyes; and morning through the window
> Reveals again within their blue-green caves
> Deep lights that do not burn for me: the words
> Are hunger and injustice and misrule,
> I spell them for you like a rival's name. . . .

(p. 39)

15. (London: Leonard and Virginia Woolf, 1934).

The conflict is that which Bernard Spencer faced when he deliberately controlled the degree to which he might let misfortune invade
his private pleasures.

The conflict between escape and commitment is once again
explicit in Rex Warner's first volume of poems: he experiences
guilt in his enjoyment of nature: in the opening sonnet of *Poems*[16]
(retained in the same position in the revised volume[17]), entitled
simply "Sonnet," he celebrates briefly the *douceur de la vivre*
associated with lambs, streams, the early thrush, mountains, and
stars. "But me my blood binds to remember man/more than birds,"
he goes on.

> Nor will my mind permit me to linger in the love,
> the motherkindness of country among ascending trees,
> knowing that love must be liberated by bleeding,
> fearing for my fellows, for the murder of man.

Stephen Spender's comment on the excesses of will in Warner's
poems is exaggerated: "He never looks at a bird or a berry or
cracks a joke without one feeling behind his lines the pressure of a
conscience determined to draw a moral and exploit a meaning."[18]
But Warner himself has said that when he tries something purely
descriptive like some of the poems on birds, "all sorts of other
things get in";[19] and we do indeed find injected into the bird poems
a melancholy not proper to their subject.

It was strictly against the principles of the men of the thirties to
fade far away into the sylvan primitivism and even temporarily
forget. Life was, after all, a social matter, to communists absolutely
and to the others to varying degrees. And engagement with the
sorrows of others became a necessary aesthetic quality, attested
to by the frequency with which poets quoted the lines from Keats's
*Hyperion*. Poetry of the highest quality could not be oblivious to
men's suffering. At the same time not all poets felt as Randall
Swingler did, that natural scenery was tolerable only as part of an

16. (London: Boriswood, 1937).
17. *Poems and Contradictions* (London: John Lane, The Bodley Head, 1945).
18. *Left Review* 3 (July 1937), 358-59.
19. *The Poet Speaks,* ed. Peter Orr (New York: Barnes and Noble, 1966), p. 262.

all-encompassing world view.[20] And aspects of the English country-side do feature as subjects for their own sake in poems that it is not always easy to distinguish from those included in Edward Marsh's anthologies.

Julian Bell's first volume, *Winter Movement,* is introduced with a poem of homage to Richard Jefferies, whose stories embodying faithful descriptions of the English countryside used to be read regularly by English children. The poem begins with Bell's indebtedness:

> You are our master, and to you
> I bring these poems. If they hold
> Some pale, faint beauty, it is due
> To gleams of your remembered gold.[21]

It closes, "The seasons . . . prepare our English paradise." Most of the volume is devoted to minute and accurate descriptions of various parts of this paradise. Bell has captured certain of the sights and sounds of the countryside with a fidelity that reminds one of D. H. Lawrence—Lawrence at his most perceptive in the *Birds, Beasts and Flowers* volume. Chaffinches, for one example out of many, are in fact exactly as Bell has seen them, in the poem so titled:

> Strong beak, bright eye, high forehead's almost crest,
> Rounded curve of a down soft, brick-red, cherry breast,
>   Apple lichen green, from nape
> Slate blue, the mantle's shoulder'd shape.
>   Black wire, neat
>   Stiff legs and feet.

Whatever the merit of the poetry, the detail is perfect. As this sample suggests, these descriptive poems are hard and virile, a quality possessed by the descriptions in Jefferies. The countryside they reflect is itself not luxurious. The poems are saved from being flat description by the varieties of meter and by their intensity.

20. "History and the Poet," *New Writing* 3, n.s. (Christmas 1939), 53.
21. *Winter Movement and Other Poems* (London: Chatto and Windus, 1930), p. 9.

Michael Roberts remarks of Bell that he writes "of the English countryside in rhythms which show that for him it means no weekend cottage or funk-hole from the town: his clearest delineations of landscape express . . . a feeling for the land itself. . . ."[22] This attributes an unduly specific meaning to rhythms; but Roberts's general drift is acceptable: unlike the Georgians, as characterized, Bell is not asking for peace and quiet.

The title poem of Julian Bell's first book, "Winter Movement," is designated "A Formal Ode," and the poet announces that "the metre of two stanzas [is] imitated from Gerard Manley Hopkins." The poem presents vignettes from the winter scene in various metrical arrangements. For much of his boyhood, Julian Bell lived at the foot of the range of hills in Sussex known as the Downs, a particularly beautiful part of a county generally beautiful. That he should wish to embody its sights and sounds in poetry, putting them to no impressive moral purpose, is natural enough. The poems of natural description, however, have a further, a Wordsworthian kind of significance. In presenting these scenes, Bell is writing out of his strong conviction, later expressed in a poem called "Autobiography,"[23] that his "country years" were a "central and certain and undoubted good" and that they had provided him with a positive moral belief about life that no future disaster or distress would be able to undermine:

> Whatever games there now remain to play
> Of love or war, of ruin or revolt,
> I cannot quite admit that world's decay
> Or undespairing wish it on its way.

These lines, written much later than the *Winter Movement* poems, explain somewhat the intense detailed appreciation of the rural scene that appears in the latter.

Of the nature verse of Clere Parsons, the friend and contemporary of Auden and the others at Oxford, who, doomed to an early

22. "Preface," *New Signatures*, p. 17.
23. *Work for the Winter and Other Poems* (London: Leonard and Virginia Woolf, 1936), p. 16.

death, "was eager above all to be contemporary,"[24] one might say what one says of Bell's—that he shows no Georgian instinct for retreat from anything in his densely packed descriptions of natural things:

> Wood ways shall soon be
> smelling earthy-clean

> And here is the generous
> almond tree whose pink
> Victorian skirt primly resists the wind. . . .[25]

Or:

> Flystung in pools kneedeep
> to cool their hooves
> Indolent and immobile the
> cows brood
> Or lazily raise listlessly
> swish
> And droop
> their tails. . . .[26]

That is nearer to E. E. Cummings, whose method he was in fact fumbling for,[27] than to Marsh's people.

In spite of the general reaction against it, the Georgian mode persisted here and there both in the passive acceptance of the rural scene and in the supineness of the style at its worst, as for example Andrew Young, who frequently presented nature in anthropomorphic terms. The Georgian mode persisted also, curiously enough, in poets who were obviously consciously interested in style. Edgar Foxall, who studded his verse with passages derived from *The Hollow Men*, could write in the characteristically vague Georgian manner:

24. Louis MacNeice, *The Strings are False: An Unfinished Autobiography* (New York: Oxford University Press, 1966), p. 114.
25. "Suburban Nature Piece," *Poems* (London: Faber and Faber, 1932), p. 11.
26. "Photogravure," *Poems*, p. 13.
27. As he informed MacNeice. *The Strings are False*, p. 114.

> There is a sense of elation in the warm air,
> A sense of rest among the lonely trees;
> There is the peace of darkness in the brown pond. . . .[28]

Then, although much later, there is David Gascoyne who, after experimenting with surrealism and surrealist effects and strong rhetoric, resorts at length to lines that would not have seemed incongruous in one of the Georgian anthologies.

When Charles Madge declared that the separatists were returning, he excepted Stephen Spender on account of lines that repudiate the city in favor of the country and strongly suggest the Georgian cop-out: "The city builds its horror in my brain./This writing is my only wings away," which come from No. XXI of *Poems, 1933.*[29] But in this matter as in many others, Spender is ambivalent: in the same volume he includes "I hear the cries of evening," which had appeared first in *Twenty Poems, 1930,* and which, as F. R. Leavis properly observed, is a Georgian poem:

> I hear the cries of evening, while the paw
> Of dark creeps up the turf;
> Sheep's bleating, swaying gulls' cry, the rook's caw,
> The hammering surf.
>
> . . . . . . . . . . . . . . . . .
>
> Town-bred, I feel the roots of each earth-cry
> Tear me apart.[30]

The city in the poem Madge quotes, however, is more metaphorical than literal: "at corners of day/Road drills explore new areas of pain"; furthermore, in one or two other places in the same volume Spender makes it clear that he recognizes the unreality of the traditional delights of the countryside and is prepared to spurn them in favor of reality or in order to second responsible urban progress. In "The Pylons," that celebrated piece concerning which

---

28. "Poem," *Water-Rat Sonata and Other Poems* (London: Fortune Press, n.d. [1940]), p. 35.

29. "Without that once clear aim, the path of flight," *Poems* (London: Faber and Faber, 1933), p. 35.

30. *Poems, 1933,* p. 16.

Spender speaks in the *Collected Poems,* of an "obligation to 'own up,'" he is at some pains to praise these ugly constructions at the expense of the old, good country features that they despoil and to which we are conventionally attracted—the stone, the "crumbling roads", the "sudden hidden villages." These are "mocked dry" and dwarfed, and the secret of the hills is betrayed by the pylons, "the concrete / That trails black wire," where "Like whips of anger/ With lightning's danger / There runs the quick perspective of the future." Once again, the poet unwittingly captures our sympathy for the traditionally poetic, which looks better than the new-fangled apparatus, the monstrous appearance of which is made worse, if that were possible, by the simile that compares its structures and their stance to "nude, giant girls that have no secret" (p. 47). Rhetorically the poet is instructing us otherwise, however: we must do as Stephen says, not as Stephen does. The other poem to be mentioned in this connection is "At the end of two months' holiday," in which the traditional beauty of the countryside is pitted to its disadvantage against the iron railway lines: The poet is dreaming that he is looking from a train:

> Like the quick spool of a film
> I watched hasten away the simple green which can heal
> All sadness. Abruptly the sign *Ferry to Wilm*
> And the cottage by the lake, were vivid, but unreal.

The countryside, the scene of the weekend escape of the bourgeoisie and of the Georgian picnic is declared unreal; the train, symbolizing progress and the "iron time," is real enough:

> Real were iron lines, and, smashing the grass
> The cars in which we ride, and real our compelled time:
> Painted on enamel beneath the moving glass
> Unreal were cows, those wave-winged storks, the lime. . . .[31]

It is odd to think of Spender's bringing himself to utter sentiments that come naturally to William Carlos Williams, to whom in temperament he was a polar opposite. In one essay Williams

31. *Poems,* 2d ed. (London: Faber and Faber, 1934), p. 16.

celebrates the Ajax Aniline Dye Works and sneers at the popular habit of taking the car out into the country, "To 'nature' to breathe her good air. Jesus Christ."[32] The two poems of Spender, while once again they arise from his own peculiar conflict, are at the same time minor documents in the contemporary repudiation of the Georgian idyll.

32. *Selected Essays* (New York: Random House, 1954), p. 66.

5

# Observations

Withdrawal into nature as an escape was *passé* for the thirties
people, but the observation of nature or other phenomena in the
solid physical world with a view to creating poetic observation,
being a more or less permanent poetic procedure everywhere, was,
of course, widely practiced. A substantial number of the poets of
the decade, as of any other, knew no substitute for sense and
offered vivid visible reports in their poems, of this and that object or
event; and sometimes the question was raised, as it should be
raised now, as to whether such observation was, in fact, used
poetically, or whether it was a mere reflection of things and nothing
more, like some of those little poems that appeared under the
permissive dispensation of Amy Lowell's brand of imagism or the red
wheelbarrow of William Carlos Williams, the most over-celebrated
vehicle in literary history.

One phenomenon of the times that was deliberately intended to be no more than a mere reflection of things was the products of Mass Observation; it was not poetry, but it was claimed that it would benefit poetry, and its main sponsor was a poet. In the words of Charles Madge, who with Tom Harrisson was its organizer, Mass Observation was "a technique for obtaining objective statements about human behavior."[1] Observers might send in, for example, a minute account of the behavior of a bus conductor at work or accounts of the way people all over Great Britain celebrated the coronation.[2] The interchange of observations was considered to be "the foundation of social consciousness." But the process was also to have usefulness in poetic matters: the observations, it was claimed, were to "produce a poetry which is not, as at present, restricted to a handful of esoteric performers. The immediate effect of MASS-OBSERVATION is to de-value considerably the status of the 'poet.' It makes the term 'poet' apply, not to his performance, but to his profession, like 'footballer.'"[3] Julian Symons was quoted to the effect that "Every poet is an *unconscious* mass-observer."[4] The process of observing raises the observer from subjectivity to objectivity.

Part of the difficulty in obtaining data, this elevation not being instantaneous, was, of course, the subjective part of the observer, who would use a style "incorporating social fantasy representative of his class environment." The reviewer for *Left Review* found, as might be expected, that the working-class observers were far more objective than the intellectuals.[5] In order to focus on the social fantasy, however, Madge and others carried out an experiment on

1. Charles Madge, "Poetic Description and Mass Observation," *New Verse*, no. 24 (Feb.–March 1937), p. 3.
2. Suggestions for further topics for observation sent in by observers included vaccination, anti-semitism, behavior at war memorials, quick and slow walkers, litter, smoking ("Note *when* people start smoking; what were they speaking about when they produced cigarettes"), depilation, gestures and shouts of motorists. Charles Madge and Tom Harrisson, *Mass Observation* (London: Frederick Muller, 1937), p. 59.
3. *New Verse*, no. 24 (Feb.-March 1937), p. 3.
4. Francis Scarfe, "Introduction," *Auden and After: The Liberation of Poetry, 1930–1941* (London: Routledge, 1942), p. xii.
5. Maurice Richardson, *Left Review* 3 (Nov. 1937): 625.

"the dominant image of the day," producing the phenomenon of the Oxford Collective Poem. Twelve undergraduates each reported the image that had most occupied them during the day, each day for three weeks. They selected the six images that appeared most, and then they each composed a single pentameter for each image; they selected the best of these. Then the lines were integrated into a unified poem, and finally emendations were made by all. The poem that emerged, Madge said, was much more a collective account of Oxford than an account by any single person in the group. It was claimed, in a word, to be an objective observation. It bore witness, Madge said, to the sense of decay and doom, responsibility and responsibility neglected. It is not a bad effusion; it is superior, I believe (as an act of faith, perhaps), to "The Meditation of IBM 7094–7040DCS."[6] The first stanza is as follows:

> Believe the iron saints who stride the floods
> Lying in red and labouring for the dawn:
> Steeples repeat their warnings; along the roads
> Memorials stand, of children force has slain;
> Expostulating with the winds they hear
> Stone kings irresolute on a marble stair.[7]

The medium in which these reports on Mass Observation and the Oxford Poem appeared was *New Verse*. *New Verse* was a "poem periodical" which ran from January 1933, to May 1939, and, except for the last two issues, could be purchased every two months for sixpence, "the price of ten Players." It was by far the most engaging and vivacious literary periodical of its day, and, no doubt, of many another day too. Its editor was Geoffrey Grigson; his poetry and criticism reveal an extraordinarily acute ear, as well as broad and intelligent perception in many areas, and an independent mind. His comments in reviews and in occasional editorials were instructive, sometimes a little over-strenuous, and sometimes refreshingly rude. Mostly straightforward, they fall, occasionally, a

6. For this prodigy, see Marie Borroff, "Computer as Poet," *Yale Alumni Magazine* 34 (January 1971): 22–25.
7. This account of the poem is taken from "The Oxford Collective Poem," *New Verse*, no. 25 (May 1937), pp. 17–19.

little short of clarity because of the refinement of the sentiment they are expressing.

*New Verse* had no political obligations; in *The Long Weekend,* Robert Graves and Alan Hodge say of this review that "it advanced no political theory. Its policy was to publish poems that dealt with observations of real objects. The observations were in general listed impressionistically and tagged with the appropriate revolutionary feelings excited in the poet by them."[8] Observations, there were, certainly; but revolutionary feelings are, in fact, rarely expressed in *New Verse.* It announced in its second number that it had no politics; "If there must be attitudes, a reasoned attitude of toryism is welcomed no less than a communist attitude."[9] Though if anything its bias was left, it was far from being partial to revolutionary poetry, as Graves and Hodge suggest; it was, as a matter of fact, reproved by a writer in Moscow[10] for Catholic propaganda about Gerard Manley Hopkins, for entering a bloc with French surrealists, and for hounding C. Day Lewis for "an excess of Communist loyalty."

*New Verse* was originated in order to provide space in which poets of its time might be published, good poets of course. In its last issue, Grigson declared that it "came into existence because of Auden." Auden was Grigson's favorite: the periodical published more poems by him than by any other poet. Louis MacNeice came a close second. Others published included Bernard Spencer, Charles Madge, Ruthven Todd, Norman Cameron, C. Day Lewis, Dylan Thomas, Rex Warner, George Barker, Gavin Ewart, Randall Swingler, William Empson, R. B. Fuller, Kenneth Allott, Bernard Gutteridge, A. J. M. Smith, Herbert Read, Edwin Muir, K. J. Raine, and Stephen Spender; better, perhaps, to say who of that British generation now remembered was not represented by a specimen of his verse: Roy Campbell; John Lehmann. Of Americans represented there were John Crowe Ransom, Allen Tate, Frederic Prokosch, Archibald MacLeish, Theodore Roethke (4 lines), Oscar Williams.

8. Robert Graves and Alan Hodge, *The Long Weekend: A Social History of Great Britain 1918–1939* (London: Faber and Faber, 1940), p. 300.

9. "Politics: And a Request, " *New Verse,* no. 2 (March 1933), p. 1.

10. D. Mirsky, *International Literature,* no. 10 (1936). Reported in "New Verse Goes Trotskyite?" *New Verse,* no. 23 (Christmas 1936), p. 24.

*New Verse* reviewing was trenchant: Roy Campbell's *Flowering Rifle*, 1939, it says, "sounds like a hyena, ambitious to be a lion, howling away to itself (and to Mr. Edmund Blunden, who has crept out of his hole to praise it) in the middle of a lonely and extensive sewage farm."[11] It reminds us in another place that one should realize "the downright badness of Day Lewis's verse, in manner and totality of manner and meaning."[12] Of George Barker, Grigson wrote: "Why has anyone published, does anyone praise, does anyone read, the verse of Mr. George Barker?..."[13] Randall Swingler, Grigson found dull and ill-read, and he thought he should "give up poetry for politics or prose."[14] Rayner Heppenstall was "absolutely a BORE." Persons and institutions in more or less perpetual editorial umbrage included the Georgians and the BBC, Edmund Blunden, Sir John Squire and *The London Mercury* of which he was editor and which had been host to the Georgians, the literary phalanx of *The New Statesman and Nation,* Clive Bell and the "Bloomsburies," St. John Ervine, and *Poetry* (Chicago), of which Grigson asks, "Why not die?"

Later, in his autobiography,[15] Grigson regretted some of the asperity of his *New Verse* dicta. Surely no one else did, except perhaps Dame Edith Sitwell, who, under the nickname "The Old Jane," was the most frequent target for the *gamin* stone-throwing of *New Verse,* presumably because she was more deserving than other available candidates. Quite frequently her dicta, taken out of context (though context would scarcely have saved them) and used as fillers, contributed to the verve that the pages of this periodical never lacked: under the title, "Spare Parts," "'... my senses are like those of primitive peoples, at once acute and uncovered—and they are interchangeable.' The Old Jane."[16] Under the title

11. "Rum Tum Tum on a Broken Drum," *New Verse* 1, n.s. (May 1939): 54.
12. "New Verse Goes Trotskyite," p. 24.
13. "Nertz," *New Verse,* no. 15 (June 1935), pp. 17–18 ("Nertz" is polite for nuts, with its anatomical meaning).
14. "Two First Books," *New Verse,* no. 7 (February 1934), p. 20.
15. *The Crest on the Silver: An Autobiography* (London: Cresset, 1950), p. 162. See also for afterthoughts about *New Verse,* "A Conversation With Geoffrey Grigson," *the Review,* no. 22 (June 1970), pp. 18–19 and *passim.*
16. No. 22 (Aug.–September 1936), p. 19.

"Cuckoo," "'I was born by the wildest seas that England knows
. . .' The Old Jane."[17] Grigson's first volume of poems, *Several
Observations,*[18] was dedicated "For Bertschy. And on second
thoughts, also for my publicity manager, Edith Sitwell, with love
and thanks." Julian Symons, editor of *Twentieth Century Verse,*
also made use of Sitwellisms for fillers, printing occasional oddities
from Edith and her brothers. The following "Note on Eminence,"
though it has been quoted before, is as Symons said, "too good
to be lost" and is worth reproducing here:

> *The New Coterie* (no. 1, Nov. 1935) printed this letter, in reply
> to a circular sent out to a number of writers and artists, asking
> them to send work:
> "Sir,
>     I am requested by Miss Edith Sitwell to return the enclosed
> communication, which was doubtless sent to her by mistake.
> Writers of Miss Sitwell's standing do not 'submit' their works
> for approval. . . . Miss Sitwell asks me to assure you that she does
> not suspect you of deliberate bad manners; your mistake is
> possibly the result of lack of experience in dealing with writers of
> eminence.
>
> Yours faithfully,<br>M. Grogan.<br>(for Miss Sitwell)."
>
> This is much too good to be lost.[19]

As Robin Skelton remarks, "Miss Sitwell presented to the public
an image of the poet which was far more effective theatrically than
anything a thirties man could dare to invent, and also opposed in
every way to that image of the poet in society which the thirties
generation was busy trying to clarify."[20] She was useful as a symbol
for the outmoded, the alexandrian, and the precious, as is suggested

    17. No. 21 (June–July 1938), p. 22.
    18. *Several Observations: Thirty-Five Poems* (London: Cresset, [1938]).
    19. *Twentieth Century Verse,* no. 10 (May 1938), p. 45. Quoted by Robin Skelton,
Introduction to *Poetry of the Thirties* (Harmondsworth, Middlesex: Penguin Books,
1964), pp. 28–29.
    20. Skelton, p. 29.

by the reviewer in *Twentieth Century Verse* who designates the phrase *husky sunsets,* in a poem of Laura Riding's, as "a mescaline Edithism."[21]

A number of the people Grigson criticized so severely were contributors, some of them regular contributors to *New Verse*. The question, "Why has anyone published George Barker?" he should have addressed to himself, as in a later comment he shows himself to have been aware. But nobody was sacrosanct; even Auden was not quite unscathed by magisterial disfavor, though the criticism in this case is carefully tempered: on his acceptance of the Royal Medal for poetry, "We rather regret that Mr. Auden has taken it. . . ."[22] On account of his remarks about the painter William Coldstream, Grigson tactfully recommends that Auden keep quiet.[23]

Grigson's praise, however, could be no less intense than his blame. Here are parts of a tribute to Auden:

I do not know any poems written in the last forty years by Yeats, or Eliot, or any Englishman which are superior to some of the best of Auden's recent poems. . . .

[T]here are many people who might quote of Auden: *"To you I owe the first development of my imagination; to you I owe the withdrawing of my mind from the low brutal part of my nature, to the lofty, the pure and the perpetual."* Auden is . . . something good and creative in European life in a time of the very greatest evil.[24]

The second paragraph quoted must be one of the most extraordinary accolades in literary criticism. And Auden was shortly to write, "Poetry makes nothing happen!"

21. Hugh Gordon Porteus, "Reading and Riding," *Twentieth Century Verse,* no. 14 (December 1938), p. 131.

22. "Remarks," *New Verse,* no. 28 (Jan. 1938), p. 14. Later, Grigson sent Auden to Coventry for the offense of the medal!

23. "Remarks on Painting and Mr. Auden, " *New Verse* 1, n.s. (January 1939): 18.

24. "Twenty Seven Sonnets," review of Auden's sonnets in *Journey to a War* by W. H. Auden and Christopher Isherwood (London: Faber and Faber, 1939), *New Verse* 1, n.s. (May 1939): 49.

In his autobiography, Stephen Spender recalls that early on he had differed from Auden in their concepts of poetry:

> When Auden said at one of our earliest meetings, "The subject of a poem is a peg to hang the poetry on," he had indicated what I gradually realized to be another basic difference between our attitudes. For I could not accept the idea that the poetic experience in reality, which led into a poem, was then, as it were, left behind, while the poem developed according to verbal needs of its own which had no relation to the experience.[25]

This makes curious reading now, because the attitude attributed to Auden here better fits Spender's work and the one Spender claims for himself fits Auden's. Auden, for his part, reviewing Herbert Read's book on Shelley, declares that he expects literature to have "plenty of news" in it, and that a lack of interest in objects of the outside world is destructive.[26] "News," in Auden's early poems at least, as has often been remarked, easily becomes symbol or synecdoche.

The predilection for news and objects, among many other features, appealed no doubt to Geoffrey Grigson. His own first volume of poems announced on its dust jacket that he had "always favoured a poetry *about objects* and poets who mention things"; "his own poems," the blurb says, "are objective reporting."[27] This is, no doubt, a publisher's simplification; Grigson writes as follows:

> There is a world outside and there is a world inside, a world of objects and a world of the traditions and achievements and phantasies of the mind. It is impossible for a writer to acknowledge only the exterior world, or only the interior world; and it is fatal to treat the exterior world as a kind of handwriting, the

---

25. *World Within World: The Autobiography of Stephen Spender* (London: Hamish Hamilton, 1951), p. 59.

26. "Psychology and Criticism," *New Verse,* no. 20, (April–May 1936), p. 24.

27. Quoted from Roy Fuller, "Poems by Editors," *Twentieth Century Verse,* no. 17 (April/May 1934), p. 25.

only use of which is to make the interior world legible. The world of objects is our constant discipline.[28]

Grigson's admiration for Louis MacNeice springs similarly from this poet's abilities as a poetic observer. MacNeice believed that the poet's first business was mentioning things; he had a marvelous sense for living among concrete objects. Love called him to the things of this world, he preferred Aristotle to Plato, and his poetry celebrates not *mere* things but things in their human relations, though to say so is perhaps to say no more than that he was a poet.

In 1938 Grigson was willing to allow that in some ways MacNeice was superior to Auden: he had more style; "there is no other poet in England who is such a good *writer* (Auden may be on a bigger scale altogether, but at present he does very often make a mannerism of his own inventions)." These discriminations are made in a review of *The Earth Compels,* which reveals a little of what lies behind Grigson's approval. MacNeice's earliest poems, Grigson thought, were unattractive: "they shone with a bric-a-brac gleam." They suggested that the poet might have followed the Sitwells or the Bloomsbury circle. But he "had enough morality for his elegance. He was intelligent. He could see and sense things with too much passion." Grigson says, you can't see "a rhododendron or a word clearly and then hobnob with Miss Sitwell or Mrs. Woolf for very long; and perhaps the more passionately you see things without twist or mistake the lonelier you are, and need to remain." His poems are "the experiences of a lonely contemplative person, occupied with himself and with the world we share, with his environment of colour and shape"; they are marked by "the certainty and peculiarity and delicacy of the rhythm."[29]

There are various ways in which observations of the world may be made poetic; there is, for one thing, a difference in the degree to which, of themselves, they speak; and these considerations as

28. "Lonely, But Not Lonely Enough," *New Verse,* nos. 31 and 32 (Autumn 1938), p. 16.
29. "New Poems by MacNeice and Prokosch," *New Verse,* no. 30 (Summer 1938), pp. 17 and 18.

they apply to Spender's contemporaries are glanced at below. The idiom may vary between one critic and another. Grigson rightly recognizes the danger of preciosity in the early verse that might have led MacNeice into the Sitwell orbit, where Grigson, with his intense dislike of aestheticism, would not want him to be. "And we dally and dip our spoons in the golden tea," for example, a line taken from what MacNeice subsequently called juvenilia. Grigson, who is strongly affected by the niceties of rhythm, is right also about its importance in MacNeice. MacNeice was master of both rhyme and rhythm, and he could make extraordinary gains from their use and also from declining their use at the right moment: the avoiding of an expected rhyme or an expected pause— the use of enjambement, for instance—has an effect on this poet's voice like that of the sudden cessation of all other conversation in a room. One example, because the effect has sometimes been destroyed in reprinting by the addition of a period, may be quoted; that is the lovely enjambement across the break between the last two stanzas of "The Sunlight on the Garden":

> The earth compels
> We are dying, Egypt, dying
>
> And not expecting pardon,
> Hardened in heart anew. . . .[30]

MacNeice was able to get this and other kinds of striking effect with rhyme or rhythm.

There is a good deal of objective reporting in Grigson's own poems. Roy Fuller, reviewing his first volume, *Several Observations*,[31] says that Grigson arrays objects as in a catalogue and not organized as a poem: "they are interesting and significant in their uniqueness (shape, colour, price, utility) or in their relation to the other items (the 1d. black followed by the $1\frac{1}{2}$d. magenta). Ultimately this sort of poetry is a private poetry. . . ."[32] There is some-

30. *The Earth Compels* (London: Faber and Faber, 1938), p. 10.
31. *Several Observations: Thirty Five Poems* (London: Cresset, 1938).
32. Roy Fuller, "Poems by Editors," *Twentieth Century Verse*, no. 17 (April / May 1939), pp. 24–26.

thing in this. Possibly Grigson veers toward the excessively specific and thus the somewhat private image in his distaste for the trite and the obvious (which he condemns in Rex Warner and Randall Swingler respectively[33]). When he offers the items of a catalogue, however, there is occasionally an explicit comment, or an oblique one arising from nuances provided by rhythm or tone, which must not be missed. "Each poem," says Grigson, "was made vocally aloud, was made as a unit of personal speech for reading and feeling aloud."[34] At the same time, his predilection for painting would make him sympathetic to a poetic kind in which all the ideas were in things: in the preface to his *Collected Poems*, he says

> such a remark as "A white stone," by itself or extended into a poem isn't necessarily either *description* or *nature verse*. Images (so I think) should retract into themselves, be involved in themselves, and shouldn't be extended too much into explanation—a white stone *because it is hard, heavy, white, conspicuous, dead, lonely, cold, different, indifferent*, et cetera, et cetera.[35]

Conrad Aiken, scorning the poetic code in which the "I" is lost and subjectivity is taboo, quotes a sentence of Grigson's and attributes it to a complete psychological misunderstanding. Grigson had called on poets to avoid "that poetic inflation, which follows when a poet mistakes the product of the conflicts in himself for the gift, inspired in him, mysteriously, by some outside agent."[36] Aiken remarks: "the poor ego, with its conflicts—that actual *fons et origo* of *everything*, absolutely everything—is set up as a sort of anathema or antichrist."[37]

Grigson's verse, whatever his precepts, is richer in ego than this. There are a number of poems that are almost or exclusively pure

33. G. E. G., "Rex Warner," *New Verse*, no. 28 (Jan. 1938), p. 22 and "Two First Books," *New Verse*, no. 7 (February 1934), p. 20.
34. Preface to *Collected Poems of 1924–1962* (London: Phoenix House, 1963), p. 7.
35. *Collected Poems of 1924–1962*, p. 7.
36. "Preface" *New Verse Anthology* (London: Faber and Faber, 1939), p. 15.
37. Conrad Aiken, "Back to Poetry," *Collected Criticism*, ed. Rufus A. Blanshard (New York: Oxford University Press, 1968), p. 99.

scene, relaxed and casual disseminations of details, the importance of the physical sensibility being notified by frequent imperatives, like "See," "O watch," "Consider," or "Complete the natural history of this view." But at the same time these are *made* poems: they don't bear evidence of the uncut edges of reality as the poems of D. H. Lawrence often do or those of William Carlos Williams. Grigson's comment about the latter distinguishes them from his own: "not poems, but little knocked off bits of unmade poems."[38]

Frequently enough, Grigson's own poems make a comment by means of the observations. The comment may be only in the title, or it may, as mentioned, be distilled in its minor nonrhetorical features. "The Non-Interveners" has three short sections: the first describes features of two English statesmen: one "with the second/and a half chin and his heart-shaped mind/hanging on his thin watch-chain"; the other "with gout who shaves low on his holly-stem neck." The second section presents a few natural details of Spain—things that remain as they are: olives, trees, sea-hedgehogs; and also some things that the war has ravaged: "the arterial blood/squirting into the curious future." The third section describes the English newspaper, "with its/indifferent headline, its news from our own/correspondent away from the fighting"; and it presents some of the familiar things of nature—trees and birds. "Non-Intervention" was the term used to describe the much-debated British policy with regard to the Spanish Civil War, and non-intervention statesmen were the frequent victims of leftist satire[39] and abuse. Here the term covers not only statesmen but natural things too, even shed blood. And the juxtaposition of these things provides the comment. The poem appears in the same volume as "And Forgetful of Europe," in which we have seen the wealth of implicit meaning arising from the observed details.

There are other poems of Grigson's in which the meaning to be elicited from the catalogues is in doubt or is subject to change. In "Ucello on the Heath," what we may call the donnée may give

---

38. "Two Poets," *New Verse,* no. 8, (April 1934), p. 18.
39. An eminent example is Edgell Rickword's poem, "To the Wife of Any Non-Intervention Statesman," *Poems for Spain* (London: Hogarth, 1939), p. 74.

rise to a pastoral scene or, with "analysis" to a "rich battle scene."[40]
"Under the Cliff: November" begins with the display of buddleia
and Michaelmas daisies, and the tassels of a table cloth, but develops
into a terrifying cry for help against the grotesque forces of the
mind that corrupt what is sweet and trivial.[41]

The poetization of objects persists with strange and compelling
effectiveness into a series of love poems, *Legenda Suecana,*[42]
addressed to Suzanne. Perhaps these are a product of Grigson's
own voice along with the influences of *Modern Love* and John
Donne. (Today they are a little reminiscent of W. D. Snodgrass's
*Heart's Needle,* itself reminiscent of Meredith.) In many of the
poems it is once again the details of the scene that give the action
or the sentiment its poignance. Or they may give even more, as
when the poet, called upon to "Describe Suzanne" in the fourth
poem, "The Room," appeals not to "red nailed hands / Or brushed
back hair," but to "some room / That lacks you where I wait."
Objects here, clearly, present meaning not immediately (as would
the nails and hair) but by indirection.

In reviewing Grigson's poems, Roy Fuller was conscious of the
problem adumbrated above: when does the observation of detail
become poetic observation? In Fuller's own poems, one is aware
of a concern along these lines. In the first volume, *Poems,*[43] many
of them, short or long, have a narrative content. And they show
something of the influences of Graves and Auden, though perhaps
the Graves influence is at second hand, Fuller having recently
remarked that it was "the talented imitator [Norman Cameron]
who struck home rather than the more elderly original."[44] The
Graves-Cameron influence is to be observed partly in the grotesque
and sinister material, in an occasional allegory or nightmare, and
partly in the terse, close-lipped voice—the short, unjoined staccato
clauses—that Fuller occasionally uses. Poem Number II describes

40. *Several Observations,* p. 15.
41. *Under the Cliff and Other Poems* (London: Routledge, 1943), p. 34.
42. Twenty five copies printed for the author by Chiswick Press, London, 1953.
43. Roy Fuller, *Poems* (London: Fortune Press, [1940]).
44. "Norman Cameron—Four Views," *the Review,* nos. 27–28 (Autumn–Winter
1971–72), p. 18.

in eight lines how a murdered man had been "rumoured up again";
then the corpse is exhumed and found "lying with the rumour,
murdered." In Poem no. VI, a man travels all day to a tumbledown
Gothic mansion, which he enters to wrestle with a fiend; in another
poem a thriller writer (such as Fuller himself is) smooths his hair
and finds his hand smeared with crimson. In Poem no. XI the
noble JA, a figure like one of Graves's grotesques, sits "Bearded
with seaweed and his elephant's legs/Crossed in the droppings."
Graves's terse voice is heard thus in Fuller:

> The leader denied his men were discontented:
> He'd doled them riches from the latest spoil,
> A few lieutenants rented private villas,
> And lusty shouts of greeting showed control.[45]

It is in Fuller's second and third volumes, *The Middle of a War*[46]
and *A Lost Season*,[47] that the role of the observation is called in
question. There are a number of sketches and extended descriptions
of war scenes; among the latter are scenes from Africa (including
the animals), where Fuller served. Often the comment that concludes such descriptions is minimal. But there is a strong sense of
the shame and the boredom and the terror of war, and this sense is
evoked to some extent by Fuller's admitted failure to find images
for it. In "The Coast" after a series of bright images, the poet says,
"... I think of things/For which these are inadequate images."
Then follows another bright image, and then:

> There is no substitute for the harsh and terrible
> Facts of the time, which only longing
> And sadness cloak,
> And which have grown meaningless and commonplace.[48]

Even earlier than this poem, Fuller plays with the idea that codifica-
tion by words or otherwise is a falsification: in "YMCA Writing

45. *Poems* (London: Fortune Press, 1940), p. 22.
46. (London: Hogarth Press, 1942).
47. (London: Hogarth Press, 1944).
48. *A Lost Season*, p. 41.

Room," he attributes to a map a "lying order and compression";
and at the end of the poem he says,

> These words are false as the returning Spring
> From which this March history has made subtraction:
> The spirit has gone and left the marble thing.[49]

In the same volume he is as contemptuous as Hemingway of words
like Freedom, God, and Duty—an "obscure, remote communication" perpetrated by the chaplain. Later in "Rhetoric of a Journey,"
in *Counterparts,* he confirms the sentiments about the failure of
words, and indeed art, and their betrayal of the facts, renouncing
what is neat and finished in favor of what is fragmentary, enigmatic,
or vague. Already in line with this sentiment, the verses in *Epitaphs
and Occasions* had become lighter, occasional, even trivial, nursery
rhymes, ballads, bawdry: the "obituary of R. Fuller," for example;
the secret of "Byron's foot and James's privates"; the pitch of
"Than the outlook of the ulcer/Nothing could be falser." The
shift to the fun of such things reminds us of Auden's similar relaxa-
tion in the fifties; and a remark of Fuller's in "Virtue"[50] may apply
to both: "What offends / Or kills can in its simplest ends, / Being
human, also bless." We are reminded also of the move away from
official poetry on the part of many American poets, following the
ceaseless guerrilla activity against the establishment conducted
by William Carlos Williams and his sons: the distrust of the fixed
and formal, "the cooked," as D. H. Lawrence had expressed it
much earlier; the elevation to rank and dignity of the thumbnail
sketch, the spontaneous thought unmediated through professional
tranquillity. Fuller's distrust of the formalities of art proceeds into
the later volumes, where he does not cease to employ it. But if he
condemns the distortion involved in neatness, he would still rather
have it than its romantic opposite.[51]

49. *The Middle of a War,* p. 41.
50. *Epitaphs and Occasions* (London: John Lehmann, 1949), p. 31.
51. See Ian Hamilton, review of *Buff* by Roy Fuller, *London Magazine* 5, n.s.
(June 1965): 67–70.

One poem of Fuller's that has been justly praised,[52] "The Statue," suggests a conflict between what is living and what is codified and frozen, life versus art, or history, perhaps, which is comparable with the conflict seen in the later Spender, in his poem "Returning to Vienna, 1947,"[53] between destructive life, on the one hand, and the historical art works of Vienna on the other. Spender's sympathies go, in the end, to the former, but they are balanced; Fuller's go to life. There is a statue at the entry to the harbor; it is not this, however, but a figure of a man seen by the poet, smoking and contemplating "his great wan/And dirty feet. . . ." that "dominated this sea's threshold and this night."

Bernard Spencer, published frequently in *New Verse,* is a brilliant scene painter in his later poems. The scenes seem at first to be painted for their own sakes, but the poet is concerned with a relationship between scene and mind. He is conscious of the need to relate the inner to the outer world, a need that is strongly felt by Spender, who finds authority for the procedure in Rilke. Spencer is aware that his scene is too brilliant: in a poem called "Cage," he finds satisfaction in a correlation between his own situation and the antics of his canary exploring the bars: "I lunge to left, I lunge out to right," he says, "And hit no bars that way, only mists' pretence. . . ." But: "the likeness stays:/Much of my life will go to exploring my fence."[54] Most often, however, Spencer records a failure in the relationship between scene and mind: he is surprised at the discord struck by the mind and the environment, as in "Greek Excavations," where he unearths the ordinary kitchen trappings of ordinary life and confesses he was looking for coins, busts, or vases: "My mind was never turned the way/Of the classic of the just and the unjust" (p. 8). Or again, the ship in the poem so titled is "so lucid and so brave" that neither the poet nor painter could "find one jot to add . . ." (p. 19). But "the imperfect is so hot in us" (in the phrase of Wallace Stevens), the mind finds this scenery

52. Anon., "Poet of the Political Animal," *Times Literary Supplement,* August 31, 1962.
53. *The Edge of Being* (New York: Random House, 1949), pp. 19–25.
54. *Aegean Islands and Other Poems* (London: Editions Poetry London, 1946), p. 41.

"bland"; it is at home more with another kind: "our loves being mostly natives of a land/mountainous, hung with forests, loud with storms. . . ."

The burden of "Aegean Islands 1940–41" is that the memories of the islands, which constitute the bulk of the poem, speak of a happiness the poet can hardly believe in any more. In "Yachts on the Nile," he finds the ships "terrible [in] their perfection" (p. 22); in "Salonica June 1940" we get a similar feeling, with a difference:

The dancing, the bathing, the order of the market, and as day
Cools into night, boys playing in the square;
Island boats and lemon-peel tang and the timeless café crowd,
And the outcry of dice on wood

(p. 9)

—these are all, in a sense, too good, too good to risk destroying: he would lock them away because they are vulnerable, like everything else, including love, to the gunfire of the world war.

Ruthven Todd is another poet from whose descriptions meanings are subtly precipitated. "On Hampstead Heath" offers contrasting details from the Heath and from the northern islands of the poet's past. There is practically no commentary; only, "In these two places, I am the constant factor / That can see the difference and compare the likeness. . . ."[55] We are not easily able to prefer the one place to the other, or to find preference in the poet. Hampstead offers flints, "rotten birches," twisted privet and laurel leaves, "the scum of half-formed ice," gulls; the north offers "snipe trapped by their beaks in the ice," the drowned ewe, numb fingers, the smack of a gun. There is the echo, however, of Robert Graves— "the monotonous voices of idiot boys repeating/The orders they were given, to clean the byre,/Build up the dung-heap by the stable and feed the heifer"; and we settle for what Graves would settle for—the hard northern life rather than that of the "soft burghers," Graves's characters, of the Heath, "where the walkers/Are always within easy reach of home and the cars / Come noisily along the frozen dividing roads." The interest of the poem is in the obliquity

55. *Until Now: Poems* (London: Fortune Press, [1942]), p. 14.

of its message: the shifting proportions of repulsion and attraction exerted respectively by each series of images.

A meaningful assembly of details is presented in "An Autobiography," which is flawed a little by a conclusion of bare statement— "I myself am not so purely simple." The body of the poem consists of various memories, some of which easily lend themselves to symbolic use—"Trains running ceaselessly along the single track, /Proved that a journey without possible return"; "death/Was a grey mouse by the roadside, squashed/By the iron-shod wheel of a haycart"; others remain local individual memories in the gritty texture of boyhood:

> That was at Hunter's Quay, where one night
> The guns spoke often, briefer than thunder
> And the next morning David, my brother,
> Returned dirty from the pebbly beach
> His plump face smeared with diesel-oil;
> Evidence concerning a vanished submarine.

The simple contrast of scenes with undeclared resolution, as in "On Hampstead Heath," is one form of this poet's most successful tactic in *Until Now*: repeatedly he contrasts one place with another, the past with the present, the real with the romantic.

Stephen Spender, at Oxford, felt that his concept of poetry differed from Auden's inasmuch as he didn't conceive of the subject of the poem as a mere peg on which to hang the poetry. But as suggested above, his poetic practice would certainly lead his reader to believe that whatever of the outside world had fired his poetic activity into operation, by the time it had become the manifest poetic content, had been refined, sometimes refined out of recognition. He gives an interesting instance of the refining process in "The Making of a Poem". He is demonstrating the play of memory; but what emerges most remarkably from the example is how remote the poetry is from the experience from which it arose. The poem is merely a fragment:

> . . . Knowledge of a full sun
> That runs up his big sky, above

The hill, then in those trees and throws
His smiling on the turf.

Spender says

> That is an incomplete idea of fifteen years ago, and I remember
> exactly a balcony of a house facing a road, and, on the other side
> of the road, pine trees, beyond which lay the sea. Every morning
> the sun sprang up, first of all above the horizon of the sea, then it
> climbed to the tops of the trees and shone on my window.[56]

The poem has come some way from the sharp, sensuous particularity
of the perception. All in all, Spender manifests a much stronger
fidelity to art than to the world of which art is normally representative and from which it takes its raw materials.

The process illustrated here is quite at odds with the way the
poets mentioned above have dealt with their sensuous experience:
these for the most part have rendered their observations objectively
—in the way Charles Madge desiderated for poetry in his comments
about Mass Observation, that it might be saved from the esoteric.
To some extent, as we have seen, they have attempted to make the
objects and events speak; to some extent their observations have
been specific rather than general—details from Mlini in Grigson,
details from Scotland in Todd, for instance, which of themselves,
given their respective dispositions in the poem, obliquely convey
meaning. This way is not Spender's, not regularly. Spender tended,
in the words he himself used in connection with the last section
of *Ruins and Visions,* to seek "universal experience through subjective contemplation."[57] Rather than reflect back into the poem
the sensuously observed objects as they are, he submits them to
inward processes from which they emerge as images, remolded
to conform to the shape his artistic consciousness demands of them:
his canvases tend to contain a superabundance of pure rhythms,
shadows, and balances in proportion to the defined and recognizable
figures on them.

Spender had learned from Rilke that it was the poet's job to

56. *The Making of a Poem* (London: Hamish Hamilton, 1955), p. 56.
57. *Poetry Since 1939* (London: Longmans, Green, 1946), p. 34.

transform external phenomena so that they symbolize inner experience. "Ideally," says Spender, "the artist should transform the environment into his own world." And we repeatedly find him using the outside world for inward symbolic purposes, covertly or overtly.

When Bernard Spencer seeks a correlation between mind and world, he leaves the real world the way it is. But it must be observed of Spender that he is profoundly uncertain about the reality of the outside world: his poetry and prose repeatedly show that no fact about it is bare and obvious to him, no idea about it is unmuddied by complexity, no sensation is clear, and permanence is an illusion.

We see more closely into Spender's motives in this matter when he points out the failings of Rex Warner's procedures in his review of Warner's poems. His emphasis is on the failure to relate the objective experience to an inward source. He is referring to Warner's willed effort to get some social or political comment into his poems: instead of consulting the "world of his unique inner experience," Warner draws on the world of textbooks and economics, "which he endeavours to translate back into the language of his own authentic inner experience."[58] The inner experience, one notes, is authentic; and Warner ought to have referred his external materials to it. "The poet is committed to what he can really feel with his imagination . . . and if the paths of imagination do not lead back to this social conscience there is nothing to be done about it." Spender himself had experienced, quite recently, or indeed was at the time of this review experiencing a similar dilemma in poetry, "stating a public emotion which . . . never became completely [his] own inner experience. . . ."[59]

All that Spender says may, indeed, be so. If not for others, it was apparently the way he himself went about the making of a poem. There are other principles that come into play, but we may describe as Spender's method in general the submission of external observation to an inward center, the unique inner experience, as he calls it, with its reissuance in images that conform, not to the recognizable

58. Review of *Poems*, by Rex Warner, *Left Review* 3 (July 1937): 358–59.
59. *World Within World*, p. 191.

world but to the present needs of a poem. Repeatedly we read the
same images: suns, bars of light, wires, cages, strings; often enough
the images are literal, in the sense that they refer only to other parts
of the poem; and often enough the poem is what one may call
pure as opposed to descriptive. It just doesn't seem to have much
news in it.

# 6

# Technique, Imitation, and Self-Consciousness

It has been claimed for the poets of the thirties that their interest in politics precluded any interest in poetic techniques. But if that had been entirely so, some strenuous efforts and some indifferent poetic effects might have been happily avoided. *New Signatures* is an anthology of poetry that came out in 1932 and included work from poets who were then beginning to be published: W. H. Auden, Julian Bell, C. Day Lewis, Richard Eberhart, William Empson, John Lehmann, William Plomer, Stephen Spender, and A. S. J. Tessimond. In the preface, the editor, Michael Roberts, shows some interest in techniques. He calls for new ones: "The poet who, using an obsolete technique, attempts to express his whole conception is compelled to be partly insincere or be content with slovenly thought and sentimental feeling."[1] The poems in *New*

1. "Preface," *New Signatures: Poems by Several Hands,* ed. Michael Roberts (London : Leonard and Virginia Woolf, 1932), p. 7.

*Signatures,* says Robert, were, a "clear reaction against esoteric poetry in which it is necessary for the reader to catch each recondite allusion."[2] The obscurity of Empson, he points out lamely enough, is due to compression; not "accidental association." New poetic possibilities, he says, are opened up by the fact that each poet represented in the anthology has, "without recourse to any external system of belief," resolved some of the contradictions that humanity is heir to. Roberts proceeds to illustrate how C. Day Lewis had solved the problem (as had Auden and Spender also) of spontaneously using the material of modern civilization in imagery. These poets had also discovered rhythms not alien to the movement of English speech but, like earlier formal meters, definite enough to allow variations to be perceptible.

Industrial imagery is used by Lewis and to a less extent by Spender partly because the new society of the accepted vision relied upon machinery to make life better for all—hence Spender's pylons and Lewis's dynamos and other equipment. Such imagery is also put to use in simile and metaphor to conceive of the strength of the workers. Spender, more notably than Lewis, tries to give lyrical status to industrial objects, like the mothlike air liner and the train, "gliding like a queen." Louis MacNeice, on the other hand, uses industrial images almost solely to suggest the squalor of the world of the lower classes. All of them, and Auden too, use imagery of decayed industrial equipment as parts of their pictures of England's economic and social distress.

The claim of originality made for the new poetry was not entirely due: as D. E. S. Maxwell has pointed out, Eliot had already introduced an unconventional imagery derived from our quotidian lives, as he had also, under the tutorship of Pound no doubt, retreated from free verse into the quatrains modeled on Gautier.[3] It may be true of these poets, as Roberts says, that their rhythms are close (or not alien) to English speech; but then there is no poetic innovator in the history of literature for whom that claim has not been made. Nor does Roberts quite squarely face the matter of

2. *Ibid.,* p. 12.
3. *Poets of the Thirties* (London: Routledge and Kegan Paul, 1969), pp. 43–44.

obscurity when he writes as if obscurity, or the only kind that mattered, were due necessarily to "recondite allusion." Auden and Lewis were both on occasion deeply obscure for different reasons; Spender is frequently opaque; it is hard to imagine that Auden, for example, had the least concern for his reader or an attitude less "contemptuous" than that which Roberts so designates in his predecessors, when he compiles poems out of the accumulation of odd lines that pleased Isherwood or plays the private Mortmere games in public. Also, as Leavis noted, in trying to exculpate Empson in the matter of obscurity, Roberts goes too far, when in spite of Empson's avowed aims to puzzle the reader, he makes him a champion in the campaign to "remove the difficulties which have stood between the poet and the writing of popular poetry."

In the preface to his next collection, *New Country*,[4] Roberts starts out with some gusto to proclaim the immediate need for a proletarian revolution which, he assured his middle-class readers, would save the things worth saving in England. He goes on to say that there is no time now for "literary writing—writing, that is produced under the stimulus of reading"; and then he says that, whereas poets of the previous generation had mastered material that was sordid, his own generation had found "that seaplanes and mountains, derricks, greyhounds and jessamine, all excited in them the same lyrical enthusiasm."

Two years before he declared in *New Signatures* that the traditional poetic coinage was debased, Roberts had published his first volume of poems, *These Our Matins*,[5] the first part of which might have served as an exhibit for his brief. It consists of conventional pieces in conventional and uninteresting meters. The poems are mostly in tight quatrains with old and tired rhymes:

---

4. *New Country: Prose and Poetry by the Authors of "New Signatures"* (London: Leonard and Virginia Woolf, 1933). The list of authors was not quite the same: there are no poems from Bell, Empson, Eberhart, or Plomer, who had appeared in the earlier collection; but there are poems by Richard Goodman, Charles Madge, Michael Roberts, and Rex Warner, who had not. There are essays, sketches, or stories by Lewis, Spender, Christopher Isherwood, Plomer, Roberts, Edward Upward, and others.

5. (London: Elkin Matthews and Marrot, 1930).

boulders-shoulders, ringing-singing, fountains-mountains, youth-truth. The diction is equally shop soiled: "dim crags," a "broken dream," a "starry night," "some far chorus," and "the dust that once was" something else of minor interest. Even in *These Our Matins*, however, Roberts shows that he is making efforts to break out of the obsolete conventions: Part II is rougher and more sophisticated, and Part III a good deal more free. But in these poems, when he dispenses with the conventional meters and rhymes, he seems to dispense with poetry. His only techniques, it seems, are the old ones.

"On Reading Some Neglected Poets" is an example: it possesses a very uncertain *poetic* element: the rhythms are awkward, the alliteration without apparent significance, the metaphor confusing.

> And maybe no one will ever come,
> No other traveller passing that way,
> Therefore the load we lifted will be left
> A milestone, insignificant, alone.[6]

These lines are quoted by Janet Roberts to illustrate Roberts's idea that poetry was primarily an act not of self-expression but of exploration.[7] But it is not until later volumes that we get the sense that Roberts is using his poems for a purpose, whichever it may be; in the first volumes and frequently in *Poems*,[8] which followed it six years later, we do not receive the impression that poetry was a means for him to express or discover anything. He implies in *New Signatures* that poetry is a language in which one can think and feel,[9] but under his own hand it becomes rather a small and trifling felicity.

At the same time, there are places in *Poems* and in the last volume, *Orion Marches*,[10] where the poetic nature of his subject seems to have forced him into a poetic expression of it. Janet Roberts informs

---

6. *These Our Matins*, p. 52.
7. "Introduction," *Collected Poems: Michael Roberts* (London: Faber and Faber, 1958), p. 20.
8. (London: Cape, 1936).
9. *New Signatures*, p. 7.
10. (London: Faber and Faber, 1939).

us, for example, that Michael believed that positive results were derived from conflict of itself, and we observe this concept in a remark in *New Country*: he doesn't claim, Roberts says, that "the world which we shall help to make will be in any absolute sense 'better'"; but men were to renounce the old system as a way of life, they were "to live *by* fighting against it."[11] The concept finds embodiment in poems that are not poured into a mold for their support nor dependent upon old techniques but have poetic lives of their own. One aspect of the theory in particular seems to have brought successful poetic expression: the idea of there being a constructive product of destruction—an idea perceptible also in some of the poems of Stephen Spender. In Roberts's "Emblem," the poet addresses chaos:

> Come, you were always there, my chaos
>
> . . . . . . . . . . . . . . . . . .
> Come, it is for you always,
> Stuff of the waking and the dreaming world,
> And it is you, consolidated, hardened,
> Names in the flame, evasive nothing, you,
> The light, the darkness, you who serve
> To build the thought, the firmer skull, the structure,
> Holding the sky of love, and all his features.[12]

"They Will Come Back" promises the return of the "quiet days,/ Rosemary, myrtle, lavender," "the gentian days," and "the strenuous days." But these will not return peacefully:

> Through bombs and teargas, through the acute
> Machine-gun rattling answer, strict
> Self-knowledge, dark rebellion, death
> In the shuttered streets, through barricades,
> And doors flung open in the wind,
> They will come back.[13]

11. "Preface" *New Country*, p. 13 (italics mine).
12. *Poems*, p. 29.
13. *Ibid.*, p. 23.

The paradox appears more sharply in "The Battle," in Roberts's last volume:

> . . . the battle is peace under the stars,
> The battle is the birth of kings and flowers,
> The battle is peace deeper than the world's wars.[14]

In this volume Roberts comes into his own: he has dispensed with the trite meters and clichés and he has found frequently an individual means of being poetic without the self-defeating hand-me-downs by means of which he had at first made his middle flights. Occasionally we recognize the influences of Eliot or Graves or Auden. But they are neither strong nor frequent. His most characteristic poem uses scenery—often mountains or the mountain villages of Europe: for much of the page descriptive details are presented. But usually there are among them the hints, suggestions, or flat statements that roughen the surface and give the poem some depth beyond a mere reflection, though often the depth is not very deep, the complexities not enthralling.

Roberts's remark in *New Country* that literary writing was tolerable in a time of stale tradition, but not now, reminds us that everyone believes always that any other time is more stable than his own, whenever it may be; but in any case, if it is affected at all, stability would be enhanced by *un*originality and the imitation of others, rather than by originality. In every age, however, relatively stable or not, there have been minor poets whose style is not their own, as—the obvious analogy—there are always men whose clothes make them look as if they had stepped out of an L. L. Bean catalogue, or some other one. A number of the poets whose works I have discussed in this essay seem, to their great credit, to be unconscious of style. This is the case in two manifest ways: first, the style is the poet's own; his poems are reasonably homogeneous; early in his career he shows us his hallmarks, the features that apparently come naturally, and he doesn't later completely surprise or greatly disappoint us. Second, he is unconscious of style because he is satisfied that his substance will generate its proper effects,

---

14. *Orion Marches*, p. 49.

and he is under no necessity to augment those effects by dressing up or, so to say, *adding* style. Obviously these two conditions are too indefinite to be easily managed as criteria in discussing poems. It is possible, however, to identify a few poets to whose work they do not thoroughly apply, among them Stephen Spender.

The first condition, that a man's way of writing be his own, is particularly subject to qualification, for he must develop, and his development will call upon him to make use of characteristics as if they were his own. The problem is like that of sincerity as it is disposed of by W. H. Auden: ". . . only animals who are below civilization and the angels who are beyond it can be sincere. Human beings are, necessarily, actors who cannot become something before they have first pretended to be it. . . ."[15] Imitation, the poetic equivalent to "pretending to be it," need not invariably be a procedure that leads to self-consciousness in style, though it may often do so. It seems apparent, for example, that Norman Cameron found in Robert Graves a way of writing that he absorbed and made his own as naturally as a man assumes the patois of a locale not his own.

Cameron was at Oxford in 1927 and became the friend of Graves. Many of his few poems might have been written by Graves: there are the grotesque subjects, "Fight with a Water-Spirit,"[16] "Nunc Scio Quid Sit Amor"—"From lands where all the flowers have teeth, where half/A serpent-furlong coils round every tree . . . Has come this most outrageous foreigner,/This fierce outlander who has swooped on me . . ."(p. 1). Under the influence of Graves he sets his poems in landscapes where the natural phenomena are unwholesome, like nightmare rocks or poisonous dews. He imitates also the Gravesian use of classical situations for the generation of a moral paradox. "The Thespians at Thermopylae" presents the case of men who, unlike the putatively brave Spartans whose courage was mandatory, actually chose to be brave: "Spartans cannot retreat. Why, then, their praise/For going forward should be less

15. *The Age of Anxiety: A Baroque Eclogue* (New York: Random House, 1947), p. 109.
16. *The Winter House and Other Poems* (London: Dent, 1935), p. 5.

than others'." The similarity to situations in Graves, for example
in "The Cuirassiers of the Frontier," is perfectly clear; and so are
the echoes of his terse diction. These we hear again and again in
Cameron: in "Central Europe" (p. 7), "... fat peasants winter-
bound, / Stunned by the heat of their enormous stoves, / Whimpering
fear of baleful gods and wolves—"; or in "Meeting My Former
Self,"

> Great cliffs of chalk slope from the fishing-village
> Up to the lighthouse. Rum sold free of duty.
> Only the fishermen and lighthouse-keeper
> Beside ourselves.

These lines come from *Winter House*, Cameron's early volume.
But the Graves influence is only a little less detectable in the later
volume, *Forgive Me, Sire*, of 1950, and indeed in his translations
Cameron contrives to make parts of Villon and Rimbaud also speak
like Graves.

Cameron found in Graves a way of saying things that he wanted to
say himself, and thus he created his own style. He died young and had
a relatively small output of poetry.

Less than Cameron used Graves, Edgell Rickword used Donne
and the metaphysicals and, so it seems, Eliot. He writes quatrains in
short satiric poems, some of which, "Divagation on a Line by
Donne,"[17] for example, are reminiscent of Eliot's poems modeled on
Gautier. Donne's Satire I is the model for Rickword's "Twittingpan,
or The Encounter," which is about the gossipy social fop whom the
narrator meets about town. Twittingpan is a literary entrepreneur,
upon whom the poet has bestowed some of the features, theories, and
tastes of Wyndham Lewis. And Twittingpan has some kind words
for Lewis, which must have been less than gratifying to him. He
remarks to the narrator,

> "Lewis and Middleton Murry are, I'm sure,
> the only moderns likely to endure
> of the older crowd. . . ."

Then:

17. *Twittingpan and Some Others* (London: Wishart, 1931), p. 44.

"Don't you think Wyndham Lewis too divine?
That brute male strength he shows in every line!
I swear if he'd flogged me in his last book but one,
as some kind person informed me he has done,
I'd have forgiven him for the love of art."

(p. 13)

Lewis, Rickword thought, was like "a powerful man tormented by gnats. The apostolic fervour which the campaign for their extermination develops as it grows is a sign of a weakening of the sense of reality, of that humour which we possess, perhaps, so that we may be enabled to live in a society at all. . . ."[18]

Rickword, however, when writing like Donne, injects his own intelligence; and often his influences are inaudible. He is concerned repeatedly in his poems with the passing of daylight or with time and its ravages. He reveals an imagination whose products are not to be distorted by being crowded into an economical sentence: his sentences are often long, firmly jointed, and packed with meaning; and they trudge stubbornly forward, determined to make it:

The tragedy of human habitations
is subject for the eloquence of Gibbon,
I meditate private disasters only,
and, among these, Time's treachery to women;
the faint cosmetic mask grain by grain stolen
till their moon-faces wane and no light fills
with thin romantic foliage lips' dry valleys.[19]

On the other hand Rickword can be beautifully urbane, as he is in the only poem of his that actually belongs to the thirties, "To The Wife of a Non-Interventionist Statesman." There are some perfectly chiseled passages of cooled anger—

18. Edgell Rickword, "Wyndham Lewis," in *Scrutinies by Various Writers*, Vol. II, Collected by Edgell Rickword (London: Wishart, 1931), p. 161.
19. "In Sight of Chaos," *Collected Poems of Edgell Rickword* (London: The Bodley Head, 1947), p. 50.

> Spain bleeds, and England wildly gambles
> to bribe the butcher in the shambles. . . .
> because our ruling clique's pretences
> rob loyal Spain of her defences,
> the chaser planes and ack-ack guns
> from which the prudent Fascist runs.
>                                    (pp. 78–79)

The voice of Marvell is heard in this last line. What is particularly interesting about this poem is the completely successful conjunction of the public and the private things, adumbrated in the title and made the major theme of the poem: can a woman sleep with a man whose policies have wrought evil? The poem ends,

> Would not his breath reek of the tomb
> and with cold horror seal her womb?
> Could a true woman bear his brat?
> The millions wouldn't.
>                                    Thanks, my hat.

The conjunction between public and private worlds is interesting to us inasmuch as Spender attempts it much more elaborately in *Vienna*, where it fails. And C. Day Lewis's poem *From Feathers to Iron*, a series of meditations on a private theme concerning childbirth, had a public meaning imposed upon it by readers.

The slim volume of posthumous poetry of Christopher Caudwell, the deeply committed communist, is more than half given over to a long dramatic poem, "Orestes." This contains curious and, in places, clearly conscious echoes of Shakespeare, "Lycidas," Tennyson, and Arnold. Among the shorter poems is one in the Graves manner and voice, "Tierra del Fuego," a grotesque incident in which a Christian ship's company misuses the savages:

> A few we spitted on our swords; the rest
> Our priests whipped till they owned the Christ; one girl
> Ape-faced, but breasted well, our captain took.

The provenance of another short poem, "Classic Encounter," in which the poet encounters souls of those slain in a classic battle, is Thomas Hardy and perhaps Wilfred Owen's "Strange Meeting."

The strongest influence, however, on Christopher Caudwell's poetry is that of Donne: it pervades the volume. The volume opens with "The Hair," in which the metaphysical conceits and the direct debt to images from *Songs and Sonnets* are paraded:

> This hair. I took it first for tidiness
> And then for love (for it is valueless)
> And knotting it around my button said:
> When you and I are dead
> This hair may still be living. They'll not find
> What Donne prospected, round the bare bone twined
> This filament; it may be anywhere.[20]

As in Donne, all the possible improbable relationships of the hair are tried out. The poem steadily maintains the tenor which, like this sampling, is intense, homogeneous, and economical. Donne's influence, along with other Elizabethans', is at work also through a sequence called "Twenty Sonnets of Wm. Smith," partly in the attitude and partly in the texture of the poetry. The narrator is bent upon celebrating the physical accoutrements of love at the expense of romantic stage properties, the nightingales, roses, and stars of convention. Sonnet II begins and ends as follows

> Before us all who worked this leaping oar
> Contrived to drench the handle with perfume
> But we in Love's hot galley load the grain
> With natural sweat that bites the kissing palm. . . .
> . . . sailors in their rough and tarry mode
> Announce what grand extraordinary sights
> Are to their nest of stinking cabins owed
>> Concealing not the thing by which they move.
>> Old body, faithful vessel of our love.
>> (pp. 26–27)

John Donne's narrator in "The Extasie" was likewise at pains to explain that "pure lovers' souls" must

20. *Poems* (London: Lawrence and Wishart, 1965), p. 9.

> descend
> T'affections, and to faculties,
> Which sense may reach and apprehend,
> Else a great Prince in prison lies.

Caudwell, like Donne, is celebrating the vehicles of love but is not, on that account, denying the existence of cargo. In the last sonnet of the Wm. Smith sequence, rose, nightingale, and moon, duly cut down to size, are readmitted to the master bedroom:

> Yes, even the wood's great pimp the nightingale
> In the full flood of meretricious song
> Set on by his unholy bawd the moon
> May be permitted to observe our love. . . .

It must be remarked that Donne's influence in these sonnets has been thoroughly assimilated by Caudwell. There is much in them that is not specifically Donne's: there are, indeed, sonnets closer but not very close to Shakespeare. What is impressive about them and, indeed, about the whole volume is simply the achievement and maintenance throughout of a high standard of verse. Caudwell takes risks, goes out after original ambitious effects, and he is not flawless. But it is surprising to find such strength and so few lapses from it in a volume that has remained inconspicuous for thirty years.

Another long, robust poem of Caudwell's, "The Art of Dying," is written in a predominantly eighteenth-century style—the heroic couplet, the formally declared metaphors and similes, the strong consciousness of the prepared moral. Yet it is studded with metaphysical conceits that recall Donne; some of these are exquisite: "The burning ghats / In whose smoke body imitates its breath"; "If you are proud, think ere that second birth / You now would own, but then will be the earth." "I think that flesh which fits me like a glove / Must all be slipped off at the last remove."

It is interesting that Caudwell, the most strongly committed communist poet-critic of this decade, should have written such poetry as this. There is less explicit political comment in this volume than in those of many men who were less committed, in spite of the fact that, according to D. E. S. Maxwell, most of it was written in

1935 while Caudwell was reading Marxism preparatory to joining
the Communist Party.[21] Maxwell's comment on the Marxism and
the poetry is nice:

> Marxism, as it impinged on Caudwell's consciousness, did not
> obstruct his poetry with idealised comrades, ranting calls to sol-
> idarity and action, diatribes against the horrors of capitalism.
> Gradually a point of view emerges, compatible with marxism but
> not overtly announced. The poems seem, indeed, the work of a
> man for whom marxism had become a habit of thought, not a
> system of ideas to be applied to experience with finicking cir-
> cumspection.[22]

One could say much the same, in passing, for the poems of Roy
Fuller, who believed in Marxism as a view of reality in poetry and
that it provided what R. P. Blackmur had found magic providing
for Yeats, Christianity for Eliot, and ironic fatalism for Hardy,
"'a connection between the poem and its subject matter and . . . an
adequate mechanism of meaning and value.'"[23] The phrase "habit
of thought" applied to Marxism reminds us that, introducing a
collection of Caudwell's essays, Edgell Rickword observes that one
of their leading themes is the unity of thinking and doing. Having
grasped the clue from Marx, he says, Caudwell found that the other
knowledge he had fell into place and proportion; what had been an
accumulation, "'A monstrously detailed collection of facts,'"
became capable of organization and vitality. He didn't merely
grasp Marxism intellectually and emotionally: he thought in it.[24]
Marxism provided him with a unified system, a ground from which,
in *Illusion and Reality* and in his miscellaneous essays, he could
assail all areas of illusionary bourgeois thought and practice:
poetry, prose fiction, liberty, science, religion, aesthetics, history,
psychology, and philosophy.

21. Maxwell, p. 66.
22. *Ibid.*, p. 82.
23. "The Audience and Politics," *Twentieth Century Verse,* no. 18 (June/July 1939),
p. 50.
24. Preface, Christopher Caudwell, *Further Studies in a Dying Culture,* ed. Edgell
Rickword (London: John Lane, The Bodley Head, 1949).

It is unity that Caudwell prizes. It is the failure in unity, the lack of integrity in the bourgeois revolutionary poets, raising their un-calloused hands in the workers' salute, that underlies his critical attack on the Auden group. He desiderates for them a unity of sentiment and intellect. And so for himself, what model for poetry would more naturally present itself than that of John Donne, the recently acclaimed champion of the undissociated sensibility?

Imitation as practiced by Cameron, Caudwell, and some others is not a self-conscious act that produced an artificial style. And there is much imitation of this kind in the poetry of the thirties, though it is less extensive than in Cameron or Caudwell. Many of the poets were, after all, university graduates; not a few had come via the English tripos. Auden, however, not yet material for the schools, was the strong magnetic north of this time and territory; and to the attraction he exerted many poets responded, many repeatedly, in phrase, or line, or longer passage, and in attitude and subject matter. Gavin Ewart in his early work was one of Auden's closest conscious imitators. Later, he writes

> Let me see the map.
> All these roads are Auden's old chap.
> I've been over them once, following his tracks. . . .[25]

Auden, however, was a very usable influence in both rhetorical techniques and attitudes: his ellipses, his catalogues, metonymies and synecdoches, his symbols, his awareness, paradoxically vivid, of the boring and the dull, his brilliant treatment of quotidian things, the "usual" things, in his own familiar terminology. Kenneth Allott has harvested quite a few of these characteristics in his own verse: "those before whom the handwashing maitre d'hotel/Smirks and walks backward"; "those to whom charitable appeals / Are always directed"; and the images from suburban living of aspidistras, privet hedge, milk on the steps in the morning, and lime marmalade.[26] Roy Fuller writes, "Beneath the usual sky / The

25. "Journey," *New Verse*, no. 8 (April 1934), p. 8.
26. Kenneth Allott, *Poems* (London: Hogarth, 1938) and *The Ventriloquist's Doll* (London: Cresset Press, 1943).

pleasure towns where most / Have come to live or die"[27] (and, though much later, "the others have always some excuse / To be absent from the shooting, to be at home / Curled up with a book or at the dentist's,"[28] which not only catches the cadence of Auden, but his repeated habit of dwelling in his later poems not on the major action but on what is going on in the wings). Randall Swingler drops articles and relative pronouns, combines abstractions with concretes, and achieves a long muscular sentence. Auden's "Petition" seems particularly to have been ringing in his mind as he wrote the "Envoi" to his poem "Ode : To a Plane Above the City" and also when he wrote "Instructions to Hermes." The former begins:

> Father, whose debt of love is our
> desire, speak to us in the power
> of the indifferent beeches. Ridicule
> our life's denial, our pitiful pretence.[29]

The latter begins:

> O Lord of luck, the airy
> lad who laughs out care
> our domineering uncle, hence
> be aggravating in our pit of sense,
> stirring stormwise the outward passion
> abroad into creative hands
> productive loins and quisitive eyes,
> with sharpness turning. . . .[30]

Rex Warner imitates Auden in a sequence called "Chorus," of which the first poem begins, "What night darker / that idle to go to dogs unwanted by men?" Then shortly follows another Audenesque passage:

> Facing our wives,
> whether pausing at a stairturn, lamp lifted, or suddenly seeing,
> hand on a table, perhaps, across the unwashed china,

27. Roy Fuller, *Poems* (London: Fortune Press, 1940), p. 30.
28. Roy Fuller, *Counterparts* (London: Derek Verschoyle, 1954), p. 10.
29. *Reconstruction* (Oxford: Blackwell, 1933), p. 7.
30. *Difficult Morning* (London: Methuen, 1933), p. 5.

we read a kind of derision in their eyes.
No zest in the bed since loyal they are lying,
and suspect that, with ghosts.[31]

Then follows a reference to Colonel Humphries—"What has
happened to Colonel Humphries?"—reminiscent of Auden's officer
of lower rank, Captain Ferguson, of "Taller Today We Remember
Similar Evenings."

In many imitations, one feels that Auden has been absorbed
naturally: he has become a way of talking, a mouth. But in Swingler
and Warner the imitation seems a bit forced; it seems much more so
in C. Day Lewis in *The Magnetic Mountain.* No one in this period
had a better ear for poetic voices than Lewis, as he demonstrates
especially in "Florence: Works of Art," in *An Italian Visit,* where
in separate poems he flawlessly adopts the voices of Hardy, Yeats,
Frost, Auden, and Dylan Thomas. This same talent is often of no
advantage, however, when it manifests itself in some of the earlier
works: it is only a meretricious wrapping that does not come
naturally and necessarily from the interaction of man and subject
draws attention to the saying rather than to what is said. In *The
Magnetic Mountain,* for example, there is a great deal of Auden[32]—
in the attack on the press lords, for example, or in those places where
articles and relative pronouns have been dropped and an Anglo-
Saxon echo is heard, or in catalogues. The underlying image of the
journey in this poem is probably derived from the gang myth,
mutually owned by Auden, Isherwood, and the others.[33] Also
there is more Hopkins in Lewis than in anybody else in the period.
Hopkins, as Lewis himself recognized in *A Hope for Poetry,* is not

31. *Poems* (London: Boriswood, 1937), pp. 56–57. Tambimuttu observes the
Auden influence in Julian Symons by quoting the beginnings of three consecutive
poems in his *Confusions about X*: "Night is as fatal as home," "This summer evening
and particular death Let us consider," "Let us applaud this and the other evenings
When darkness comes at half-past seven" ("Mr. Symons in His Nursery," *Poetry*
[London], no. 2 [April 1939]).
32. Francis Scarfe repeats the possibility that the Mountain *is* Auden! "The
Development of Day Lewis," *Auden and After: The Liberation of Poetry 1930–1941*
(London: Routledge, 1942), p. 7.
33. See Justin Replogle, *Auden's Poetry* (Seattle: University of Washington Press,
1969), pp. 16–21.

easily absorbed; and in *The Magnetic Mountain* the imitation smacks of virtuosity. It was more possible in those days to write naturally like Auden when to some extent at least poets were writing about the same things as he and attaching to them similar feelings. But Hopkins's rhapsodies are another matter: of no one, surely, could it be said that he lisped in Hopkins, for the Hopkins came. Lewis writes:

> Look west, Wystan, lone flyer, birdman, my bully boy!
> Plague of locusts, creeping barrage, has left earth bare:
> Suckling and centenarian are up in air,
> No wing-room for Wystan, no joke for kestrel joy.[34]

This is not very agreeable to read.

Lewis has his own lyric voice, which may be heard in *The Magnetic Mountain* as elsewhere:

> Not hate nor love, but say
> Refreshment after rain,
> A lucid hour; though this
> Need not occur again.
>
> (p. 99)

Or

> Tempt me no more; for I
> Have known the lightning's hour,
> The poet's inward pride,
> The certainty of power.
>
> (p. 105)

Or

> Look where the ranks of crocuses
> Their rebel colours will display
> Coming with quick fire to redress
> The balance of a wintry day.
>
> (p. 110)

He departs from this fine lyrical voice more often than not in *The Magnetic Mountain*, partly because the poem is dramatic. But there is perhaps another factor at work: Lewis felt that the lyric, with its characteristic total demands upon the poet which secluded him and excluded all else, was not a genre suitable for that period. Such

34. *Collected Poems*, p. 97.

demands were incompatible with the responsibilities that the times laid upon the poet: "In a state of society where it is unusually difficult for him not to be aware of the large tracts of experience outside his immediate environment and to feel that these demand some attitude from him, as a man, the lyric irresponsibility of the artist is hard to achieve."[35] Objection might be made once again to the somewhat special case Lewis makes of his own milieu; but it is of interest that he saw the situation of the lyric poet in this light. We have seen how poets showed their sense of responsibility by resisting the Georgian drift and rejecting certain subject matter; here responsibility rejects the lyric genre. We shall see below its influence upon style.

In the thirties early and late, Lewis seems to have reacted to the state of his society by avoiding lyric, except as it made up a part of a longer poem, and using rather the dramatic, incorporating voices other than his own, *First Enemy*, *Second Enemy*, and so forth. In addition, he wrote short poems in which he used the forms of other poets or images, rhythms, diction, and meters, recognizably derived, as a means of saying things without involving himself in the culpable purity of the apparently spontaneous lyric. In *From Feathers to Iron*, for instance, the third poem opens as follows:

> Back to the countryside
> That will not lose its pride
> When the green flags of summer all are taken,
> Having no mind to force
> The seasons from their course
> And no remorse for a front line forsaken.[36]

The rest of the poem has the same stanzaic structure, which has its own beauty. But the effect of the echoes of Milton's "Nativity Ode" is to alter the pitch of the lyric: we receive as a part of the experience it offers the consciousness of the poet's consciousness of style, his dexterity. Or again in "The Poet," which appeared in *Folios of New Writing*, 1940, Lewis writes in the style of the Yeats of "Easter, 1916" and "The Tower":

35. *A Hope for Poetry* (Oxford: Blackwell, 1934), p. 67.
36. *Collected Poems*, p. 55.

> I have learned to count each day
> Minute by breathing minute—
> Birds that lightly begin it,
> Shadows muting its end. . . .
>
> All I have felt or sung
> Seems now but the moon's fitful
> Sleep on a clouded bay,
> Swan's maiden flight, or the climb
> To a tremulous, hare-bell crest.[37]

In each of these examples, the "real" lyric "itself," as it were, is moved a little off center in our attention, like the meanings of the words that Henry James puts in quotation marks: something comes between the reader and the thing. And purity, total absorption in the lyric on the part of the poet, is avoided.

If this accounts for Lewis's repeated repression of his own good lyric voice, we have a situation similar to that which we shall see in Stephen Spender, who also muted his singing upon the pressures of opposing demands. And Auden ought also to be mentioned in this connection; though the cause is not quite the same, it could be conceived in terms of responsibility and irresponsibility. Poet and Antipoet, like the opposing impulses in both Lewis and Spender, often battle in Auden's poems. Justin Replogle, who covers their long campaign, says that in the 1930s especially the Antipoet believed that art might be an escape from life; the Poet preferred art to anything else. The Poet "remained aloof and superior, and spoke in a tongue far removed from lifelike speech." But, "Lofty poetic flights threatened to attract the Antipoet, who enjoyed tumbling his opponent from the heights by pelting him with coarse chunks of Life, mocking, laughing, deriding, deflating his pretensions."[38]

The ear of C. Day Lewis for poetic voices other than his own was perhaps unsurpassed in the thirties. But Ronald Bottrall goes beyond him in the extent to which he uses his models; and his use is more fundamental. As we have seen, Auden, Graves, Donne, Hopkins,

---

37. *Ibid.*, pp. 223–4.
38. Justin Replogle, *Auden's Poetry*, p. 95.

and others are recognizably imitated here and there throughout the decade; but the use made of them, though it may be extensive, is slight compared with that which Bottrall makes of Ezra Pound, whom he uses practically as an organizing principle. Bottrall had some distinction in the thirties: he was named by T. S. Eliot in 1932 along with Auden, Spender, and MacNeice as one of the four most important younger poets;[39] he was reviewed repeatedly and at some length in *Scrutiny*; and he was appreciatively criticized by F. R. Leavis in *New Bearings*.[40] He is less known now than he was in the thirties and forties. His first volume, *The Loosening*,[41] is a paradoxical combination of originality and dependence; except for Basil Bunting there was hardly anybody else in England who had taken Ezra Pound as a model; and not even his American disciples had come so close to catching Pound's voice in their own work. Leavis believed that Bottrall had absorbed Pound; his debt, he says, "serves to bring out his own strong originality."[42]

In the first volume, "Arion Anadyomenos, A Sequence" consists of nine poems that repeatedly echo *Hugh Selwyn Mauberley* in rhythms, phrasing, diction, tone, and subject matter, which is a complaint at the condition of poetry, of the poet, and of the age. The following passages, each from separate poems, will give something of the flavor of the indebtedness:

No culminating strength urges to assay 'the sublime'. . . .
— "Frustration"
Microscopic anatomy of ephemerides. . . .
— "The Thyrsis Retipped"
The future is not for us. . . .
— "The Future is not For Us"

---

39. Charles Tomlinson, "Introduction," *The Collected Poems of Ronald Bottrall* (London: Sidgwick and Jackson, 1961). p. iii.
40. F. R. Leavis, *New Bearings in English Poetry: A Study of the Contemporary Situation* (Ann Arbor: University of Michigan Press, 1960); paperback ed., pp. 201–11.
41. *The Loosening and Other Poems* (Cambridge: Minority Press, 1931).
42. *New Bearings*, p. 202.

a black row of sycamores . . .
Saddled, however, by no Zaccheus
To incite attention from the Paraclete . . .
                                    —"Arion Anadyomenos"[43]

Hopkins is also present, as F. R. Leavis observed, in "The soul has precipices, slippery footholds." And there are a number of Hopkins's curiosities, such as "The black/slithering—through—undersea projectile," in "Terns and Cormorant." There is also some Eliot, from those early poems of Eliot's that were modeled after Gautier ("We do not lack our testament and creed / We have our umbrellas and our A.B.C.'s").

The voices of Bottrall's masters are clear enough, and the poet obviously had no intention of concealing them. He announced in 1933 that he owed "more to Pound than to any other living poet."[44] Subsequently he has remarked that reading *Hugh Selwyn Mauberley* for the first time, "the scales fell from my eyes and I saw, or thought I saw, how contemporary verse should be written."[45]

The title poem of Bottrall's second volume, *Festivals of Fire*,[46] contains four parts, each headed by musical instructions. We are told in a note that for the idea of the ground plan and for certain details of the first three sections the poet owes much to *Balder the Beautiful*, Part VII of *The Golden Bough*. The Pound of the *Mauberley* sequence has been dropped, but the influence of the *Cantos* appears in the rhythm and in the structural method of the poem, which presents superficially unrelated details in juxtaposition and offers the kind of anachronisms familiar in Pound.

In his following volume, *The Turning Path*,[47] Bottrall has divested himself of most of his models, except for an occasional echo of Hopkins. He asks in the preface that the book be read as a whole, not as a collection of detached pieces; he announces what each of the three major divisions of the volume presents; and then

43. *The Loosening*, pp. 3–13.
44. "*XXX Cantos* of Ezra Pound," *Scrutiny* 2 (September 1933): 122.
45. Quoted in Tomlinson, p. iii.
46. (London: Faber and Faber, 1934).
47. (London: Arthur Barker, 1939).

he calls attention to his technique: "In section I a method of linked imagery is used. Four strands of images, each containing opposed terms, are woven together. All the strands illustrate an opposition of growth and decay."[48] The "linked imagery" is unremarkable, but Bottrall's note draws attention to his unusual interest in technique.

Edith Sitwell remarked that Bottrall was a born technician. And it is some credit to him that he could draw praise from both Dame Sitwell and F. R. Leavis, who rarely saw eye to eye about literary figures. In him they both admire the same major feature of his work, the "positive energy" of his rhythms in Leavis's words, the "articulate muscles" in Sitwell's. She also praises him for feelings and meanings arising from the merest scruples of sound: she says, "the thick dissonances of *cosmos*, and 'the *close*/Of our long progress is hinted by the *crass*' these give an actual feeling of a surrounding fog pressing upon us"[49]—a feeling perceptible, surely, to Dame Sitwell alone.

What is admirable in Bottrall's work is his unhesitant grip on metaphor, with which he is like a climber who has absolute certainty that each outrageous handhold is perfectly secure and does not pause. At his best he can reach heights that resist critical description: "So may the disjoint / Time resolve itself and raise up dolphins backed/Like whales to waft us where a confident sea/Is ever breaking, never spent." But the technical mastery with which he is properly credited ought to result in lucidity, which is a quality he does not always achieve.

In *The Turning Path* it has been observed that his style is hypertrophied relative to his subject. R. O. C. Winkler quotes some lines from a poem "To a Chinese Girl"; they are, he says, "so clearly contrived from the outside that it is impossible even to begin to apprehend them until a careful paraphrase has been made, and then one finds no subtlety of experience to justify the superficial complexity. . . ." The words, he adds, "seem intended to obscure rather than to express the meaning." A further observation should be quoted: of "Prologue," the first poem in the volume, the same

48. *Turning Path*, p. viii.
49. *Collected Poems*, p. viii.

critic says that it outlines the dichotomy between primitive sources of reality and ramifications of intellect that characterizes a mechanistic culture. But this, he finds, is too often a statement of Bottrall's own case: "His verse is characteristically either an intellectual construction that describes, without expressing, the problem or situation, or a realization of directionless experience in the solar-plexus."[50]

To turn to Spender: in his work, one would say, poetry from the solar plexus is remarkable for its complete absence. There is certainly none of his poetry that is not intellectual, there is very little that is not complex, and there is much that is obscure. This last quality may fall under the suspicion, as it does in Bottrall, of being deliberate or half intended at least. That is to say, it often seems that Spender would rather fail to be understood than to be crudely misunderstood. He speaks from a scrupulous sensibility; he gives the impression frequently that he has purposely twisted a poem out of the straight, turning it inward upon itself, to prevent it from delivering too easy a message, or a statement too crudely descriptive of the world. On the other hand it is conceivable that obscurity in Spender may be due to his misjudgment of what the reader can be expected to deduce from oblique notification in a poem. In "The Making of a Poem," he speaks of his poem "Seascape" as follows:

> The sea represents death and eternity, the land represents the brief life of the summer and of one human generation which passes into the sea of eternity. But let me here say at once that although the poet may be conscious of this aspect of his vision, it is exactly what he wants to avoid stating, or even being too concerned with. His job is to recreate his vision, and let it speak its moral for itself. The poet must distinguish clearly in his own mind between that which most definitely must be said and that which must not be said. The unsaid inner meaning is revealed in the music and the tonality of the poem, and the poet is conscious of it in his knowledge that a certain tone of voice, a certain rhythm, are necessary.[51]

50. R. O. C. Winkler, "Ronald Bottrall," *Scrutiny* 8 (1939–40): 215–18.
51. *The Making of a Poem* (London: Hamish Hamilton, 1955), p. 51.

It is a curious pronouncement: it is true that there are things that "must not be said"—"said," that is, literally. But although all things are not conveyed in the same manner, all must be conveyed somehow or other—some things in direct statement, some obliquely through tone, rhythm, connotative and other effects. But, to look at the poem itself, the idea of eternity in the sea is not in fact conveyed at all; and symbolic equivalences in any poem, such as sea equals death and land equals life in this poem, are not in fact conveyed, as Spender declares, by its "music and . . . tonality" or its rhythms. It is possible that some of the obscurity here and there in Spender is to be attributed to his faulty assessment of just how much the various available poetic techniques might be made to express and which of them was appropriate for any particular part of the experience to be conveyed.

As we proceed through Bottrall's volumes, there is an increasing sense of style as something the poet uses to add complexity and excitement to material inherently deficient in it. Similarly, in the poems of George Barker it is difficult not to think of style as an additive and, therefore, as a blemish. Barker, beginning in 1933 at the age of twenty, has by now published extensively. Unlike many of the poets considered in this chapter, he has been fairly widely reviewed; but many of the reviews have been harsh. Of the first volume,[52] Hugh Gordon Porteus says, "His malady is an ingrowing soul. . . ." and, "It may be hoped that when he has finished sweating out his latinisms he will 'donate' . . . some of his attention to his worst vice—exploitation of his own pathos."[53] On the second volume, *Poems*,[54] Geoffrey Grigson wrote his piece, "Nertz,"[55] which has already been quoted, suggesting that Barker's narcissism manifests itself in the overwrought style. Of the third volume, a single long poem, *Calamiterror*,[56] H. A. Mason reports that the interest in Barker's political awakening, purported to be celebrated in this work, "lies not so much in the world outside as in himself.

---

52. *Thirty Preliminary Poems* (London: Parton Press, 1933).
53. *Scrutiny* 3 (June 1934): 84.
54. (London: Faber and Faber, 1935).
55. *New Verse*, no. 15 (June 1935), pp. 17–18.
56. (London: Faber and Faber, 1937).

For he claims that he has rid himself of his life-long pre-occupation with himself." But, says Mason, the whole of the poem gives him the lie: "Thirty four of the fifty three pages are taken up with the theme of himself coming to birth." For all the violence and profusion, he adds, nothing of importance is said.[57]

In a poem called "Tract," the American poet William Carlos Williams describes the good style in the metaphor of a farm wagon: it is to be old, unpainted, weathered, generally beat-up. For Barker the equivalent vehicle would have chrome—the hubcaps, badges, bars, fake ventilators, and exhausts that embellish the automated transportation of youth. Francis Scarfe compares Barker's style to the lavish brushwork of Van Gogh, saying that the public "has not yet realized that a poetry can also be written which is predominantly sensational, the emotions existing raw and natural almost in a pure state."[58] The pure state of the emotions in Barker, however, is a matter of some uncertainty. He writes his poems as if he understood that intensity, not permitted to arise of its own accord, as it were, from the deployment of images or the facts of the subject itself, had somehow to be added, like fortification to ordinary wine. Barker came to poetry when many new techniques had recently become available, thanks to Eliot, to his and Sir Herbert Grierson's revaluation of Donne, to the innovations of Auden, and to the publication of the work of Gerard Manley Hopkins. The work of Hopkins shows, says Leavis, and "intensity of 'doing'" and a limitation in "the stuff of experience he commanded for poetry."[59] And Barker's poetry shows somewhat similar symptoms. It is a little like some recent films, whose directors, flush with all kinds of novel techniques to hand, have bedazzled us into taking their work seriously by concealing its emptiness under the new devices they have just fallen heir to. "Technique is a monstrously hard thing to acquire," said Geoffrey Grigson, "but to think too much about it, divorced from its only purpose, is debilitating." One reviewer,

57. *Scrutiny* 6 (1937–38): 81.
58. "George Barker: A Pure Poet," *Auden and After*, p. 118.
59. *New Bearings in English Poetry: A Study of the Contemporary Situation*, with "Retrospect 1950" (Harmondsworth, Middlesex: Penguin Books, 1963), p. 192.

comparing Barker with the early Yeats, proclaims that pretentious-
ness is "wrongly treated as an unqualified vice." He had hopes for
the future: "these men," he says of Yeats and Barker, "make themselves into considerable poets by sheer pertinacity, by a slow and
laborious transfiguration of youthful unchastities."[60]

The characteristics of unchaste excess in Barker are, first, the
overstatement: "Avalanched with immaculate quietude"; "the
interminable grieving of the sea." There are puns and near puns:
"Wondering one, wandering on"; "I mourn him. Him I mourn from
morn to morning"; "That she will move from mourning into
morning" (the last line and only flaw in a sonnet to the poet's mother
that is curiously free from the besetting addictions under discussion
here), "the trepanned/the trespassers prosecuted"; meaningless
alliterations, assonances, internal rhymes, cute misquotations—
"how can his word sleep in his hand," for example. While these
little cadenzas are being performed the progress of the poem is
held up: "Awful the tall walls consorting that direction/From which
like traps appalling fungus falls/Athwart my throat. . . ." One
reviewer praises particularly the use of internal rhymes and the
interlocking by rhyme of the end and beginning of successive lines
as signs of Barker's technical originality.[61] But though they may be
original, such devices are more often meretricious ornamentation
than a contribution to meaning.

Quite a lot of the self-conscious stylishness in Barker is the
imitation of other poets: Edith Sitwell, Blake, Donne, Eliot, Yeats,
Hopkins, and Dylan Thomas. Barker seems to have felt, for one
thing, that a poem about a poet, a kind he frequently makes, ought
to be embellished with a little of the other's style. In his sonnet
to Hopkins we get this:

> He is for ever his feathers of sunset shedding,
>    Bedding all beautiful in the far harder and softer
> Breath of his word, bird in a thrash alighting
>    All claws for the world that his heart is after. . . .[62]

60. A. Desmond Hawkins, Review of *Calamiterror, Twentieth Century Verse*,
no. 4 (June/July 1937), p. 78.

61. Anon., *Times Literary Supplement*, March 23, 1940.

62. *Collected Poems, 1930–1955* (London: Faber & Faber, 1957), pp. 174–75.

In a poem for Dylan Thomas, the echoes of "A Refusal to Mourn . . ." do what the poet says he cannot do:

> I cannot take, even for such a purpose
> As to honour this death by an act of passion,
> The word that wore the ring of his married breath.
>
> I will not . . .
> . . . . . . . . . . . . . . . . . . . .
> Vex his cold nurse with a fragmentation of heart.
>
> (p. 206)

"The Death of Yeats" begins "That dolphin-torn, that gong-tormented face. . . ."

Meaning is sometimes come at with difficulty through the jungle of the wordplay, and one needs to be fairly general in identifying it. A reviewer of *Calamiterror* instructs us that the theme is "the finding of an objective, adequate view of the world,"[63] and this fits Barker's own assessment. But one couldn't say that this was *not* the theme of *Hamlet, The Ambassadors*, Pound's *Cantos, Lord Jim*, and *Howl*.

This style and others in the same general category of the highly self-conscious are the indulgence only of those writers with an overweening love of words, as Grigson points out in the passage quoted above in connection with Dylan Thomas. Poems are made with words—this we have all heard often; and Barker's response to a query about his attitude to poetry was that it was an "amorous" one.[64] One does not have to go far to find praise for his verbal magic, accompanied sometimes perhaps with an admission of intellectual thinness. "His individual tropes and symbols . . . would be ludicrous were it not for the magnificent rhetoric. . . ."[65] Or "every single poem contains a suspension, an intensity and drama, a discovery,

63. X, in *New Verse*, no. 28 (July 1938), pp. 20–21. Francis Scarfe says it can be "read as a sort of imaginative autobiography, a struggle from darkness to the light" ("George Barker: A Pure Poet," *Auden and After*, p. 126).

64. Quoted in Stanley Kunitz and Vineta Colby, eds., *Twentieth Century Authors: A Biographical Dictionary of Modern Literature* (New York: Wilson, 1955), p. 46.

65. F. C. Golfing, "Mr. Barker and His Critics," *Poetry* 72 (April 1948): 37.

a vitality. . . ."[66] Scarfe finds *Calamiterror* "perhaps" the most successful long poem of the thirties. And David Daiches has perceptively exhibited the function of connotations, diction, and symbols in Barker's poem "The Amazons."[67] As already seen, Stephen Spender admired Barker's *Calamiterror* because the poet showed he had no determined character like Rex Warner's and was vulnerable to imagination experience and totally involved with it.

The lack of "determined 'character'" Spender mentions is a condition like that at which the surrealists arrived when they attempted to present their unconscious impulses without inhibition from the conscious mind. English writers and painters took an increasing interest in surrealism during the thirties, which came to a high point when the surrealist exhibition in London in 1936 touched off a temporary but fairly widespread enthusiasm for surrealist poetry. It made quite an impact on the little periodicals, one or two of which issued surrealist numbers or a double number devoted to such poetry. Most of them devoted editorial space to the arrival of this curious immigrant, even the institutional *London Mercury.* Two editors declared themselves against it: Tambimuttu of *Poetry* (London)[68] and Julian Symons of *Twentieth Century Verse.*[69] The periodical most hospitable to surrealist poetry was *Contemporary Poetry and Prose,* edited by Roger Roughton, which printed work by an extraordinarily wide range of writers, a few of whom are thought of as surrealists regularly, some never, and some part of the time: besides Roughton himself there were Gavin Ewart, E. E. Cummings, Kenneth Allott, Wallace Stevens ("Farewell to

66. Harvey Breit, "View of the World," *Poetry* 59 (December 1941): 160.

67. David Daiches, "The Lyricism of George Barker," *Poetry* 69 (March 1947): 336–39.

68. "Life and the understanding of it is surrealist, but writing about it is intellectual. Therefore it is futile to practice surrealism purposively" ("First Letter," *Poetry* [London]1 [February 1939]).

69. No. 3 (April/May 1937), p. 42: "because it is a movement of 'literary' painters and poets who use words as if they were separate blobs of colour to be stuck on a canvas, not words to be made into a poem: because it has no standards of craftsmanship, but automatic standards, so that surrealists disagree about what is genuine and every crackpot can write a poem that may be called surrealist: because it has become a political movement: because art, finally, is made by individuals and not by groups."

Florida"), Dylan Thomas, Ruthven Todd, Kerker Quinn, George Barker, Roy Fuller, Hugh Sykes Davies, A. J. M. Smith, and David Gascoyne; in translation, Salvador Dali ("Cradled Pamphlet": two stanzas exactly identical linked with the remark, "Yes I will repeat it a thousand times"), René Char, Alfred Jarry, Paul Eluard, and others.

David Gascoyne's book, *A Short Survey of Surrealism*, had appeared in 1935. It included André Breton's definition: "Surrealism, n. Pure psychic automatism, by which it is intended to express, verbally, in writing, or by other means, the real process of thought. Thought's dictation, in the absence of all control exercised by the reason and outside all aesthetic or moral preoccupations."[70]

Some poems of Charles Madge present a juxtaposition of images almost as fortuitous as the famous chance meeting of the sewing machine and the umbrella on the dissecting table:

> The little sun fled backward through the sky
> The airy cloudy cumulus split every way
> The remote sea was with the remote fish.
>
> Merciless into morsels
> She cut her young brother and cast them
> On the sea where each a battleship became
> In whitest blossom decked.[71]

And in a recent declaration about poetic creation Madge acknowledges that he gives a pretty free rein to the "something" that "dictates itself in the poem": "I am not really free to choose whether I write poetry or not. This is something which is decided for me. And therefore what comes out of it is also to some extent decided for me."[72] But in Madge we are more often impressed with manifestations of formal control, even though this may fail to render the work lucid. Madge believed that English poets should not follow the French slavishly in this matter of surrealism. He re-

70. *A Short Survey of Surrealism* ([London]: Cobden Sanderson, 1935), p. 61.
71. "The Hours of the Planets," *The Disappearing Castle* (London: Faber and Faber, 1937), p. 25.
72. *The Poet Speaks,* ed. Peter Orr (New York: Barnes and Noble, 1966), p. 140.

commended to the young poet some remarks by Edward Young, author of "Night Thoughts": "'. . . in the ode . . . the imagination, like a very beautiful mistress, is indulged in the appearance of domineering; though the judgment, like an artful lover in reality carries its point, and the less it is suspected of it, it shows the more masterly conduct and deserves the greater commendation.'"[73] Madge is prepared to permit some rein to imagination, particularly in conflict and contradiction. Some English and French critical sources he quotes are in agreement in this matter. "The theory of metaphor and the double image—Young's 'connexion exquisite of distant worlds' and Lautréamont's 'rencontre fortuite sur une table de dissection d'une machine à coudre et d'un parapluie'— should guide the poet to development of his own tradition, the product of his own environment."[74]

It would be expected that the poetry of Charles Madge, co-creator of Mass-Observation, would be dense with observations about such fair sociological game as the bus conductor or the coronation. But this is not the case. Madge's poetry makes a long stride away from naturalism, and it is more remarkable as a technical exercise than as a reflection of recognizable life; it is as esoteric as anyone could wish, and we recall that Madge went to Cambridge and admired William Empson (both were Winchester and Magdelene— some years apart).[75] The least esoteric poems are those in which Madge declaims against the corruption of the present time or anticipates the birth of a new world.

> We have no home. Our bourgeois home is wrecked.
> We seek instead the shadowy consolation
> Of glimmering alcohol. . . .[76]

> We shall be differently aware, we shall see all things new
> Not as a craze or a surprise, but hard, naked, true.[77]

73. "Surrealism for the English." *New Verse*, no. 6 (December 1933), p. 15.
74. *Ibid.*, p. 17.
75. Kenneth Allott, *The Penguin Book of Contemporary Verse* (Harmondsworth, Middlesex: Penguin Books, 1950), p. 199.
76. *Disappearing Castle*, p. 50.
77. "Instructions," *New Verse*, no. 2 (March 1933).

Except for the pejorative use of the word bourgeois, these poems have little or no explicit marxist sentiment. A number of the esoteric poems convey a vague sense of the loss of Eden, or its possible reclamation in a fantasy of the imagination — this followed by a mortifying realization of error.

> Lulled by the waves, no mortal heart resists
> The gaudy scenery of the noble bay,
> That paradisal image which persists
> In all its brightness to the present day.[78]

These lines have more lucidity than is usual in Madge. The poems repeatedly use images of angels, the traveler, the exile, things vertical standing upon things horizontal, light, stone, and houses. Most of the poems in *The Disappearing Castle* and *The Father Found* are impenetrably obscure. The collocation of images sometimes suggests surrealism; but if they were arrived at by the short-circuiting of conscious control, they are very frequently subject to a fairly firm meter—quatrains or *terza rima* or other. It is possible that Madge has consciously suppressed the straightforward in order that the effects of the sounds of the poem may play their part unmasked by mere prose sense (unlike Eliot, who offered the reader meaning as a bone offered the housedog by the burglar, so that poetry would work on him thus distracted) and perhaps with the intention of keeping the poem open to whatever incidental unpremeditated meaning might enter. Spender says the poems of *The Disappearing Castle* enable Madge "to slide from one elusive mental position to another." He goes on, "His poems have no rhetoric, they say little or nothing, they have a clear, exact imagery, a beautiful music, and they leave often the impression of something colourless and transparent. Technically, his poems seem to stand midway between the imagists and the surrealists."[79] Two of the four triads of "In Sua Voluntade" may serve as a brief illustration:

78. *Disappearing Castle*, p. 52.
79. "New Poetry," *Left Review* 3 (July 1937): 361.

Fly, life, in quiet despair of empty air
Between the two-fold freezing of the poles
As still as eyesight. Fly and be found, where

The cloud-coloured sea soft over the shoals
Breaks like fine hands on the numb sands.
. . . I am broken. The air is full of holes.[80]

The clever deployment of sounds will be remarked and with it the uncertainty of the sense. It is not an entirely unsatisfactory artifact, but it is a far remove from observation and the lucidity it was hoped that mass-observation would bring.

Dylan Thomas, also, writes at times as though he were practicing surrealism; but he has disclaimed that procedure, describing his own method and giving some emphasis both to the presiding rational control and, like Madge, to conflict;[81] we know from his worksheets of his extensive labor of the file. Grigson remarks, "Pure, deliberate Surrealist poems (if that is not a contradiction) which aim at no meaning are acceptable enough; but many of these poems by [George] Barker and [Dylan] Thomas were not of that kind. They were half-aimed at meaning but missed it, or achieved it imperfectly."[82]

Most of David Gascoyne's first volume, *Roman Balcony*,[83] produced at the age of sixteen, is devoted to brief poems, each composed of a few images. These are fresh, and they are freely presented; the poet does not seem anxious to put his perceptions to any moral use, simply to offer them. But the poems are coherent

80. *Disappearing Castle*, p. 15. Elision in last line quoted is in the text.
81. "A poem by myself needs a host of images. I make one image, though 'make' is not the word: I let, perhaps, an image be made emotionally in me and then apply to it what intellectual and critical forces I possess; let it breed another; let that image contradict the first, make, of the third image, bred out of the other two together, a fourth contradictory image, and let them all, within my imposed formal limits, conflict" (Quoted in Henry Treece, *Dylan Thomas 'Dog Among the Fairies'* [London: Lindsay Drummond, 1949], p. 32).
82. Introduction, *Poetry of the Present: An Anthology of the Thirties and After* (London: Phoenix House, 1949), p. 21. In the interview quoted above Barker remarks that "The Surrealist idea was certainly the most exciting idea around then."
83. (London: Temple Bar, 1932).

in the way surrealist poems are not. His next volume, *Man's Life Is This Meat*,[84] consists largely of what Grigson would call, "pure deliberate Surrealist poems." One or two betray the operation of the reason, though it may be a minimal operation, hardly limiting at all the autonomy of what the unconscious has delivered forth. By the time this volume had appeared, however, Gascoyne had renounced surrealism.[85]

There is, of course, a difference between the completely surrealist poem—the whole thing welling up, image by image, uncensored from our unknown depths—and the contrived poem in which, well within the poet's control, are smaller elements which, though in themselves they may have come unbidden and illogically to the poet's mind, have been deliberately attached to the framework of the poem. There is, in fact, little poetry of the former kind in the period; there is an appreciable amount of successful work of the latter kind.

Some of the poems of Spender give an impression like the one he himself derived from Madge's work—they are abstracted away from meaning into transparency, and lie in the territory between imagism and surrealism. Others may seem to employ imagery that has been provided by the unconscious without being a completely unconscious product but having suffered minimal inspection by the conscious mind, or they may seem to have brought together imagery in such a haphazard way. If surrealism, as defined, is not the *method* of such practice, the practice of surrealism is perhaps the *sanction*. Here are two examples from Spender where an image is consciously arrived at, one supposes, but where the *effect* is surrealistic: "Our eyes, fish wrapped in newspaper," in the poem "Perhaps,"[86] where the poet is bombarded with news to the extent that he feels all he sees is the newspaper, so that, in turn, his eyes are in effect "wrapped" in them and thus, newspapers being the usual wrapping

84. (London: Parton Press, 1936).
85. "The Surrealists themselves have a definite justification for writing in this way, but for an English poet with continually growing political convictions it must soon become impossible." (*New Verse*, no. 11 [October 1934]. Quoted by Robin Skelton, in his introduction to *The Collected Poems of David Gascoyne*, ed. Robin Skelton [London: Oxford University Press, 1965], p. xii.)
86. *Collected Poems* (London: Faber and Faber, 1955), p. 51.

for fish in England, are like fish. Then, second, "the wall-paper/
blowing smoke-wreaths of roses. . . ."[87] is an image of which the
stages in its fabrication may be traced: first there is wallpaper with
roses in wreath form; second, the word *wreath* reminds the poet of
wreaths of smoke and leads to the combination. Not surrealist in
origin, it is a product like the surrealist. If surrealism is a style of the
greatest degree of purity and unconsciousness, its effect arrived at
otherwise will be contrived and excessively conscious.

It seems that in this decade there were more cute reflections and
clever imitations of predecessors than in other decades: Barker's
imitation of Yeats, quoted above, is of this kind; Bottrall's imitation
of Yeats, Donne, and others in his later volume; C. Day Lewis's
imitation of Milton, Hopkins, and the Rubaiyat. Edgell Rickword's
echo of Shelley is somewhat typical for its skilled trifling and the
uncertain value of its effects: "You must meet Iris, she who lives
serene/in the intense confusion of the obscene. . . ." The memory of
Shelley's "Letter to Maria Gisborne," "You will see Coleridge—he
who sits obscure/In the exceeding lustre and the pure/Intense
irradiation of a mind . . ." provides a qualification of tone, brings
the clever personality of the speaker into the lights, and upstages the
subject.

The decade also, however, makes a more profound use of its
mentors and models, where these are sometimes hardly identifiable
and yet in a subtle way may be felt. It is possible to open a volume of
poems or a review upon a couple of stanzas and, without making
accurate attributions of indebtedness for image or idea or each
element of diction or rhythm, know perfectly well that without
Hopkins, Eliot, Graves, or Auden, and perhaps without the surrealist interest, the lines printed there would not be as they are. The
following lines, for instance, are taken at random, as that term is
usually used, from *New Verse*; they are not literally a communal
effort like the Oxford Poem, but they manifest the product of an
assemblage of the best genes of the time:

87. "Thoughts During an Air Raid," *Collected Poems*, p. 96.

Cries in the head were making him light,
He found it difficult sleeping at night,
The warmth of the women was a shocking reward,
And their unfortunate wishes were growing weird.
There was no kind of good in staying on
When the delight was gone.

O where did he head for? The wind in the wood,
And the goat on the tether was coughing up blood,
The clock on the church was pointing at ten
As he passed by the women and left the men.
There was no kind . . .[88]
                                    (refrain)

The following lines too show a similar composite parentage:

Now, evening and lilacs and honey can magnetize
The rose and the crocus speak for history:
Time for the act with the sun and the wonderful skies,
There is time for lolling cool in valley streams
Hearing the innocent airman's roars.[89]

Risking the awful and inevitable dangers of generalization, one
might say that these are the kinds of poem you get in the thirties.

88. E. V. Swart, "Casey Jones," *New Verse*, no. 21 (June–July 1936), p. 4.
89. Hugh Chisholm, "Ode," *New Verse* 1 (January 1939): 8.

## 7

# Spender's Volumes of Verse

Spender's first poems appeared in 1928, printed on his own small hand press at No. 10 Frognal, Hampstead, London, N. W. 3, in an edition of 500 copies. The press was also used for printing chemists' labels and the earliest edition of Auden's poems (1928). In the middle of producing these, however, it collapsed.[1] The volume of his own work is entitled *Nine Experiments: Being Poems Written at the Age of Eighteen*. Spender says he subsequently rounded up and destroyed as many copies as he could. None of the poems is later reprinted.

The volume opens with "Invocation," which sounds as if it were inspired by Shelley's "Ode to the West Wind":

1. Stephen Spender, Foreword to Fascimile of *Nine Experiments: Being Poems Written at the Age of Eighteen* (Cincinatti: University of Cincinatti, 1944).

> Blow forever in my head!
> And ever let the violins, tempest-sworn
> Lash out their hurricane. . . .

The prevalence of imagery related to light in this volume, such as "sun" and "eye," is also reminiscent of Shelley; and since it is a regular feature of all Spender's subsequent poetry, his early susceptibility to light is worth remarking. He makes more use here than later of the repetition of individual words, though it is always among his stock techniques; much of it here is a matter of trifling. There is also a certain playfulness in rhyming, which may be what he refers to when he says, "When I wrote NINE EXPERIMENTS, I was still in the stage of putting my money on an appearance of madness in my poems" (p. x). Thus in "Gilles" he writes,

> Gilles de Rais'
> > FACE,
> How blue the fringes shone!
> The tassels were
> > Torn from the air,
> (The sky is made of silk there). . . .

And "Ovation for Spring" goes

> The nineteenth time, from bough to bough
> I see the mocking fires of spring;
> And twice I've rhymed the name with 'king',
> But I am grown more *blasé* now.

He is very blasé and very self-conscious throughout. One doesn't want to pin too much solemn deduction on a few instances of self-consciousness and play. But it would be interesting if this technique, to be superseded later by others, were a means, conscious or otherwise, of protecting a rather raw-nerved, naked engagement with the poetic object. Other poems testify in part to an impulse to shield the sensibilities. Thus, for instance, the "whorl/whirl" play in the following passage from "Evening on the Lake—*(dolce)*," acts as some sort of stiffener in an otherwise passive Shelleyan response to beauty:

Beauty cometh: See how gently
`Graven in the        Water, play
The lazy whorls, which        Whirl absently
Round the prow, and        Glide away. . . . .

Later on we shall see techniques that are apparently calculated to
break in and destroy romantic excitement or lyrical pitch, controlling
emotion by deliberately introducing bathos. So, similarly, on
certain occasions in his career, Spender dealt with his overpowering
feeling: when seeing the fascist stage effects in Rome or upon
receiving a brief glimpse of General Goering as he entered Dubrov-
nic, he burst into a high-pitched giggle.[2]

A poem called "Appeal" should be noted for it anticipates
sympathies that are to be developed further: it opens, "The voices
of the poor, like birds/that thud against a sullen pane,/Have worn
my heart. . . ." The simile too is characteristic of Spender's later
verse.

There is not a great deal of merit in these poems; Spender remarked thirty-six years after they were composed that he did not
publish anything "worth preserving" until Blackwell's came out
with his *Twenty Poems* in 1930.[3] This volume is made of more
durable stuff: fourteen of the twenty poems are reproduced in the
*Collected Poems* of 1955,[4] having appeared again before that in
both editions of *Poems,* 1933 and 1934.[5] The poems appear in the
order of composition except for the first one, "At the Edge of
Being," which was composed later than its position indicates.
Poem II, "Discovered in Mid-Ocean" (first line: "He will watch
the hawk with an indifferent eye"), is surmounted by a rubric, "The
'Marston' Poems," which, though the title is not repeated at the
top of each following page, is presumably a series that includes
numbers II to XII, for above No. XIII is the heading "Other
Poems." Only six of the Marston series were reprinted in the

2. Geoffrey Grigson, *The Crest on the Silver* (London: Cresset Press, 1950),
pp. 169–70.
3. (Oxford: Blackwell).
4. (London: Faber and Faber).
5. Both published in London by Faber and Faber. One poem from *Twenty Poems,*
"I hear the cries of evening," was dropped from the 1934 edition of *Poems.*

*Collected Poems*, and then not as a group. "Other Poems" consists of eight unrelated pieces, including "'I' Can Never Be Great Man" and "Beethoven's Death Mask," familiar to anthologies. All but one of these eight, "Always Between Hope and Fear," are reprinted in *Collected Poems*.

The "Marston" poems are related to an experience Spender describes in his autobiography.[6] Marston is the name he gives to a fellow undergraduate at Oxford, who was a boxer, skier, and pilot but who was withdrawn, Spender felt, from the other college athletes, the "hearties," as they were generally known. Spender developed an emotional attachment to him which was unilateral and frustrating:

> Rushing in room and door flung wide, I knew.
> Oh empty walls, book-carcases, blank chairs
> All splintered in my head and cried for you.[7]

His enthusiasm was met with "quiet politeness" and the indifference that seems, paradoxically, to have been Marston's most attractive quality. After the relationship was over, Spender began, he says, to write poems different from any previous ones. "A concrete situation had suddenly crystallized feelings which until then had been diffused and found no object." The Marston series begins with the superman poem, "Discovered in Mid-Ocean," in which Spender as poet has resolved the oppression of his real personal predicament by a species of amputation—making an image of the unattainable beloved as dead:

> This aristocrat, superb of all instinct,
>           With death close linked
> Had paced the enormous cloud, almost had won
>           War on the sun;
> Till now like Icarus mid-ocean-drowned,
>           Hands, wings, are found. . . .
>                   (p. 3)

6. *World Within World: The Autobiography of Stephen Spender* (London: Hamish Hamilton, 1951), pp. 64–67.
7. *Twenty Poems*, p. 7.

In another of the series, "Marston, dropping it in the grate, broke
his pipe," Spender celebrates the pipe Marston had bought on a
continental holiday, appreciating it for its associations. He is
using the poetry here as a means of taking possession of a part
of Marston's coveted activities; as in another poem, "Saying
'good morning,'" he recognizes that conversation is "a form of
possession / Like taking your wrists. . . ." In the second poem of the
series, "The Dust Made Flesh," which has not been reprinted, the
poet describes how he has created four figures. It is a creation
somewhat in the manner in which Yeats created his characters, and
Spender's lines recall the rhythms of Yeats. Marston, although
we know him to have been real, is here designated one of the poets'
creations:

> First made I Marston the superb boxer
> More than with men who dealt with death,
> Marston who ski-ed through snow,
> Curved through the whiteness, ran,
> Helmeted drove through air. . . .

After Marston came Helen, "Dark-eyed, words piercing night
like stars"; then Catherine, who "sprang in sky" and "Along the
ice-fleeced rocks shot chamois down." Finally there is Ainger, the
poet

> . . . severe, voiced raucous-reed,
> With fascinating facets of crude mind,
> An enormous percipient mass on the plain.

Spender did not in fact *make* Marston as the poem claims; and the
others are perhaps no more fictitious than he—Ainger, indeed, might
for some features be Auden, briefly sketched.[8] But they may all
be allowed to be the poet's imaginative creations; while each is
very unlike him, each perhaps embodies desirable characteristics
and is a coveted projection of himself; Spender is like Yeats again,

8. C. Day Lewis has a similar piece, but more clearly Yeatsian, in *Transitional
Poem,* in which those who have his allegiance are mustered, like the friends of Yeats
"that cannot sup with us" ("In Memory of Major Robert Gregory"): Lewis's last-
named figure is "the tow-haired poet," who breeds "a piebald strain of truth and
nonsense"—a more accurate rendering of Auden.

who summoned the image of the "most unlike" who was his anti-self.

The characters are more likely to be coveted because each of them seems all of a piece: each can be briefly epitomized in one or more swift studies of imagery. In this respect the poem anticipates a later expression of Spender's qualified admiration for people whose personalities were so unified that they could be summed up in a single image or phrase: the "truly great," for example, of the poem that begins, "I think continually of those who were truly great,"[9] who leave the air "signed with their honour." There are others who appear in the later poetry, especially in *The Still Centre,* who are of this kind of distinction. They are unlike the complex, disjointed "I" who can never be a great man, in the poem on that subject, on account of all the disparate parts, "'I eating'/'I loving,' 'I angry,' 'I excreting'"; and Spender repeatedly recognizes their appeal to him.

In the poems of the Marston series that follow "The Dust Made Flesh," only Marston appears again by name, and he in only one of them; Helen, Catherine, and Ainger are not again identifiable. The remaining poems either celebrate a man or address a person, who may be man or woman, to whom the speaker is apparently emotionally attached; in each case it is presumably Marston. The last poem in the series, "The Port," is incongruous in that it neither mentions nor addresses any single person, being only a well-packed description of a port; but perhaps the sinister imagery of graves, caves, skewed faces, lightning, and so on are an objective equivalent for the poet's feelings of frustration and grief.

One poem of this volume not in the Marston series is related to an incident in life: "Written Whilst Walking Down the Rhine," in *Collected Poems* titled "In 1929," refers to a meeting of three young men—the poet and two Germans, Joachim and Heinrich, a communist clerk. The story of Heinrich, Spender says, was a "fragment of the saga of all this German youth which had been born into war, starved in the blockade, stripped in the inflation— and which now . . . sprang like a breed of dragon's teeth . . ."[10]

9. *Poems,* 1933, p. 37.
10. *World Within World,* p. 116.

The poem looks back ten years and finds two of the three young men at war; it looks forward ten and finds Heinrich, the communist, building his world out of "our bones." There is now no prompting by the dead fathers for revenge:

> Now I suppose that the once-envious dead
> Have learned a strict philosophy of clay
> After these centuries, to haunt us no longer
> In the churchyard, or at the end of the lane
> Or howling at the edge of the city
> Beyond the last bean-rows, near the new factory.[11]

When the poem reappeared in Spender's next volume, Allen Tate pronounced it one of the finest in the century, remarking in it a clarity and a mastery of words that had been absent from English verse since Landor.

The poems in *Twenty Poems* are rich in concrete imagery. One or two of them are even descriptive as wholes: "The Port," for instance, or "I hear the cries of evening," the Georgian type of poem that describes evening in the country; and such poetry is unusual among Spender's shorter pieces. In one of the Marston poems there is also humor, which is also somewhat rare: shocked at the magnitude of his affection upon a small occasion, he thought,

> . . . if these were tricklings through a dam,
> I must have love enough to run a factory on,
> Or give a city power, or drive a train.
>                                      (p. 9)

In his autobiography, Spender mentions that Harold Nicolson offered to notice *Twenty Poems* in his column in the *Daily Express* but that he, Spender, declined the offer, saying that the volume was not for public sale, "but really out of pride and for no other reason."[12]

Spender's next volume, *Poems,* was published in 1933, by Faber and Faber. He had arrived in Russell Square. In this volume are gathered those poems for which, judging by the anthologies, he has been chiefly known throughout his poetic career. There are thirty-

11. *Twenty Poems,* p. 15.
12. *World Within World,* pp. 144–45.

three poems in all, ten of which had already appeared in *Twenty Poems*: these include five of the Marston poems, "At the Edge of Being," deprived now of its title and relegated to a position later in the volume (No. X), "'I' Can Never Be Great Man," "Different Living," "Beethoven's Death Mask," and "I hear the cries of evening." Of the other twenty-three in the new volume, seven had already appeared in 1932 in Michael Roberts's *New Signatures*.[13] These seven were the poems that first brought Spender to the attention of the public and first linked him in its mind with Auden and C. Day Lewis. The poems are "Oh Young Men," "The Prisoners," "I Think Continually," "Who Live Under the Shadow," "The Express," "My Parents" ("My parents kept me from children who were rough"), and "The Funeral." *Poems* contains in addition such familiar anthologized pieces as "What I expected," "After they have tired," "The Landscape Near an Aerodrome," "The Pylons," and "Not palaces, an era's crown." Among these are expressions of leftist sentiment which, while they were received by the doctrinaire Marxists without enthusiasm, as we have seen, have somewhat colored Spender's poetical reputation. In the introduction to *Collected Poems*, Spender says that he has included in that volume certain poems like "The Pylons" and "The Funeral" because "there seemed an obligation to 'own up'" to them, "when they were written [they] provided a particular label for some of the poetry of the 'Thirties: an embarrassment to my friends' luggage more even than to my own."[14] There are, as a matter of fact, relatively few poems that are unequivocally leftist.

*Poems*, 1933, was noticed in a bland paragraph in the *Times Literary Supplement* of July 6, 1933. The use both of the idiom of the day and also of an older vocabulary is remarked. The poet's main defect is said to be a lyrical exaggeration not always germane to the starker material, a comment that is surely an expression of the uneasiness incurred on account of the ill-assortment of the lyricism and the bathos in such poems as "Not palaces" and "The

13. *New Signatures: Poems by Several Hands,* ed. Michael Roberts (London: Leonard and Virginia Woolf, 1932).

14. *Collected Poems: 1928–1953* (London: Faber and Faber, 1955), p. 13.

Funeral." But the main impression received by the *TLS* reviewer is of gentleness and a peculiar sweetness of temperament—so far from the so-called modern world. The rhythms are found to be personal and persuasive. F. R. Leavis also noticed this volume, but in a manner a little more strenuous. He found immaturity and instability in the technique, he observed unrealized imagery, and he said Spender was given to the "glamorous-ineffable-vague." Illustrating these defects he quotes from four poems: "My parents quarrel in the neighbour room," "The Port," "I hear the cries of evening," and "Your body is stars whose million glitter here." Of the first of these, Leavis says, "Mr. Spender is unformed enough to be able to reproduce (quite unwittingly, it seems) the Meredith of *Modern Love*." The echo of Meredith is admittedly clear enough:

> My parents quarrel in the neighbour room.
> "How did you sleep last night?" "I woke at four
> To hear the wind that sulks along the floor
> Blowing up dust like ashes from the tomb."[15]

It is audible also incidentally in one of the Marston poems, "Acts passed beyond the boundary of mere wishing":

> Then once you said "Waiting was very kind"
> And looked surprised: surprising for me too
> Whose every movement had been missionary,
> A pleading tongue unheard. I had not thought
> That you, who nothing else saw, would see this.
>
> (p. 15)

Spender is not by any means alone in speaking in a voice like Meredith's: the echo of *Modern Love* is heard repeatedly throughout the decade in lyrics that poetize an emotionally charged relationship.

Leavis uses "I hear the cries of evening" to illustrate his contention that "slightly disguised in the technical modernizing, there is a good deal of the Georgian" in the volume, saying the poem might have come from one of the Georgian anthologies. The poem about parents did not reappear in Spender's later volumes; "I hear the

---

15. *Poems*, p. 22.

cries of evening," dropped from the second edition of *Poems,* turned up again in the *Collected Poems.* "The Port" and "Your body is stars" have remained.

For the second edition, nine poems were added to the first, which, with the withdrawal of the two just mentioned, made a total of forty. Three of those added had appeared in Michael Roberts's *New Country;*[16] about half of them were to appear again in *Collected Poems.* Among those added is "Van der Lubbe," which is the name of the young Dutch communist who in the year previous had been blamed for the burning of the *Reichstag.* In the defendant's laughter Spender sees reflected the madness and twisted justice of contemporary Germany. The poem was not reprinted. Another poem added, "For T. A. R. H.," is based on the poet's relationship with the young man Hyndman, which he discusses at some length in the autobiography. The poem is reprinted in *Poems* (1934), with revisions, from the *New Oxford Outlook* and appears again, with more revision, in *Collected Poems.*

> Even whilst I watch him I am remembering
> The quick laugh of the wasp gold eyes. . . .
>         . . . for love
> Is soaked in memory and says
> I have seen what I see, and I wear
> All pasts and futures like a doomed, domed sky. . . .[17]

There is much of Spender in this short poem; some of its features are characteristics that have already been mentioned; others are those that remain to be discussed. Biographically, there is the affection for another man, a kind of love of which the incidence in society is no doubt greater than the frequency with which it is discussed. It is fairly typical also inasmuch as the poem is not immediately concerned with Hyndman (its title after all is "*For* T.A.R.H.") but with Spender's own inner world in its response to Hyndman. And accordingly, in consonance with this fact, the

---

16. *New Country: Prose and Poetry by the Authors of "New Signatures,"* ed. Michael Roberts (London: Leonard and Virginia Woolf, 1933).
17. *Poems.* 2nd ed. (London: Faber and Faber, 1934), p. 36.

substance of the poem has been largely withdrawn from the facts
in the external world that gave it impetus; the imagery is relatively
insubstantial, and it has been refined into a structure where the
laws of art prevail, and sounds determine word selection:

> . . . a doomed, domed sky.
> Thus I wear always the glint of quick lids
> And the blue axel turning. . . .

In 1934, the same year as the second edition of *Poems,* Spender's
long poem, *Vienna,* appeared.[18] It celebrates certain of the details
of the defeat of the socialist insurrectionists in February 1934, in
Austria, where Spender had traveled shortly after it occurred.
This was socialism's first battle and its first defeat. But although
there is an image in a poem of Charles Madge's and a reference or
two in John Lehmann's poems, *Vienna* is the only major literary
work in English devoted to the tragedy. It uses a passage from
Wilfred Owen's "Strange Meeting" for epigraph: "They will be
swift with swiftness of the tigress,/ None will break ranks, though
nations trek from progress."

The poem is in four parts; it presents images of the political life
of Austria and details of the fighting, particularly the heroic episodes
of the capture, trial, and killing of Kaloman Wallisch, the socialist
mayor of Bruck-an-der-Mur. Then, along with this public material
and awkwardly associated with it, the poem presents certain purely
personal feelings of the poet's that are attached to an entirely
different and separate matter, a love affair he had pursued in
Austria, in the spring of the same year as the insurrection, with an
American woman, whom he calls Elizabeth in the autobiography.[19]
In the poem, no concrete details of the affair are given; only feelings,
presented expressionistically or in abstraction. In the autobiography
Spender dwells on the reason that he had imposed the private
matter upon the public: "public events had swamped our personal
lives," he writes, "and usurped our personal experiences." But

---

18. (London: Faber and Faber, 1934). Spender is mistaken in saying, in *World Within World,* that he wrote it in 1935.
19. *World Within World,* pp. 193–201.

characteristically he had hung on to his private life, and thus "a poetry which rejected private experience would have been untrue to me." He says of *Vienna* that it was intended to express his indignation at the suppression of the socialists;

> but in part also it was concerned with a love relationship. I meant to show that the two experiences were different, yet related. For both were intense, emotional and personal, although the one was public, the other private. The validity of the one was dependent on that of the other: for in a world where humanity was trampled on publicly, private affection was also undermined. (p. 192)

These things are not quite so. The validities of socialism and human love are not necessarily dependent upon one another; private affection is not undermined by the presence of inhumanity in the world at large; and things that are intense and emotional are not necessarily thereby related. The effects named are not consequent upon the causes given, unless, by fiat of his imagination, the poet, drawing all things into his personal center, effectively make them so. This was no doubt his intention, and the product was to have been one variety of this poet's pervading expressionism.

But Spender recognizes that *Vienna* was a failure; certainly the relationship he claims and the interdependence of validities quite fail to manifest themselves, and they do not assist the flimsy structure in its unequal burden of containing both the objective and the subjective elements. We may observe here, however, that Spender's poetry most characteristically strains beyond its ability to make unity where diversity is overwhelming and to make resolutions out of unresolvable conflicts. More than for most poets, for Stephen Spender throughout his work, not to have failed would be not to have assayed a sufficiently tough project, to have shortchanged the complexity of things, to have taken the simplicity of appearances too much on trust, simplicity that has not won its way through complexity not being worth having.

The first part of the poem, "Arrival at the City," describes the unwholesome *patron* of the Pension Beaurepas, who brings to the poet's mind that "many men so beautiful" lay dead while this vulgarian lived on, and he compares him implicitly with Wallisch, whom he makes the hero of the rising. The constrast between them informs the first part of the poem; but in this part also, undisciplined by the structural scheme, there is the expression of feelings, which as mentioned, are not strictly germane to the objective parts of the poem. The poetry fluctuates between description of the outside objective world and description of inward sentiments; both efforts may employ concrete imagery; and thus, the movements from one thing to another not being marked, it is obscure.

After some fragments of self-revealing dialogue from the female residents of the Pension, the poem proceeds to force the paradox that the life of the patron is a decaying wound while the wounds and the death of the hero are an "Opening to life like a flower him overarching." Of the two examples, the poet says he chooses "the wholly dead." He adds, "their courtesy/Like lamps through the orange fog, with a glazed eye/Can preach still"; and the image is a small embodiment of the idea Spender develops later in "Exiles from their Land, History their Domicile," a poem in *The Still Centre,* that the dead, in his own words, have "obtained for their lives a symbolic significance which certainly passed unnoticed when they were living" and have imposed on the imagination of posterity a "legend of their unity of being."[20]

It is not death we fear, the poem goes on, but disloyalty to an ideal memory of peace in the past and disloyalty toward the dead. The poet wants to keep the past firm; just as the dead are to appear in the unity of being with which death has endowed them, so the past should be kept inviolate, though already the "settled mountain . . . Slides its burnt slopes." So later, in Spender's play, *Trial of a Judge,* the Judge wishes to act for the sake of peace and "for the survival of a vision/Within the human memory/Of absolute justice. . . ."

A sense of the drabness of reality presides over the last thirty lines or so of this part of the poem, drabness that is momentarily escaped in the possibility of forgiveness. The poet presents first the real situation in images that point to the ordinariness of a part of the town—"Unhomely windows, floors scrubbed clean of love,/A

20. *Collected Poems,* p. 14.

waste canvas sky," and the like. These images are presumably correlative to the poet's feelings about the revolution, from which the idea of forgiveness provides temporary relief. It provides also a link with the second theme of the poem, the love affair. A sense of guilt and the need for forgiveness simply for being a member of the rentier class and being thus immune to the sorrows of the workers was regularly manifested in Spender and in some of his colleagues. But for Spender guilt arose also out of his love affair with Elizabeth, because it conflicted with his feelings and his duties toward his secretary, T.A.R. Hyndman. We learn from the autobiography that Elizabeth and Spender discussed his guilt; and he wondered whether their explanations, "which made [his] 'psychology' responsible for everything, did not actually increase [his] sense of guilt."[21]

The idea of forgiveness comes to his mind glowing, paradoxically, like the first sin of loving in Eden:

> Instantly released, in joy and sorrow they fall,
> Escaping the whole world, two separate worlds of one,
> Writing a new world with their figure 2.

But reality returns in images of murky or "difficult" light, light "dripping/On speechless pavement," "The defeated/Staring, white canal." Part I closes with the same lines as those it opened with:

> Whether the man living or the man dying,
> Whether this man's dead life, or that man's life dying.

Part II, "Parade of the Executive," is itself divided into four parts marked by marginal subtitles in italics. The first part, *The Executive,* presents the rulers, Dolfuss, Fey, and Staremberg, as waxwork models in a parade, "Looking like bad sculptures of their photographs." They are parading in their fancy dress in in order to "illustrate the truth" that they are our ancestors. We are exhorted at the very end of the poem, however, that not these representatives of order but the revolutionaries whom they crushed are in fact our ancestors. Next, presented as counterpoint, there are

21. *World Within World,* p. 197.

the unemployed, who, reduced to an attitude of basic realism, "politely" stay away from the parade. One noticeable feature in a number of Spender's poems is the manner in which he swings from one theme to its polar opposite or to another contrasting theme, then swings back: and then sometimes, but not here, he comes finally to a resolution at a midway point. In the third section of this part of *Vienna* we come back to *The Executive* with images that show the determination and the strength of this group. Then at the end of this part, the poet introduces a figure called *The Stranger,* the observer of the political scene who, unlike the poet himself, is objective and impartial. "Would he forgive us?" the poem asks, returning at the end to the obsessive guilt, of which the poet is determined to cut himself a large share:

> Would he
> Glance at a minister who smiles and smiles
> "How now! A rat? Dead for a ducat." Shoot!

In Part III, "The Death of Heroes," the poet identifies himself with the revolution, analyzes the causes of its failure, and presents vignettes of the action, some of which are quotations in prose to which he adds verse summaries. The poem describes the retreat of Wallisch to the mountains and how he was hunted down and caught by ski-patrols, then his defense in court, then his death, and finally how sympathizers brought flowers for his grave and for the graves of the other dead revolutionaries. The villain of the piece is Vice-Chancellor Fey.

Part IV is titled "Analysis and Final Statement." First, five voices whose speeches are labeled with the letters A to E make a composite commentary; the poem here totally withdraws into the world within, where the poet wants to deal with his feelings. Voices representing the participants of the conflict brought on by the love relationship all speak here. Voices A and B recognize the value in the relationship. C admits the harm it does to "a friend/Who is external," presumably Hyndman. Then D, thus introduced, who has the longest speech of the five, speaks as that friend:

It is not what they stole nor what they spoiled . . .
It is that my devotion they have spilled
And bled my veins of trust across their sport.[22]

He forgives them, but he sometimes wishes, he says, that he were

loud and angry
Without this human mind like a doomed sky
That loves, as it must enclose, all.

The image of the doomed sky is associated with Hyndman in the poem "For T.A.R.H.," published in the second edition of *Poems* in 1934 (p. 36). In the passage in *Vienna,* D is no doubt expressing Spender's own hankering after the strength of will as he sees it in powerful men, as Arnold had hankered after it in the poem Spender quotes in *Forward From Liberalism.* The Judge in *Trial of a Judge* also regrets an inability to respond to situations with animal fierceness—an inability he considers characteristic of the liberal: "I envy, I envy/Those who had faith in the past to work the good/Or evil which they willed."[23] The comment of E (to return to *Vienna*) is obscure: he or she seems to be bringing the problem into alignment with the political matter by declaring that we rely upon corruption in men inasmuch as we rely upon their own self-esteem to motivate their heroism. Such an attitude spreads the guilt wide, bringing it to inhere in our very virtues.

Following the comments of the five voices, the poet begins to draw phrases and images from the earlier part of the poem, using these presumably to knit the parts together. But between such phrases, there are still the inward explorations of the poet's own "unknown, mental country." At last, the personal data and the political are fused—"yoked by violence together," rather—in a disintegrated profusion of imagery.

The failure of the poem to bring together its components was not one of the main charges brought by reviewers, who concentrated

22. A different interpretation of this passage was made by W. H. Sellers in "Spender and Vienna," *Humanities Association Bulletin* 18 (Spring 1967): 59–68.
23. (London: Faber and Faber, 1938), p. 73.

their objections on the images. D. M. T. in *New Verse*[24] finds in certain passages and image clusters a "falsity and affected ugliness," which he attributes to the current affiliation of Spender with political poets to whom he was, temporarily it seems, lending his moral weight. Tom Wintringham would have considered such moral weight to be negligible: as we have seen, he found Spender "unable to associate himself with the living stuff of the revolution," which inability produced in *Vienna* "a remoteness a coldness of image. . . ."[25] There is, certainly, a self-conscious contrivance about Spender's images all the way through *Vienna* and elsewhere that often makes them seem remote and cold; but there is no reason to attribute this to a lack of engagement in politics. It is conceivable that if he had abandoned himself to a burning political passion he would have fused all his materials into a unity; but, for better for worse, Spender never abandoned himself to anything. He never wrote out of excitement generated in the lower levels of the soul, whence come, for example, the terrifying or ecstatic outcries of Yeats or Roethke or Robert Graves; he brought forth no poetry that was not mediated through an analytic cerebration.

All this is not to say, obviously, that he had no feelings; probably these were in fact so strong that he was at pains to suppress them. Edwin Muir, one of Spender's most sensitive critics, notes that in *Vienna* there is no natural voice and nothing seems to be felt with definiteness, such feeling as there is being muffled in the "latest kind of poetic diction." And we need not suppose that this muffling was unintentional.

*Trial of a Judge,* 1938, produced by Rupert Doone for the Group Theatre, presents again the conflict between left and right, and with it that between public and private life, conflicts which, although very much Spender's own, have from the beginning of this century become familiar by their monstrous prodigies to every household in Europe and have not ceased since then to trouble the sleep of all sensible men. The conflict in the major key in this play is engaged between blacks (fascists) and reds (communists); between these

24. No. 12 (Dec. 1934), p. 20.
25. "Artists in Uniform," *Left Review* 1 (Feb. 1935): 158 n.

two factions stands the liberal Judge. The fascists have murdered Petra, on the mistaken assumption that he was a Jew, and the Judge has condemned them to death. The communists, molested while handing out leaflets, have shot and wounded a policeman in the arm; and because the carrying of firearms is so punishable, the Judge has condemned them to death also. Hummeldorf, a minister of the government, asks the Judge to reprieve the fascists; the Judge desires the President to reprieve the communists. Power in the state moves to the right, however; and the Judge, the reds, and also Hummeldorf, now converted to the liberal position, are imprisoned.

The conflict in the minor key is that between the private life and the public, which in one particular form the poet had attempted to resolve earlier in his poem *Vienna*. The Judge champions the private against the total claims of the state, asserted by both the blackshirts and the reds. In the following passage, which has already been referred to, the city is the *res publica*; and the natural world, the "greenness," symbolizes the private life. The Judge is speaking:

> Petra's murder
> Printed in a million newspapers
> Torn and carried by the wind,
> Tugs like entrails on the blackthorn
> And fouls the edges of the city
> Where greenness first begins[26]

Part of the private life is the vision of absolute justice—a memory from the past to be kept and kept sacred like the same kind of memory in *Vienna*; again the Judge speaks:

> Then, for the sake of such a peace
> · As still does mantle sunset villages
> Where the heart may love and rest,
> Which still to Europe I may restore;
> And, for the survival of a vision

---

26. *Trial of a Judge* (London: Faber and Faber, 1938), p. 29.

> Within the human memory
> Of absolute justice accepted by consent. . . .
>
> (p. 30)

For the fascists, of course, the nation is indivisible and "Embossed beneath one iron will"—everyone bearing the same stamp. One reviewer points out that the private life receives little enough dramatization in the play;[27] but, as will appear, Spender's distribution of dramatic life in the play is altogether gratuitous.

Like a number of Spender's shorter poems, the play has a dialectical structure: blacks versus reds, as thesis and antithesis, with the Judge not so much forming a synthesis as abjuring both their houses. The Judge's quarrel with the blackshirts has its obvious causes; and theirs with him is for his liberalism and his idealism: "this Judge," says the Black Troop Leader,

> believed
> That an argument would govern the state which drew its form
> From the same sources as the symmetry of music
> Or the most sensitive arrangement of poetic words
> Or the ultimate purification of a Day of Judgment.[28]

The Judge's quarrel with the reds is that he will not condone their policy of answering violence with violence and using lies and hate in their struggle, as if the ends justified all. For using their methods

> we betray
> The achievement in ourselves; our truth
> Becomes the prisoner of necessity
> Equally with their untruth, ourselves
> Their stone and stupid opposite.
>
> (pp. 103–4)

"Yeats," says Spender elsewhere, "was perhaps the writer who best understood that public passion can 'make a stone of the

27. Janet Adam Smith, in *Criterion* 17 (July 1938): 730–34.
28. *Trial of a Judge,* p. 109.

heart.'"[29] Between the Judge and the reds also falls the idea of abstract justice,[30] which the pragmatic reds reject, as indeed they reject the very idea of abstraction: the fiancée of Petra says to the Judge

> Let your self-pitying eyes sink
> Deep into their bone wells and stare
> At the world's tragedy played out in that one skull.[31]

Louis MacNeice says that the "intended moral of the play was that liberalism today was weak and wrong, communism was strong and right. But this moral was sabotaged by [Spender's] unconscious integrity; the Liberal Judge, his example of what-not-to-be, walked away with one's sympathy."[32] One reviewer of the play calls it a morality play, and this is reasonable since we find the villains declaring their villainy as they used to do in the old drama.

> A verbal victory is awarded to the Communists with their party line of tit-for-tat against the Fascists and the notion that finally power (the power of the proletariat) is right. But all the best arguments and all the feeling speeches go into the mouth of the judge with his defence of abstract justice. . . . Spender may have intended one moral for his play and diffidently suggested another. The only moral I could find was that Stephen Spender ought not to be a Communist. As a result of this contradiction in the play the judge walks out of the mosaic and becomes a character.[33]

29.  *World Within World,* p. 191. He elaborates the idea in his discussion of Yeats's "Easter 1916" in *The Creative Element* (London: Hamish Hamilton, 1953), pp. 118–19. The "doctrine of necessity" of the communists, says Spender, "taught them not only that necessity justified bad means and individual suffering, but also that it was necessary to deny that it did" (*The Creative Element,* p. 154).

30.  Louis MacNeice describes how, at the meeting arranged by the Group Theater to discuss the play, which was attended by a "squad" of comrades, an old man announced he was worried about one thing: "of course he knew S. could not have meant it, there must have been a mistake, but the writing seemed to imply an acceptance of Abstract Justice, a thing which we know is non-existent. [Spender] deliberately towered into blasphemy. Abstract Justice, he said, of course he meant it; and what was more it existed." (*The Strings are False: An Unfinished Autobiography* [London: Faber and Faber, 1965] p. 168).

31.  *Trial of a Judge,* p. 73.

32.  *Strings are False,* p. 167.

33.  K. A., "Play for Puritans," *New Verse,* no. 30 (Summer 1938), p. 20.

This review demonstrates another instance in which Spender's "real" nature reveals itself through the ill-adjusted robes of the propagandist. The Judge seemed to Edwin Muir the most impressive figure in contemporary drama. "He is an embodiment of the spirit of man at a particular stage of history; he is a representative figure. . . . Every one needs such a figure, as an embodiment of itself and of what it wants to be."[34]

The play is not entirely dramatic, not exactly conceived as an artifact to be visible and audible on the stage: "Producers are not expected to follow too closely the details of sound (drums), lighting, scene shifting—" says the prefatory note. One stage direction runs, "raising her with a gesture which is really his own self-pity"; another, "Lighting suggesting illusion." The action of Act I, we are directed, is to suggest "that this act is a dream in the Judge's mind." Act IV involves another willing suspension of belief, being the dream of Hummeldorf. "Realism and symbolism were never quite reconciled," Gavin Ewart remarks, recording that the play opened with the Judge lying on the bier of the murdered Petra, indicating his sympathy but wrongly suggesting that he was dying.[35] Edwin Muir commented that "the actual struggle is neither between the Fascists and the Communists, nor between the Judge and the world he lives in: it takes place within himself."[36] This condition is like that which contemporaries found in Spender himself, for whom the large conflicts in the world were said to reflect a conflict within.[37] Muir goes on: "This is perhaps a defect, dramatically; and it is paralleled by a corresponding defect: that the dramatic speech, with its involution, is more suited to monologue than to dialogue. The verse has some times great beauty, but it has rarely the direct speaking quality of dramatic utterance." In addition to these factors, which tend to sap the play of its dramatic strength, the imagery, as was pointed out in *Scrutiny*,[38] does not regularly

34. *The Present Age from 1914* (London: Cresset Press, 1939), pp. 179–80.
35. "Two Views of a Play," *Twentieth Century Verse*, no. 10 (May 1938), p. 52.
36. *The Present Age*, p. 180.
37. As the reviewers of *Forward From Liberalism*, for instance, were not slow to instruct him.
38. H. A. Mason, "Mr. Spender's Play," *Scrutiny* 7 (September 1938): 222.

lead into the subject; it is often vague. There are places where it is clear and objective and reveals the poet's intended meaning of its own accord, without his curious manipulation; but these places, effective as they are, are unusual. One reviewer found nothing more convincing in the play than the objective passage of prose in which the Black Troop Leader sells himself to us as a harmless bourgeois.[39] Here the imagery is clear and offers its own message. The "harmless bourgeois" sounds like one of the knights out of *Murder in the Cathedral* who has read Auden:

> ... most of us are happily married and myself, I may add, the proud father of six. Most of us own a little scrap of harmless property, a small shop with a bell that tinkles happily to summon mother when you open the door, or an acre or so of land, perhaps even a vineyard with the soft tendrils of the grapes and the fine globular fruit clustering around the ripe cheeks of our laughing children and young wives.[40]

More often we get verse, and verse with tortured and complex imagery, more suited to monologue, as Edwin Muir pointed out, than to dialogue: Of Petra:

> They shot only his face
> That's still the face of what he is:
> Their leaden bullets against a knife edge
> Of steel, have tried to turn the blade:
> But instantly when he died, the entire knife
> Of what he thought and strove, glued to my hand.
> (p. 22)

These metaphoric equivalences would not be easily grasped in the theater. Spender even as dramatist is not content to be the mere choreographer, disposing his counters for objective vision and audition, revealing his meanings in their movements. Throughout all his work, images tend to be strained or twisted in the poet's

---

39. X., Review of *Trial of a Judge, Twentieth Century Verse*, no. 10 (May 1938).
40. *Trial of a Judge*, pp. 86–87.

restless, sophisticated effort to express the refinements and nuances of a truth that is not to be expressed by the normal blunt means of articulation. But there is a place in drama for bluntness; and in life itself there is a point at which something of the endless complexity of the truth inherent in things must be sacrificed for the sake of simplicity of expression and communication itself.

*The Still Centre,* published in May 1939, contains nearly all the poems written since the publication of the second edition of *Poems.* Many of these are about the civil war in Spain, grounded in experiences the poet had had there during 1937. The volume also contains longer poems: in the 1933 and 1934 volumes, no poem had gone much beyond thirty lines; some in *The Still Centre,* on the other hand, run to around a hundred and thirty. Among the longer ones, "The Uncreating Chaos" and "Exiles from Their Land, History Their Domicile" have been extensively revised, the poet tells us, since their first appearance, as had the shorter poem, "An Elementary School Class Room in a Slum." In his foreword Spender also says that external pressures had tended to make poets write of what was outside their own individual experiences, which had been dwarfed by the violence of the times. Therefore, he says, he has himself "deliberately turned back to a kind of writing which is more personal."

If, as he implies, Spender has now resigned his commitment to action in the "violence of the times" and presumably then also to poems bearing political burdens, he is still diversely drawn to the outer and the inner worlds respectively, and the tension is felt in many poems. The foreword includes a reference once again to the poet's need to relate the private world within to the public outer one; "Even while he is writing about the little portion of reality which is part of his experience, the poet may be conscious of a different reality outside. His problem is to relate the small truth to the sense of a wider, perhaps theoretically known, truth outside his experience."[41]

The theme that recurs most frequently in this volume is that of the achievement of unity of being or of an image of the integrated self.

41. *The Still Centre* (London: Faber and Faber, 1939), p. 10.

This has been attained to, apparently, by those who are dead, those who were (or are) "truly great," and those who exert will. Spender has suggested that the achievement is one of the "obsessive themes" that are always with him.[42] In a recent poem he recalls that as a child he thought that being grown up was "when/How they look from the outside/ Is what they have become all through."[43] In the first poem of the Marston series, in *Twenty Poems*, he shows his predilection for personalities that can be condensed each into a single image which is as clear, vivid, and uncomplex as a mere sign—in Yeats's words, "Character isolated by a deed/To engross the present and dominate memory." We learned also in Spender's early volume, in "'I' Can Never Be Great Man," that because the "I" is various, disintegrated, and not single, it can never be great.

In *The Still Centre* we find these ideas taken up again: there is the poem "Exiles from Their Land" of which Spender remarked that it was about "those who have, after their deaths, obtained for their lives a symbolic significance...."[44] In this poem death is the divinity that shapes ends and selects purposes and acts that will endow us with symbolic significance; in another poem, the poet looks forward to entering "The cloudless posthumous door/Where the slack guts are drawn into taut music."[45] But this significance, this unity of being, as Spender calls it (and Yeats before him), is not necessarily the product of death: there is also the will. Death has enshrined those exiles as great because it has made them "one with what they willed" (p. 24) or "cast / Their wills into signatory moulds. . . ."

The poet of *The Still Centre* thinks of his own will as "faltering" (p. 33); Spender wrote in his diary in Hamburg, "I have no character or will-power outside my work"[46]; in "The Human Situation" he envies figures whose wills are firm:[47] the father, the captain of

42. "Introduction," *Collected Poems,* p. 15.
43. "Draft of the First Five Selections of Part One," *Pronouns of this Time, Shenandoah* 16 (Autumn 1964): 9.
44. *Collected Poems,* p. 14.
45. *Still Centre,* p. 89.
46. *World Within World,* p. 205.
47. *Still Centre,* p. 81.

the school, heroes of legend or history, a certain woman. Will is admired also in nonhuman forms: the Midlands Express, for example, which "with unerring power" drives straight to its goal, ravishing England that lies beneath it like a woman (p. 47). Along with the admiration and the envy, however, there is firm recognition in this volume of what would be lost if the will took over, or what has been lost in circumstances where it had taken over. In "The Human Situation" the poet again observes that it would be impossible for him to enter, or imagine or wish to enter the symbolic beings of those he envies; it would be "Death to me and my way of perceiving / As much as if I became a stone," the Yeatsian image used in *Trial of a Judge* to express the result of singleminded absorption in public passion. His multivalence with all its liabilities is necessary to him. And he recognizes in others the importance of weakness as we have seen; declaring it valuable in George Barker, while the will is an obstacle to Rex Warner. In the short poem, "Houses at Edge of Railway Lines," he contemplates with favor a life of which the richness lies in the absence of effective will—a train, once more, that rushes by outside (pp. 103–4) and in a later volume, under the same metaphor, he distrusts the will and the "confident iron rails."[48] Then in *The Still Centre* again, there is Napoleon, the subject of a long poem,[49] who is "ruled / By a dead will," burdened by the fixed image of self—the kind of image that in some other poems of Spender's is devoutly to be wished.

The poet, then, calls for the strength of will to become a being of integrity and at the same time knows he needs his own essential lack of will, what he designates weakness, for his very way of life. Weakness as the opposite of will is what he refers to when he says in the foreword that he has included in his subjects "weakness and fantasy and illusion." But a recurring process in this volume is the courtship of incompatible opposites, seen in such poems as "The

48. "The Journey," *Ruins and Visions: Poems 1934–1942* (New York: Random House, 1942), p. 91.
49. *Still Centre*, pp. 96–100. (Francis Scarfe finds the figure of Napoleon untrue to the facts of history; he is, rather, an immense Spender with all the complexities and defeatisms magnified ["Stephen Spender: A Sensitive," *Auden and After*, p. 47]. Charles Madge finds the poet's own reflections about greatness and defeat projected onto Napoleon ["Spender," *Poetry* (London) 1 (Nov. 15, 1940): 85].

Human Situation," "The Separation," "The Mask," and especially "Darkness and Light." According to a reviewer in the *Times Literary Supplement*, the still center is the point from which all opposites can be reconciled.[50] Another reviewer of the book finds the still center to be a symbol for "that position from which the poet can stabilize his values and thus come to terms with his world."[51] But, no, it is a pole and not a point of equilibrium, and it cannot be the point of reconcilement: the peace at the still center, in the last stanza of "The Separation," is obtained by release from the will's error; and that is no reconcilement or compromise with the will but the removal of its influence:

> Shuttered by dark at the still centre
> Of the world's circular terror,
> O tender birth of life and mirror
> Of lips, where love at last find peace
> Released from the will's error.[52]

The still center is, surely, that residue of the self, as Spender was later to designate it, which, washed over by all tides of public occurrences, is finally untouched and lives independent of any conditioning whatsoever.

The *TLS* noticed also that "a cry for release into reality through a profound acceptance of it sounds repeatedly through these poems, a cry to be recalled 'from life's exile. . . .'"[53] The final lines of "To a Spanish Poet" are quoted, including the following passage, which reproduces once again the Keatsian sentiment that was discovered to have much relevance in the decade:

> . . . only when the terrible river
> Of grief and indignation
> Has poured through all my brain
> Can I make from lamentation
> A world of happiness. . . .

50. Anon., "The Poet's Dilemma: the Impact of Events," May 6, 1939, p. 266.
51. Robert D. Harper, "Back to the Personal," *Poetry* 57 (October 1940): 49.
52. *Still Centre*, p. 85.
53. Anon., "The Poet's Dilemma: the Impact of Events," *TLS*, May 6, 1939, p. 266.

But if the acceptance of reality sounds repeatedly throughout this volume, so too does the instinct to withdraw from it—"out of rapid day" into "the tunnel of my dream," or into "symbolic being" or to be at the still center where there is peace.

We have observed above in connection with the Marston poems a simple instance of how Spender uses the poem to resolve his own real-life quandary, the poetic death of Marston satisfying the grievous frustration Spender had incurred on being repudiated by him. "Darkness and Light" performs, no doubt, a similar act: behind the poem there presumably lies the personal problem of individuation, or at least the integration of various parts of the personality, say, the inner and outer worlds. The poem resolves that problem poetically, and, the effort at integration having grown the very habit of Spender's soul, it is not surprising that the poet uses the poem, with modifications, as epigraph for *World Within World*. It will be considered below in some detail. Meanwhile, as a poetic welding of incompatibles, it is of interest to observe it in passing as an example of the use of the poem toward the solution of an insoluble problem.

In *Ruins and Visions* and in *Poems of Dedication,* which follows it, Spender puts his art to service in assuaging the grief of two personal afflictions, the departure of his wife and the mortal illness of a beloved sister-in-law, Margaret. At the same time, however, he questions the efficacy of art in resolving problems in reality. *Ruins and Visions* (1942) consists of four parts: the first three, "A Separation," "Ironies of War," and "Deaths" constitute the ruins; Part IV is "Visions." The poems of Part I express grief at the loss of a loved woman, who is presumably a reflection of Inez, who had left Spender in 1939. The substance of most of the poems is defined and decently removed from the literal source of the grief; but there are some occasional, telling, realistic details: "She was never one to miss / The plausible happiness / Of a new experience," for example, or, addressing himself, recognizing the deficiency he shared with Matthew Arnold:

> At first you did not love enough
> And afterwards you loved too much

> And you lacked the confidence to choose
> And you have only yourself to blame.[54]

There are only a limited number of realistic touches such as these in "A Separation," but Spender seems to be concerned throughout this and the two following parts with the essential falsity of dreams, of certain thoughts, and of the artistic resolution of real problems— the kind of resolution, for example, that he created in "Darkness and Light." In "No Orpheus No Eurydice" the poet imagines his lost wife, his "pale darling," as dead, "waiting in sweet grace / For him to follow when she calls." But really she is not beautifully dead or able to "follow him back into life":

> For he is no Orpheus
> She no Eurydice
> She has truly packed and gone
> To live with someone
> Else. . . .

The poet's despair at the frailty of the poetic art in the face of an intransigent reality is seen in other poems in these earlier parts of *Ruins and Visions*. The force of an immutable reality is nowhere so powerfully felt in Spender as in this volume. One of the poems, "Wings of the Dove," which is concerned with Margaret and her incurable disease and which becomes a part of the "Elegy for Margaret" in the next volume, recognizes the frivolousness, even, of grief. "Oh but my grief is thought, a dream. . . . It does not wake every day" to the "granite facts around your bed, / Poverty-stricken hopeless ugliness / Of the fact that you will soon be dead" (p. 116). In one or two poems in the early parts, the poet is scornful of people who do not acknowledge the real, like the mother in "The Fates" who brought up her son in a climate insulated even from the news of poverty, adultery, or disease (pp. 117–22), or like the old men of the last war whose voices he mocks in "June 1940."

The poet does not give all to objective truth, however. In Part IV, "Visions," the real and manifest are subordinated to the visionary and the numinous. The section opens with a poem "At Night,"

54. *Ruins and Visions*, p. 90.

which describes the release from pressures of the real which is effected by darkness. Then elsewhere there are references to liberation from the space defined by words: birdsong takes the poet to a "space beyond words"; sleep brings men to where they see "more / Than a landscape of words." In "Dusk," as men drift into sleep, "the great lost river," which must have some atavistic meaning, "crepitates / Through creeks of their brains." Spender wrote subsequently of this part of the book that it reflected a tendency in poetry of that period, shared by the works of other poets, to turn inward to personal subjects (although this act he had already performed in *The Still Centre*, and he had so indicated in the preface). The poems of the last part of *Ruins and Visions*, he said, were "in search of universal experience through subjective contemplation."[55] This, as we have seen, tends to reverse the procedures of the rest of the book.

The last poem in *Ruins and Visions* is "To Natasha," which is the name of the woman Spender married in 1941; and this poem of union balances those of separation at the beginning of the volume. Now, once again, art, whose resolutions had been suspected in some of the other poems, is allowed to bring harmony out of chaos. "Your fingers of music," says the poet, "Pressing down a rebellion of mistakes / Raise here our devout tower of mutual prayer." But even more is to be attributed to artistic vision: "Daily through vigorous imagining / I summon my being again / Out of a chaos of nothing."[56]

Part I of *Poems of Dedication*[57] is "Elegy for Margaret," which contains six poems, versions of two of which had appeared already in *Ruins and Visions*. Part II, "Love, Birth, and Absence," consists of seven poems, ecstatic lyrical meditations on the poet's marriage, refined and insubstantial. Part III is a series, mostly sonnets, called "Spiritual Explorations," and Part IV consists of three poems, "Midsummer," "Seascape," and "Meeting."

In view of the questions raised in *Ruins and Visions* as to the ability of art to solve problems, it is interesting to observe in *Poems of*

55. *Poetry Since 1939* (London: Longmans Green, 1946), p. 34.
56. *Ruins and Visions*, p. 137.
57. (London: Faber and Faber, 1947).

*Dedication* how the poet faces the dying by cancer of his sister-in-law. For one thing, he resorts to a notion from Plato, coming to it, perhaps, by way of Shelley's "Lift Not the Painted Veil":[58] "the well," those who are healthy, that is, "are those who hide / In dreams of life painted by dying desire / From violence of our time outside. . . ." Addressing his brother, Margaret's husband, he appeals also to the idea that death bestows the legend of unity of being, which he had developed in *The Still Centre:* ". . . those we lose, we learn/ With singleness to love." He brings no consolation, he says, but ". . . to accept the worst/Is finally to revive. . . ." And, last, in an illogical, poetic resolution,

> . . . she will live who, candle-lit,
> Floats upon her final breath,
> The ceiling of the frosty night
> And her high room beneath,
> Wearing not like destruction, but
> Like a white dress, her death.[59]

In the last poem of the elegy, by means of wild and distressed imagery, the act of love is relegated from flesh to bone, and the conception of love from eros to agape: ". . . to love means to bless/ Everything and everyone." The reduction from flesh to bone is a part of a pervading motif in this volume, which appears especially as a stripping down to nakedness, or in one poem as a passing beyond nakedness. The main theme of the sequence "Spiritual Explorations," eight poems, mostly sonnets, that constitute Part III of *Poems of Dedication,* if indeed it may be spoken of as having a theme, is this descent into some pure, basic condition that underlies most of the phenomena of existence, where "Each circular life gnaws round its little leaf / Of here and now." Beneath all these is the immortal spirit. Spender says the sequence is an attempt to penetrate "the very

58. Lift not the painted veil which those who live
    Call Life: though unreal shapes be pictured there,
    And it but mimic all we would believe
    With colours idly spread,—behind, lurk Fear
    And Hope, twin Destinies. . . .
59. *Poems of Dedication*, p. 15.

nature of human existence";[60] the means of the attempt seems to be that of exploring the words, their potential ambiguities and paradoxes, that describe our condition: "All that I am I am not," for instance, or "I who say I call that eye I."[61]

There is some word play too in the opening poem of *The Edge of Being*,[62] "O Omega, Invocation." It dwells on the familiar motif of getting beyond present sensations now; indeed, the poet would proceed "beyond silence," in one place. The motif appears throughout the volume:

> . . . O, whose black
> Hoop, circling on white
> Paper, vanishes where the eye
> Springs through thee, O,
> Beyond space silence image,
> O thou, word of beginning
> Oh with what wordless end.[63]

Other poems in this volume dwell on the idea of withdrawing beyond the worlds of sense: in "Judas Iscariot," a slightly dramatic monologue, Judas posits himself and Christ as eternal opposites beyond the world of "hypocrite eyes"; or in "The Angel," there is a hankering for the "inviolate instants where we are / Solid happiness hewn from day, set apart / From others far"; " . . . the real is the terrible," declares the angel. This poem begins with the assertion that "each is involved in the tears and blood of all," the sentiment Spender had adopted in the thirties along with all the other poets who abided by the Keatsian exhortation in *Hyperion*. But now in this late volume the poet hardly conceals his wishes that it were otherwise. In *Vienna,* 1934, he had tried to fuse the story of the workers with the story of his own love affair, and this effort had failed. Now in a long poem in *The Edge of Being*, "Returning to Vienna, 1947," he recognizes that his mind will not, in Eliot's

60. *Poetry Since 1939* (London: Longmans Green, 1946), p. 37.
61. *Poems of Dedication*, p. 44.
62. (New York: Random House, 1949).
63. *Edge of Being*, pp. 9–10.

famous phrase, digest such "disparate experiences": the crystal
bowl of the love affair is flawed by the reality, the unemployed:

> There was reality, the flaw
> Within the golden crystal bowl, where life
> Was not entirely love nor even
> Baroque frozen in dolphin attitudes
> But was the unemployed who starved. . . .

(p. 21)

The antitheses notified here introduce us to new terms for the conflict that Spender's foregoing volumes have variously revealed.
It is, in general, the same conflict; it finds new terms and new images:
in the early poems there are the traditionally good and lovely things,
nature and culture, on the one hand, and progress and communism
on the other; there is the world of will and that of sensibility, say,
in *The Still Centre;* there is the ruined world and the visionary in
*Ruins and Visions;* and now, at least related, is a conflict between
the gilt statuary and the destructive dust. It will be recalled that in
*Vienna* he had wanted to keep the past inviolate; but it is not to be
so. "Returning to Vienna" proceeds to link the love affair with the
architecture and sculpture of the old city; but the "seeming permanence was an illusion," and

> . . . what was real was transitory dust
> True to our time dust blowing into dust
> The dust a vital inward spring with power
> To shatter history-frozen visions
> And burst through cities and break down their walls. . . .

In other poems of this volume dust appears again as the destroyer.
(One recalls the showers of acrid dust that followed the explosion
of bombs in air raids that Spender witnessed as a fireman at the
time of the writing of some of these poems.) In "We Cannot Hold
onto the World" the poet describes two deaths, that of an athlete
who has been shot and that of Virginia Woolf; then he says in
conclusion: "Who shall regain / The concentrated mind / From
blowing dust outside, and seas, and driving rain?" (p. 54). In the
last stanza of the last poem of the volume, "Time in Our Time,"

the poet writes, "Oh save me in this day, when Now / Is a towering pillar of dust which sucks / The ruin of a world into its column" (p. 56).

The title of this volume, derived from the poem that Spender had set at the forefront of his first published work, is apt enough for a group of poems in which his wishes to be suspended between the concrete being and the abstract nonbeing are once again made manifest. "I was cast naked out of non-existence," he says. And in another poem, "Speaking to the Dead in the Language of the Dead," he contrasts the dead who have arrived at being—"the perfecting dead. Their night / Is words and statues"—with us, we, who under Yeatsian "blood and mire," are suffering on "the harsh edge of existence" (p. 52). Throughout, anticipated by the opening poem in which the eye springs through the word on paper, there is homage paid to the unreified. In "Rejoice in the Abyss," with echoes of Owen's "Strange Meeting" and stronger echoes of Eliot's "compound ghost" in *Little Gidding,* the poet is instructed after an air raid to rejoice in the abyss and to accept emptiness:

> Unless your minds accept that emptiness
> As the centre of your building and your love,
> . . . . . . . . . . . . . . .
> All human aims are stupefied denial. . . .
>
> (p. 31)

In his lines on Virginia Woolf the poet dwells on the "un": "Her mind unstrung—mirror unspoken / Thoughts (white now as her bones) / Pages of an unwritten book."

In the last poem of the volume, from which quotation has been made above, Spender seems to want some kind of fusion between being and nonbeing of the order he conceived in the fusion between darkness and light in *The Still Centre.* The poem sets up men's past and future as fixities "pivoted / On the irreducible secret diamond / His Now." He concludes

> . . . may all that was
> Once idea integrated into stone
> Enter my secret mind at the whirling centre
> Of the external storm: and combine with

A love which penetrates through falling flesh
To paint the image in my heart
Of that past greatness and that once-willed Future,
Beyond the storm, which still can make a world.

*Collected Poems*[64] adds a handful of poems that had not previously appeared in the volumes. What is of more interest than the
poems added is the fact that, of the one hundred and eleven poems
printed, a large proportion are poems that Spender wrote in the
thirties. Of the first edition of *Poems* (1933), only two poems are
not reproduced, "Those fireballs, those ashes" and "My parents
quarrel in the neighbour room," the poem in which F. R. Leavis
had heard the strong echoes of *Modern Love*. The space devoted to
this one part of his poetic output up to that date is interesting. In
addition, the poems about the Spanish Civil War, which had
appeared in *The Still Centre,* are very fully represented. So that,
even discounting his compulsion to "own up," as he says in the
introduction, to certain poems of the period, it seems that Spender
saw himself in 1955 predominantly as a poet of the thirties, or at
least supposed that that is how his public saw him and was not
displeased with the image.

Second, the changes the poet has made or has not made are interesting, though they do not demonstrate a single principle at work.
Many of the earlier poems reappear with only minor changes; "A
temptation I have guarded against," he says, "is that of making more
than a discreet and almost unnoticeable minimum of technical
tidyings up. . . . [T]he technical flaw in an early poem may reflect
a true inadequacy to impose a finished form upon an incomplete
experience. It may even . . . have a certain beauty in realizing the
rightness of such an incompleteness."[65] There is, of course, no
attempt made in the *Collected Poems* to change the image of the
poet from that of a communist to that of a humanist by deft manipulation here and there of the diction in the earlier poems.

Apart from the changes made in those poems in which the poet
has, in his own phrase, reinvented the ideas—"Exiles from their

64. (London: Faber and Faber, 1955).
65. "Introduction," p. 15.

Land, History their Domicile," for example,—changes tend sometimes simply to make for clarity in rhetorical statement. For instance, lines from "Perhaps" in the second edition of *Poems* are
altered to release a metaphor and substitute abstract terms with more
precise meaning and a simile: "is it leviathan, that revolution / hugely
nosing at edge of antarctic?" (p. 50) becomes "Is it The Shape of
Things to Come, that revolution / nosing whale-like at Antarctic
edge?"[66] Or ". . . rays / Where our eyes fuse the rainbow of their
gaze," in *Poems of Dedication* (p. 55), becomes ". . . rays / In
which our eyes meet when, near or far, they gaze."[67] A number
of such changes purchase clarity at the slight cost, sometimes, of
richness.

His poetry often being so little dependent upon the descriptive
function of its words, Spender is occasionally not loth to substitute
words that change the literal meaning of a sentence, slightly or
entirely. Thus, in "Perhaps" again, from the second edition of
*Poems,*

> Out there
> perhaps growth of humanity above the plain
> hangs: not the timed explosion, oh but Time
> monstrous with stillness like himalayan range

becomes (p. 5)

> Out there
> Perhaps it is the dead above the plain
> who grow; not our time bombs but Time
> monstrous with stillness like that Alpine range.[68]

Other examples of such changes abound in poems that have been
"reinvented."

Sometimes changes augment rather than reduce the richness of a
poem. The greatest number of this kind are accounted for by the aim
to increase the concretion of an image, to give a line particularity,
or to make what was literal metaphorical. The last change quoted
above shows Spender calling upon his wartime experiences and

66. *Collected Poems*, p. 52.
67. *Ibid.,* p. 177.
68. *Ibid.,* p. 52.

introducing the time bomb, with which as a fireman he had no doubt become acquainted. Another war experience feeds a poem that Spender changes in the direction of enrichment of image and increasing power of metaphor: the version in *The Edge of Being* of "Epilogue to a Human Drama" reads

> The City burned with unsentimental dignity
> Of resigned wisdom: those stores and churches
> Which had glittered emptily in gold and silk,
> Stood near the crowning dome of the cathedral
> Like courtiers round the Royal Martyr.
>
> (p. 28)

The *Collected Poems* version reads,

> London burned with unsentimental dignity
> Of resigned kingship: those stores and Churches
> Which had glittered century-long in dusty gold
> Stood near the throne of domed St. Paul's
> Like courtiers round the Royal sainted martyr.
>
> (p. 145)

The earlier and later renderings of two passages from "Elegy for Margaret" may be compared:

> ... a villain
> Seizes on the pastures of your life
> Then gives you back some pounds of flesh, only again
> To twist you on that rack of pain. ...[69]

in *Collected Poems:*

> ... a villain,
> Seizes on the pastures of your flesh,
> Then gives you back some acres, soon again
> To set you on that rack of pain. ...
>
> (p. 155)

> Since, darling, there is never a night
> But the restored prime of your youth
> With all its flags does not float
> Upon my sleep like a boat. ...[70]

69. *Poems of Dedication*, p. 11.
70. *Ibid.*, p. 17.

becomes in *Collected Poems:*

> Since, Margaret, there is never a night,
> But the beflagged pride of your youth
> In all its joy, does not float
> Upon my sleep, as on a boat.
>
> (p. 157)

Finally, a change increasing the vividness of a poem suggests that an unconscious borrowing (or perhaps a borrowing back of what was once loaned) has influenced the modification: The *Still Centre* version of "An Elementary School Class Room in a Slum" closes as follows:

> ... show the children to the fields and all their world
> Azure on their sands, to let their tongues
> Run naked into books, the white and green leaves open
> The history theirs whose language is the sun.
>
> (p. 29)

The *Collected Poems* version has enriched the imagery:

> ... show the children to green fields, and make their world
> Run azure on gold sands, and let their tongues
> Run naked into books, the white and green leaves open
> History theirs whose language is the sun.
>
> (p. 81)

The "green" and "gold" additions to the description of the children running into grace remind us of Dylan Thomas's children, "green and golden" themselves who depart from grace in "Fern Hill," which had appeared in *Horizon* after the first but before the second version of Spender's poem.

Much of Spender's familiar imagery is repeated in his latest poems: eyes, winds, suns, waves, nets, and light, whole or broken, in all forms. Poems dwell upon children—the poet's son and his grandchild; and they also recall people from the past, some of whom are now dead and others, living, are changed. Some of the poems are still concerned with the old question of being: the poet is absorbed with the concept of the separate being of the child, for instance: "His glance is grave / Already with some secret hidden from me / . . . . My one my own endlessly far from me."[71] Or again, in "One More New Botched Beginning," the boy doesn't see his father but, absorbed in a study of some hens, he becomes a "bird boy" (p. 32).

More often than the separate beings of children, however, Spender is concerned in these recent poems with the identities of those dead or of those who have changed through the years. "On a Photograph of a Friend, Dead" explores the matter of the subject's unity and whether the subject can be represented by a single image like the figures in "The Dust Made Flesh," in the Marston poems in Spender's earliest work. "Your gaze oblique under sun-sculptured lids / Endlessly asks me: 'Is this all we have?'" Other poems also show concern about the past and about the identities of figures therefrom, living or dead: in "One More New Botched Beginning," the poet remembers walking with Merleau-Ponty, who though dead is no more irrevocable, says the poet, "than the I that day who was / Beside him"—and the poet himself is still living. Then again in the same poem, he recalls Louis MacNeice, Bernard Spencer, and himself exchanging poems. The other two are dead. "Their lives are now those poems that were / Pointers to the poems to be their lives." The meaning isn't clear, but the lines are apparently concerned with the identity of men's works and their lives "Auden Aetat XX, LX" rehearses the well-known memories of Auden at Oxford (including the war-games) and then sets against these the present image of the poet with sixty winters on his head:

> Forty years later now, benevolent
> In carpet slippers, you still make devices,
> Sitting at table like one playing patience
> Grumpily fitting our lives to your game,
> Whose rules are dogma of objective Love.[72]

The longest poem that Spender has attempted since *Vienna* is *Pronouns of This Time*, from which I have quoted earlier; and,

71. "Mein Kind Kam Heim," *The Generous Days* (New York: Random House, 1971), p. 20.
72. *Shenandoah* 18 (Winter 1967): 5.

judging by the first section,[73] it also is to be concerned with identity. It opens with a memory of childhood, the boy lying awake in his attic room at night watching the stars and ruminating on his selfhood. He reduces himself beneath the stars to nothingness, which renders him identical with everyone:

> ... I lay under that pane of glass
> Covered with stars,
> . . . . . . . . . . . . . . .
> And knew then: "I am nothing
> But also everyone
> Outside me, knows he's nothing
> But knowing he is 'I'.
> And knowing this I know
> The being everyone
> Within his dark heart knows
> Awake at night alone."

He thinks of others—the cook and the maids and his father; but he can only imagine their daytime selves, the persons, supposedly, of will and world, their inner realities masked.

> I could not think my father even
> Except at breakfast with *The Times*
> Spread out behind an egg. . . .

Earlier poems concerned with identity dwelt upon fragmentation and/or unification within the single person. The identity of all is a new concept, but it seems to be governed to some extent by familiar rules. Spender exercises the concept in this developing poem by considering the identity of himself as an unathletic boy with that of another boy of a very different type, the captain of cricket, each reduced by night time to nothing. Tomorrow

---

73. *Shenandoah* 16 (Autumn 1964): 5–20. A note reads: "The poem is planned to be in three parts. Part one: *Thou and I*. Part two: *We*. Part three: *They*. These sections form approximately half of Part one."

> he must go
> Out on to the field, assume
> Fresh muscle and new eye:
> Attired in pads and flannels
> Be Templar, win our praise.
> In bed now, he is I. . . .

The poet works on the idea: there must have been a time when the communal selfhood was recognized by all, a time divided from us by a fault: "Something had gone wrong." But he will declare to people that they are one. The prelapsarian community, however, is an inward thing, both creating and depending upon "the world within":

> "In thee, in each of these,
> Differently the same,
> Light separates from dark
> And thou art Adam seeing
> Eden each day the first
> Created in his sight—
>
> "And not by thy sole seeing
> But by addition of those others
> Thy world within is made. . . ."

And once again, the will is the anathema:

> "Therefore whoever casts
> His will, a shadow over
> Another's life, his own,
> Plucks out the hidden nerve
> That is his own eye's seeing. . . ."

Along with the poems, we may glance at some things in the five stories that comprise the volume, *The Burning Cactus* (1936): "The Dead Island," which is a novelette, "The Cousins," the title story, "Two Deaths," and "By the Lake." These stories are of a kind of narrative different from that of *The Backward Son,* Spender's conventional boarding-school novel, full of happening and people, or that of the later novelettes: the stories are closer in style to the poems, using some of the same techniques and showing similar features. Very occasionally the prose gives way to verse with no appreciable jolt. They reveal more of Spender than do the poems: everything he writes, he says, is a fragment of autobiography; but the stories bring us closer, even if not very close at that, to the man himself behind the artifacts. 'And a brief study of them, noticing certain repeated techniques, will begin to reveal something of the main features of the cast of mind of their author, anticipating and introducing the matter of the final chapter of this essay.

There is, for example, in each story a manifestation of the need of one human for another. There are different kinds of need, but they are not social. In "By the Lake" two boys at a pensionnat "for the backward and nervous sons of rich people," such, perhaps, as Spender attended himself as a boy, develop a friendship that satisfies familiar adolescent needs. In other stories there is a more covert need on the part of one character for another by means of whom he can define himself, and this feature is not merely a technique of the telling. In "Two Deaths," for example, the character of the narrator is in part revealed to him and displayed to the reader by the description of another man, a Dr. Mur, a phoney. "But if I could think of Dr. Mur as a ghost, what was I, leading this life divided between the sanatorium, my endless exploration of the streets, and my meals at a boarding house full of old ladies?"[74] This is a fairly clear case of what takes place in other stories a little less overtly—in "The Cousins," for instance, where Werner, the hero, as well as the reader, sees more certainly what Werner is by seeing in his cousins what he is not.

The hero in most of these stories is apt to be sick in body or mind or both, and he is gravely misunderstood. He is often a double personality. The adolescent hero in "By the Lake" is broad minded and progressive, and he argues quite hotly in favor of contraception; but he is embarrassed at overhearing the bawdy reminiscence of a fellow passenger on a steamer: "Richard flushed. Yet even whilst he despised this talk, he felt it was illogical that he was shocked" (p. 226). Others have more profound divisions in

74. *The Burning Cactus* (London: Faber and Faber, 1936), p. 193.

themselves: the "dear boy," so designated, in "The Dead Island," is a Dr. Jekyll who conceals within himself a Mr. Hyde who robs a bank and scatters the banknotes among the prostitutes in a brothel; the protagonist of "The Burning Cactus" is told that when he is unhappy he is a "different person . . . like a primitive savage, or a hunted animal" (p. 171).

The sick and misunderstood heroes are related to rooms, those they actually inhabit and, for contrast, those they do not but sometimes aspire to. Similarly, a room, often a lighted room, features quite frequently in the poems. In "The Cousins," Werner lives in a bed-sitting room in Victoria (London), to which he has recently escaped from the "dark" house of his earlier years; and these are in contrast to the house where the story is set, especially the "airy white room whose tall windows with window seats on either side of the bow window opened directly on to the cropped lawn" a room which, along with its inhabitants, tells him he is unhappy. Till, of "The Burning Cactus," lives in a "small clean room with metal walls," once light but now darkened by a new building that has been put up in front of it; and the diminished light symbolizes the decline in Till's sense of well-being from the time that he had come to the house; contrasted to this room is that of his friends, Pearl and Roger, who follow a relatively unhaunted and sensual existence in a room with arsenic green wallpaper. In "The Dead Island" the male youth seeking identity with the woman symbolically takes possession of her by daily sweeping her room.

One feature of these stories that has its equivalent in the poems and is felt throughout is the author's unconcern about the sheer objective action in the external world; things happen, often for symbolic effect, which the reader cannot visualize as happening. The clearest example is in "The Cousins," when a rook is shot by one of the cousins because, he says, rooks are vermin. The action is symbolic: Werner, the progressive liberal who "felt he represented international socialism and the arts," who writes poetry and is emancipated from conventional behavior with women, is to be disposed of as obnoxious by the wealthy philistine family with its large aim of self-preservation and its traditional code. Beyond its symbolic significance, the incident doesn't interest the author and he doesn't expect it to interest us: thus, although when shot it "came flapping and planing down," half a dozen lines below we are instructed that the bird "had fallen like a black rotten weighted fruit." Other incidents confirm that the dramatic facts themselves are insignificant to Spender. He is awkward in the way he moves people across rooms, has them introduced, and gets glasses of sherry into their hands; characters always have special looks on their faces, and it is what lies behind these that he is anxious to engage us with. He likes to pin significance upon insignificant details: in "The Cousins," again, Werner fumbles the catch of the card table and the incident is made to bear much symbolic weight. Throughout the stories, people are always liable to do things that people don't do, like Till in the title story, who puts a match to a cactus.

Physical description, whether of persons or things, is sometimes flawed for the same reason—that the author is far more interested in what is not purely objective fact. We learn, for instance, that one hero "noticed under the warm skin the movement of tender bones at the base of [another's] neck: there was a nervous, spilt eagerness about them." Of another we read, "One hand was now pressed to his head, whilst the other clutched at his thigh with coarse exhibitionism, giving his whole body an expression of excluding mountain, port, sea and sky, while pointing singly to the speaker's own personality" (pp. 154–55); of yet another, "it was so easy to read on the rounded flesh of her smiling face framed by the raven hair, that she had made her power and happiness all of one unshatterable shining coloured piece, apprehended from the sea . . ." (p. 48). These things are not to be perceived by our muddy human senses: who has ever discerned spilt eagerness in cervical vertebrae? Sometimes description is lost in a simile that is only dimly apprehensible: "his dark brown eyes, shot with the red blood smeared across their whites, were threatening like the light of street lamp discs struggling redly through yellow fog." There are places, however, where description is objective and clear and not emasculated by the ideas that have invaded it; but it is most often bestowed upon scenes that have no essential parts in the stories and persons who don't matter. Such description is often vivid. We are shown Dolfuss, for example, who is not one of the principal figures in the story he enters: "A very short man with round boyish peasant eyes, full lips, snub nose, a small moustache and a very high forehead rather pathetically and prematurely lined, with the hair brushed back above it . . ." (p. 200) and Fey, "with a face white and creased like a dirty handkerchief, shot through with bloodless lips and eyes like bullets"; though the latter picture is not without the marks of the author's attitude. A woman walking through a Mediterranean port sees "a bearded nomad from a Turkish village who had spread some coloured carpets on the pavement in front of the hotel, and hung others on a lattice fence: she could see holes of blue sky through those that were hung up" (p. 63); she sees the "lithe hotel porter . . . with a springing step and a smile on his broad mongol face," "a sailing ship . . . being unloaded by five peasants whose dungarees, hands and faces were whitened by the cargo of meal," and so on.

The symbolism in the stories is sometimes presented as such: "'The life I lead here is like that cactus,'" says Till as he sets it alight. "'It's dry and bitter and cutting'" (p. 157). When the boys buy chocolate in "By the Lake," we learn that "This was one of those symbolic actions . . . which made them both return to their childhood" (p. 243). The symbolism is not always explicit; more often it is covert, and sometimes its presence is revealed by dramatic awkwardness, as in the instance of the shot bird. It is perhaps already apparent that the characters in these stories, whether they are the sensitive protagonists or their philistine opposites, all tend to respond to the symbolic values of actions, sometimes accepting things exclusively for their inward meanings. So the cousins, in their story, respond to Werner's fumbling of the catch on the card table.

It is partly with the aid of symbolism that the dialectic comes to be felt in certain stories. In "By the Lake" the adolescent boys are conscious on the one hand of their own youth, its innocence and ignorance and swift passage, and on the other of maturity, experience, knowledge, and evil. The incidents and discussions in the story constitute overt confrontations, but the structure is enriched by situations such as the following:

. . . they watched the near shore go past fast and the shore of the other side of the lake with its huge mountains seem not to move. Richard noticed such things closely and he noticed himself noticing them. On the far shore were the mountains, but on the near shore towards Lausanne and Vevey there were only slopes, terraced for vineyards. Occasionally rising from the verge of the lake were old villages with roofs recalling Dürer engravings. (pp. 226–27)

The symbolic values of islands and mountain suggest a dialectic. Others are more overtly displayed: the ruling class and the non-committed in "The Cousins," the two sides of Till's character in "The Burning Cactus."

The pervasive sensibility and the use of symbols and imagery with less-than-precise symbolic equivalence give these stories a pitch that reminds us of the poems. We are reminded of them too by such an occasional overwrought figure as we see in the poetry: "The conversation, like a wave striking a sunny rock, exploded into a million atoms of spray, some of which formed rainbows" (p. 115). The reader's mind, an instinctive cerebrator, crossword solver, code-breaker, and de-allegorizer, looks up for the meaning of the rainbow and is not fed. But what above all stamps these stories with the same imprint as the poems is the height of the stage on which both are enacted. In a word, it is elevated above the ground where objects, deeds, speeches, and feelings actually belong, to where thoughts and ideas interact, where high and subtle dramas flicker in the penumbra, and what Spender calls "moral interests" are compared. This is no doubt the nature of a good deal of fiction; but normally today the elevated drama grows by hint and insinuation or by the subtle interplay of symbol out of the muscular, physical things that are happening where we watch; and the writer behaves only as an impresario between objective facts on the one hand and the reader's active intelligence on the other. Spender's way is not this: the physical drama is a bare sequence, the author having observed in the rich ground level of reality only those details that will thrust the mental drama upon us, passive spectators. Occasionally reality makes itself felt, especially in "Two Deaths," where there are details that smack strongly of reality, of objective truth. But Spender's more usual practice, in these stories as in the poems, is to refine the blunt sensory experience and to render it again in terms of the categories of his own mind. Thus it comes about that, in these stories as in the poems, whatever the setting, images of light, whiteness, and eyes abound.

# 8

# Stephen Spender

Of the world outside himself, Spender seems to have maintained a chronic doubt as to the reality, let alone the significance. His father, he tells us, had despoiled this world with a Midas touch: he "turned everything into rhetorical abstraction, in which there was no concreteness, no accuracy."[1] So the son, in another way, tends to devalue the appearance of what most people think of as real, always wanting to see beyond it to the transcendent reality of which it is or may be made symbolic. He could not answer simple questions at school because he could not believe that the correct answers were so obvious; throughout later life he has avoided or mistrusted his immediate sensations, seeking always something he thought lay behind them. His responses to poetry recorded in

1. *World Within World: The Autobiography of Stephen Spender* (London: Hamish Hamilton, 1951), p. 7.

*World Within World* characterize his general predilections: Auden could remember poems, Spender could not: "I wanted to remember not the words and the lines, but a line beyond the lines, a sensuous quality which went, as it were, into the lines before they were written by the poet and which remained after I, the reader, had forgotten them" (p. 58). To the lines of Cleopatra,

> Peace, peace
> Dost thou not see my baby at my breast
> That sucks the nurse asleep,

he makes the most curiously ascetic response: "I found a burning away of the human condition contained within the dramatic situation, and then a penetration into a world of pure imagination beyond it. (p. 71).

Serious question about the value of the material world was not, of course, a useful attribute for the avowed dialectical materialist; nor is it useful for all poets: it was no doubt to his own immeasurable advantage that Yeats, for example, came to practice his art in a manner diametrically opposed to Spender's: "Players and painted stage took all my love, / And not those things that they were emblems of,"[2] although the "real" may have been embodied in the latter. Wallace Stevens, though endlessly equivocal on such matters, says, "You do not pierce an actor's make-up: you go to see and enjoy the make-up; you do not bother about the face beneath." He adds, "The poem is the poem, not its paraphrase."[3] For Spender, on the other hand, appearances are uncertain. Indeed, surfaces may divert the viewer from realities, and thus the daylight may reveal less than the darkness does:

> During day's foursquare light
> All is measured by eyes from the outside,
> Windows look and classify the clothes
> Walking upon their scaffolding of world.

2. "The Circus Animals' Desertion."
3. *The Letters of Wallace Stevens,* ed. Holly Stevens (New York: Knopf, 1966), p. 362.

> But at night
> Structures are melted in a soft pond
> Of darkness. . . . [4]

The darkness appeals to Spender because it renders the objective world malleable, and his great aim is to transform this world into the inner world. Where the relationship between inner and outer breaks down, in cultural life or in poetry itself, Spender sees crisis. He sees the problem in our contemporary cultural life arising because "an almost autonomous outside world of science, invention, and power, evolving and revolving according to laws of economics, etc., . . . has become unimaginable within the individual consciousness." [5] Spender sometimes speaks of the inward thing as "truth" and the outer as "reality." The poet's business was to render as much reality into truth as he was able: hence in the preface to *The Still Centre,* the remark quoted above about the need "to relate the small truth to the sense of a wider, perhaps theoretically known, truth outside [the poet's] experience"; and hence again the recent remark from "Imagination Means Individuation":

> The ideal and often evoked task for the poet in society is to personalize in his work the greatest possible amount and intensity of interest outside his private concerns. A world of external impersonal forces must be sacrificially reinvented as the poet's inner personal world, so that, for his readers, the impersonal modern world may be personalized in poetry. [6]

The work of Whitman, Spender felt, was a good example of the fulfillment of this task.

When poets failed to turn an external reality into an inward truth, Spender envisaged the kind of breakdown that may be illustrated by his view of the failings in Rex Warner's poems, which

4. "At Night," *Ruins and Visions 1934-1942* (New York, Random House, 1942), p. 123.
5. "The Imagination as Verb," *The Imagination in the Modern World* (Washington: Library of Congress, 1962), p. 4.
6. "Imagination Means Individuation," *ibid.,* p. 32.

has been cited in an earlier chapter: Warner had adopted the external political matters; and without internalizing them (not Spender's term) he had thrust them into poems. Spender suggests there was nothing in Warner's own imagination to accommodate the external political material. "The poet is committed to what he can really feel with his imagination . . . and if the paths of imagination do not lead back to his social conscience there is nothing to be done about it."[7] The deficiency Spender finds here is related probably to what he finds in Allen Ginsberg, who suffers from "journalistic immediacy."

In the matter of relating the world to the inward imagination, one of his mentors is Rilke, whom Spender quotes to the effect that the *Elegies* were "the work of the perpetual transformation of beloved and tangible things into the invisible vibration and excitability of our nature, which introduces new 'frequencies' into the pulsing fields of the universe."[8]

But even back in the days when he was at Oxford he had discovered that poetry was "a use of language which revealed external actuality as symbolic inner consciousness." He had felt that such expressionistic use of language was characteristic of the literary art of the twentieth century: Joyce, Eliot, Virginia Woolf, Graves, Laura Riding, Hemingway, the three Sitwells, Pound, Henry Green, and Herbert Read—these all saw themselves thinking; they all had "made the external world an object of interior sensibility."[9] Later Spender described artists as going from observation to invention or from invention to observation: if the artist moved from romantic inventiveness to observation of outer reality, the romantic symbols of the first period will be used as symbols for the newly discovered reality—a process to be seen in Yeats. If he began with observations, fragments of what was observed would be used as symbols for presenting the inner life.[10]

7. "New Poetry," *Left Review* 3 (July 1937): 358-59.

8. "The Imagination as Verb," p. 9.

9. *World Within World*, p. 96.

10. *The Creative Element* (London: Hamish Hamilton, 1935), pp. 113–15. Compare Christopher Caudwell in *Illusion and Reality* (London: Lawrence and Wishart, 1966), pp. 183-84: "It is possible to concentrate on the reality of feeling-tone, and dissolve the crystal of external reality. This does not mean that external reality

In his own poetry Spender consistently seems to transmute concrete experiences and to render them subjectively. But we are not really to know for sure whether subjective symbols of the inner life have distorted the image of an objective landscape or whether objective images in the memory have been used compositely to body forth features of the inward life. "Sirmione Peninsula" is an interesting poem to consider with this matter in mind. The objective scene is exactly given: the lake surrounded by mountains, "an almost perfect O," broken into by the peninsula "like one spoke thrusting to the centre." But to what extent, we ask, is the scene as reproduced in the poem objective and to what extent a symbol of the poet's own dramatic concept of himself at the time of his earlier visit with which the poem is dealing? He records that on the earlier visit his new wife seemed sad, "Seeing me self-enclosed in my view of the view/That shut her out from me. . . ." It is this memory, perhaps, that insists on the detail of the topography, which whether or not the peninsula is to be interpreted as a symbol for the self, spoiling the unity of the circle, seems pretty clearly to have a subjective *raison d'être* as well as objective facticity. So too another broken circle, the one in "Port Bou," surely has implications beyond mere topography. "In 'Port Bou,'" it has been pointed out, "one does get at first the feel of a setting, but on closer inspection the description of the harbour and firing practice turns out to be another of those carefully plotted internal landscapes. . . ."[11]

Ubiquitously in Spender's work we find the poet covertly or overtly using the outside world for inward symbolic purposes; or, on the other hand, a process that may be indistinguishable in practice, he endows the objective world with his own subjective

---

disappears; it means that external reality is manipulated not primarily according to its own laws but according to instinctive and subjective laws. Hence the plasticity of dream is retained, but the waking reality of subjective consciousness is injected into dream to enrich it. . . .

"Or it is possible to concentrate on the reality of the object and dissolve the nucleus of internal reality. This does not mean that the 'I', the observer, disappears; it means that the 'I' is manipulated not according to its own desires but according to the necessity of external reality. Once again the plasticity of dream is retained, but the reality of the waking environment is brought into the world of dream to stiffen it."

11. Peter Lowbridge, "The Spanish Civil War," *the Review*, nos. 11–12, p. 48.

206       STEPHEN SPENDER AND THE THIRTIES

coloring. Looking, for example, from a train, as he so often does, he
explicitly searches for reflections of the self:

> I look and look to read a sign,
> Through errors of light and eyes of water
> Beneath the land's will, of a fear
> And the memory of chaos,
> As man behind his mask still wears a child.[12]

Or in "The Human Situation" he contracts the world into the
glasses of his eyes, making it entirely subjective: his

> . . . single pair of eyes
> Contain the universe they see;
> Their mirrored multiplicity
> Is packed into a hollow body
> Where I reflect the many, in my one.

Sometimes, complementarily, a poem expresses the need of the
inward self for what the outer world supplies: Beethoven for
instance, being deaf and lacking the ability to make connection, is
"prisoned, masked, shut off from being;/Life like a fountain he
sees leap—outside."[13]

Other poets also body forth the external world as it has been
metamorphosed in their imaginations. But, unlike that of most
others, Spender's work has often quite lost the hallmarks of the
external world; the shaping into art that the material has undergone
may have left it with few recognizable objective features. These
have become reduced to the terms that he recognizes as truth,
appearing often in Shelleyan imagery: the shafts of light, eyes,
worlds, suns, and so forth that have already been remarked.

"Certain artists," says Spender, "are purists in their work," and
he proceeds to describe a process in which he himself often engages,
although he is not speaking of himself. "By this we mean that the
human experience which their art springs out of, is completely

12. "View from a Train," *The Still Centre* (London: Faber and Faber, 1939), p. 46.
13. "Beethoven's Death Mask," *Poems* (London: Faber and Faber, 1933), p. 19.

transformed in the work itself, which exists only in terms of its medium, paint, or notes, or words, isolated as far as possible from the reality which the work is *about*. The aim of the pure artist is to create a thing out of his artistic material and to separate it from ideas, messages, emotions which gave rise to the work."[14] He had in mind, perhaps, poems such as those of Charles Madge, of which he had observed that "they say little or nothing . . . and they leave often the impression of something colourless and transparent."[15]

As we have seen, Spender is ambivalent as to whether a poem *ought* to be pure, refined from its mundane origins. But his own often are. One good example is "I think continually of those who were truly great."[16] Geoffrey Grigson reports that Spender did, in fact, while at Oxford, think continually about those who were frequently photographed and longed for their acquaintance. But the poem itself has refined away its expression of this sentiment and contains, in fact, very little news at all: the great have become the "truly great." The first and third of its three stanzas celebrate the truly great in imagery that associates them with fire and, more particularly, with the sun; and they have very little descriptive meaning. The middle stanza consists of three prescriptions; whether they are prescriptions *for* greatness or whether they are simply offered in the light of contemplated greatness is not clear: ". . . never to forget / The essential delight of the / blood," never to deny its pleasures, and never to allow the traffic to smother the flowering of the spirit. Stanzas 1 and 3 consist of lyrical passages with literal meanings, relating only to other elements within the poem. It would thus be hard to substantiate the claims for the poem of C. Day Lewis, who attempts to make too much of its flimsy linkages with the outside world and sees it as ". . . a successful attempt to re-establish communication with the past, a minor miracle of healing." It takes, he says, "the form of ancestor worship." But it is not, in fact, nearly so palpable as this suggests.

14. "The Painter as Poet," *The Making of a Poem* (London: Hamish Hamilton, 1955), p. 139.
15. "New Poetry," *Left Review* 3 (July 1937): 361.
16. *Poems*, 1933, p. 37.

> Those who were great
> . . . remembered the soul's history
> Through corridors of light where hours are suns,
> Endless and singing.

They "hoarded from the Spring branches/The desires falling across their bodies like blossoms"; in the "highest fields" their names were "feted by the waving grass"; finally, "Born of the sun, they travelled a short while toward the sun / And left the vivid air signed with their honour." In its exquisite phrasing, the poem sings mainly to itself, reflecting upon itself in its own structure and delivering only the vaguest kind of intelligence. One is reminded of an anecdote in *World Within World,* when at an outdoor restaurant in Greece Spender hears a young man reciting from the *Agamemnon* the address of the watchman to the night: "I did not understand the lines, but the Greek words in the clear English voice were filled with the stars, the seas and the mountains. This is the effect which was my idea of pure poetry, an invocation which one understands imperfectly but which is yet expressed exactly, filled with the stars, the mountains, the tables, and the chairs (p. 94). "I think continually" is a lyric meditation of the inward self, a canvas with rhythm, colors, delineating only the most shadowy outlines of the objective world. And the use of the image of the "waving grass" in the high fields, which as we have seen is later associated with the still center, is perhaps no coincidence.

There are other poems of this kind, in which the song is unimpeded by the intrusion of the outside world and the sensibility is uncorrupted by the will. One need not, in fact, assume that this or any other poem is an artifact that has been refined from its source in the world: it may indeed have originated in the realm of art and not be description at all. The following passage from one of Spender's essays suggests that, on certain occasions at least, the poem arises as an autonomous thing and certainly not as a medium for communicating description or any news:

> Sometimes, when I lie in a state of half-waking and half-sleeping, I am conscious of a stream of words which seem to pass through my mind, without their having a meaning, but they have a sound,

a sound of passion, or a sound recalling poetry that I know. Again sometimes when I am writing, the music of the words I am trying to shape takes me far beyond the words, I am aware of a rhythm, a dance, a fury, which is as yet empty of words.[17]

To this and to other kinds of highly original sources, Spender's originality is often to be attributed. It tends to be like Shelley's, as Herbert Read sums this up: "not influenced by anything outside the poet's own consciousness . . . the direct product of his individual mind and individual feeling."[18] C. Day Lewis says Spender is one of those "whose voice seems to come out of the blue, reminding us of nothing we have heard before."[19]

One may speak of Spender's imagination, his subjectivity, when it is not completely rejecting the outside world in favor of its own independent joyous creation, as reflecting or rendering that world in its own terms. But we must observe also that the poetry manifests frequently the failure of the imagination in this work of domestication: frequently the poet does not, in fact, as he so often proposes, bring the refractory world into his own world, "sacrificially reinvented as the poet's inner personal world," as he puts it. He fails, not only with the driving belts and the political programs and ideas, but with other parts of life, on account of a fundamental conflict in himself.

As observed above, the conflict shows itself variously and continually in the different parts of his canon as Spender deliberately keeps it alive. Its principals appear respectively as the outer and the inner, the will and the imagination, responsibility and the senses, the ruined world and the visionary, or, in the one or two places, the images of circumference and center. Generally the will, on the one hand, works in the outside world, E. M. Forster's world of telegrams and anger; and the imagination or the senses, on the other hand, work in their own leisure to spell out the lyrical poetry. More particularly, with the will is associated the descriptive poem, of which there are few in Spender, or the descriptive elements, and

17. "The Making of a Poem," p. 60.
18. *In Defense of Shelley* (London: Heinemann, 1936), p. 80.
19. *A Hope for Poetry* (Oxford: Blackwell, 1934), p. 7.

the structure, the form of the poem. Associated with the center are the senses, the spontaneous lyric impulse, the nondescriptive or literal poem or images that do not primarily reflect the world, the poet's withdrawn self—his self at the "still centre," to use his own term, or what in a political discussion, in defiance of the Marxist theory of the economic control of the intellect, he calls that margin of freedom which no system can deny where there is room always for "pure states of being."[20] And, finally, associated with this pole of the personality, is what seems to be a species of negative capability that in one important poem the poet designates his weakness. If in Milton or Dante the colossal informing will is the chief agent of the poetry, it is not so in the lyrical poetry of Spender, for whom the will opposes the poetry. "Within this inner world [the "kingdom of creative imagination"] even weakness could become a kind of strength." One may note, however, that the purest lyrical talent of the century in English has never been entirely liberated from the conscience, the call of duty, the structural needs of the poem, and the world itself to issue its own spontaneous utterances.

Nowhere are the poet's north and south so clearly manifested as in "Not palaces, an era's crown," where the respective values are brought into direct opposition. As already observed the poem has a political message, and the conflict here has a political coloration which is incidental to our immediate interests. But the poem presents in more or less fundamental terms the two poles between the respective influences of which the poetry is largely composed. The poet instructs the senses—his reader's or his own—to leave their "gardens" and their "singing feasts" and submit themselves to the purposes of the will. The lines have been anthologized often enough, but I quote them here again because they speak so immediately to principles sometimes underlying and sometimes strongly evident in much of the poetry.

> Drink from here energy and only energy,
> As from the electric charge of a battery,
> To will this Time's change.

20. *Life and the Poet* (London: Secker and Warburg, 1942), p. 35.

Eye, gazelle, delicate wanderer,
Drinker of horizon's fluid line;
Ear that suspends on a chord
The spirit drinking timelessness;
Touch, love, all senses;
Leave your gardens, your singing feasts,
Your dreams of suns circling before our sun,
Of heaven after our world.
Instead, watch images of flashing brass
That strike the outward sense, the polished will
Flag of our purpose which the wind engraves.[21]

We have seen in *The Still Centre* how Spender considered that too great an exercise of will would be detrimental to his poetic processes; and we have seen also that he had earlier found that the will in Rex Warner, the "determined 'character,'" had crushed sensibility and had ossified his work. Similarly, of John Cornford's poems, he says they seem to be written from the will, while most contemporary literature seems to be written from the sensibility.[22] Wordsworth, on the other hand, had "turned away from the town to seek out the sources of being and feeling as against those of will and reason."

If, however, it opposes the lyrical utterance, it is the will that supplies the form of a poem, as indeed it supplies the form for a total life. At one point in an argument, speaking of poets' various characteristics, Spender says, "My mind is not clear, my will is weak, I suffer from . . . a weak sense of form."[23] Sometimes he seems to be guarding himself and his poem against the claims of form—he wants to get round it:

form does not lie simply in the correct observance of rules. It lies in the struggle of certain living material to achieve itself within a pattern. The very refusal of a poet to sacrifice what he means to a perfectly correct rhyme, for example, can more powerfully suggest the rhyme than correctness would.

21. *Poems* (London: Faber and Faber, 1933), p. 56.
22. "Introduction," *Poems for Spain,* ed. Stephen Spender and John Lehmann (London: Hogarth, 1939), p. 12.
23. "The Making of a Poem, " *The Making of a Poem,* p. 49.

How dubious that is! And how typical of Spender to find the reality of what is not there more compelling than the reality of what is and, as he proceeds, to be seeking to apprehend a form beyond the form:

> For it reveals the struggle towards the form, which because it has direction and movement, and is indeed an expression of will, projects the idea of an ideal form towards which the poem is moving, reaching even beyond the form itself.[24]

In "Not palaces," the poet's two poles make themselves felt. In "Darkness and Light" they are in explicit conflict, although the terms of that conflict are abstracted from the tangible outside world. Whereas in "Not palaces" the imagery is related to the world of the senses, in the later poem it points to things we conceive of rather than what we see. The poem as a whole tends to be literal—literal in the sense that the elements do not designate things outside the poem but refer to other elements within. In Spender's own phrase, such a poem "resists the flow of things." It is faithful to its form, a loose sestina; and one must forbear from making a paraphrase that merely substitutes another meaningless formula for its own. It may be said, however, that it records the poet's incompatible wishes: to live in the still center of his being, the dark, and to preserve this center but also at the same time to live at the circumference in the world, in "the world's circular terror" (as he phrases it in another poem, "The Separation") where it is light and where the will is effective. The first two stanzas play variations upon a limited number of images and references: dark and light, center and circumference, eye, violence, curve, and stone. In the first stanza, the inward self is straining outward toward the light of the external world:

> To break out of the chaos of my darkness
> Into a lucid day is all my will.
> My words like eyes in night, stare to reach
> A centre for their light: and my acts thrown
> To distant places by impatient violence

24. *World Within World* (London: Hamish Hamilton, 1951), pp. 313-14.

> Yet lock together to mould a path of stone
> Out of my darkness into a lucid day.[25]

The second stanza negates the first:

> Yet, equally, to avoid that lucid day
> And to preserve my darkness, is all my will.

His words avoid the light; his acts shatter the path. Following thesis and antithesis is a synthesis, discovered in the poet's weakness, more particularly in his fears. But his weakness is now identified, somehow, with will—that which nourishes the center with that which promotes the willed external personality:

> To break out of my darkness towards the centre
> Illumines my own weakness, when I fail;
> The iron arc of the avoiding journey
> Curves back upon my weakness at the end . . .
> . . . . . . . . . . . . . . . .
> Centre and circumference are both my weakness.
> O strange identity of my will and weakness!

The poem formally resolves its oppositions. But the resolution resists paraphrase: the poet is perhaps envisioning arrival at a condition like that enjoyed by Rilke's angels, in which the normal human contradictions are reconciled. But the words, repetitions, rhymes, and the dialectic do their duty mainly to the form of the poem as an autonomous entity. In life the conflict is not to be resolved. "Throughout these years," says Spender, referring to the early thirties, "I had always the sense of living on the circumference of a circle at whose centre I could never be."[26] The union of the will and the self-in-the-world, on the one hand, with the self of the center, on the other, is a process of individuation fulfilled in the form of the poem only. The poem is not reporting, but merely fulfilling art's function to assimilate our profound waywardnesses into a unity whose speciousness the reader or the artist himself is momentarily pleased to overlook.

25. *Still Centre*, p. 77.
26. *World Within World*, p. 192.

In many an off-the-cuff remark in poems or elsewhere, Spender shows that he favors the center over the circumference in his psychomachia. At the same time, by one device or another, he repeatedly throttles the expression of the lyrical part of the self in spontaneous song at the prompting of the opposite part. There is the injury or destruction of the lyrical pitch by calculated crudity, of which the prosaic "guts" and "skewers" in the following two passages are examples:

> To the hanging despair of eyes in the street, offer
> Your making hands, and your guts on skewers of pity.[27]

> All their perceptions in one instant,
> And his true gaze, the sun of present,
> Saw his guts lie beneath the trees.
>                    (pp. 59-60)

The crudity lies not in the anatomical location of the thing but in the sharp concrete designation among the insubstantial substantives; the same effect that is gained in "The Funeral" when "laughter on their lips and winds blowing round them" gives way without warning to "this one excelled all others in making driving belts."

In other poems the lyrical pitch is destroyed by the crude assertion of structure. Structure, which belongs to the will, is imposed upon some poems, distressing the lyrical imagery or argument and producing bathos. In "Responsibility: The Pilots Who Destroyed Germany, Spring, 1945,"[28] a later poem, we observe the forced recapitulation of imagery as a means of imposing a curious kind of wooden unity. First, the poet sees the bombers as weaving a cage—the favorite image:

> I stood on a roof-top and they wove their cage,
> Their murmuring, throbbing cage, in the air of blue crystal,
> I saw them gleam above the town like diamond bolts
> Conjoining invisible struts of wire,
> Carrying through the sky their squadrons' cage
> Woven by instincts delicate as a shoal of flashing fish.

27. *The Still Centre,* p. 30.
28. *The Edge of Being* (New York: Random House, 1949), p. 36.

Then the planes go, leaving silence and a network, now material and visible, of vapor trails, which melt into "satin ribbons / Falling over heaven's terraces near the sun." The planes, says the poet, had "carried [his] will" and bombed the German city. The imagery is linked up in the last stanza as follows:

Now I tie the ribbons torn down from those terraces
Around the most hidden image in my lines,
And my life, which never paid the price of their wounds,
Turns thoughts over and over like a propeller,
Assumes their guilt, honours, repents, prays for them.

One uses ribbons to make a presentation, a gift, perhaps, made to assuage a sense of guilt, or a wreath; and the image is related to the "satin ribbons," the vapor trails, earlier in the poem. And the propellers to which the turning thoughts are likened are those of the planes which went over in the first stanza. But thoughts simply do not turn over like propellers, and the effort to imagine them doing so injures the pitch. At the same time the repetition provides a kind of forced unity, such as Spender imposes upon an appreciable number of his poems, early and late. But we may recall the first word of the title: "Responsibility" and observe that the crude simile, inasmuch as it controls the lyrical feeling and keeps down the singing pitch, performs, no doubt, the function that the will requires of it. And in providing structural unity for the poem, the will operates as it does in Spender's notions of psychology: it purveys unity of being while impairing the poetry-making faculty.

Perhaps more remarkable and more frequent in Spender than the sudden onset of crudity and the imposition of a wooden unity is the destructive device of elaborating a metaphor or a simile to the point where it becomes ludicrous. It is a ubiquitous practice: the simile of the thoughts turning over like a propeller is one example. Others are:

... threw words like stones ...[29]
... your heart fretted by winds like rocks at Land's End ...[30]

29. *Poems,* 1933, p. 23.
30. *Still Centre,* p. 31.

. . . vivid longings/Gnaw the flesh, like minnows.[31]

Hearts wound up with love, like little watch springs.

(p. 71)

. . . whose cries, like wild birds,
Settle upon the nearest roofs . . .[32]

. . . fills her linen night-gown
As the air fills a balloon.[33]

With songs buried beneath the ground like rotted leaves
To spring as cucumbers . . .[34]

Then your happiness bound cords
Around his treasured glance, like a blue bow.[35]

These passages come from early and late poems; some come from poems that have since been revised and altered. In all of them, a lyrical pitch has been destroyed by an elaboration of the vehicle of the simile. In that elaboration, the figure becomes subject to too close a scrutiny: one might accept that vivid longings gnaw the flesh, but with the addition of "like minnows" the poem suddenly becomes an animated cartoon; similarly, with the addition of "like little watch springs" one has difficulty in living with the fiction that the heart is wound up; "cries, like wild birds" is a lovely conceit, quite spoiled with the addition; and so forth. The practice does not enrich the poem by adding a complexity to be fused into it; what is added is, as it were, a voice from another dimension, striking the poem at an angle, making it absurd. The sequence of the establishment of lyrical pitch and the destruction of it results from the two impulses, the lyrical and the prosaic. And, maintaining the terms Spender uses in the poem "Darkness and Light," we may say that these are derived respectively from his dark inner self and the light outer one. Keats, we are told, was forever contriving to

31. *Collected Poems*, p. 40.
32. *Poems*, 1933, p. 46.
33. *Still Centre*, p. 104.
34. *Vienna* (New York: Random House, 1935), p. 11.
35. *Collected Poems*, p. 142.

maneuver himself out of sensuous enjoyment into misery; and, in many poems, Spender shows an analogous kind of shift: it is as if a stern voice from the pragmatic world were calling him back from his lyrical trip.

At the same time there are other devices by means of which the poetry seems to move in the opposite direction, as if evading the structure and organization of the pragmatic world and registering the poet's distrust of its reality. Imagery, for example, that is descriptive of the world may become insubstantial, a movement in the opposite direction from that which ended with "guts" and "skewers": "voices / Murmured at night from the garden, as if flowering from water";[36]

> Belsen Theresenstadt Buchenwald where
> Faces were clenched fists of prayer
> Knocking at the bird-song-fretted air[37]

As well as by imagery that loses contact with our senses, the poet may detach himself from the world of will by means of conceptions so intricate as to be inconceivable. Instances may be adduced from the earlier and the later poems, for the practice is one of Spender's most characteristic features: of a debauchee poet of the last century, for instance, he writes,

> . . . that sigh, which hovers
> Through spaces between letters, white and far,
> Is on his page the print of what we are.
> (p. 50)
> . . . the entire knife
> Of what he thought and strove, glued to my hand.[38]

> for whom her printed page
> Is heaven on which their wills write worlds.[39]

36. *Poems*, p. 55.
37. *Edge of Being*, p. 48.
38. *Trial of a Judge* (London: Faber and Faber, 1938) pp. 22-23.
39. *Collected Poems*, p. 77.

> . . . extremes of love
> Reach the Arctic Pole of the white bone
> Where panic fills the nights in which we are alone.
>
> (p. 158)

The concepts do not spring fully armed into recognition.

To suggest, however, as I have, that the devices move the poem, momentarily at least, away from the outside world and restore it to the center may be only a crude adumbration, upon which a refinement may be tentatively suggested: that the inconceivable complexities into which the poems proceed are not exactly a device by means of which Spender is escaping the real world, but one by which the truth of that world is the more scrupulously presented. Poems do not avoid life for art, one may suggest; they refine a vision of life to the point where it is not distinguishable from art. These are merely hints and guesses: Spender is perhaps of a persuasion similar to that of his hero in *Trial of a Judge,* who was said to believe

> That an argument would govern the state drew its form
> From the same sources as the symmetry of music
> Or the most sensitive arrangement of poetic words. . . .[40]

Presumably, if it were so, the conflict between center and circumference would be a minor poetic tension.

In "Darkness and Light" the center is designated weakness, but the poet makes it pretty clear through the rest of the volume, *The Still Centre,* that this weakness is his strength. It is a kind of negative capability, which, for example, Spender seems to have thought that George Barker possessed, that will-less condition that made him able to respond with his total personality to the disasters in Spain. Perhaps Spender recognized the affinity of his own genius with the quality of negative capability that Keats described, since he speaks so lyrically of Keats in this connection:

> When Keats writes of the "negative capability" which Shakespeare possessed so enormously, a condition "when a man is capable of being in uncertainties, mysteries, doubts, without

40. *Trial of a Judge,* p. 109.

any irritable reaching after fact and reason," we have the sense of a magnetic needle pulled towards the molten core of Shakespearean truth. Critical insight has become visionary, poetic statement.[41]

Probably this quality, more than any other, the very absence of "will like a dividing spear," to use Matthew Arnold's simile, has brought to the various volumes of Spender's poetry the reviewers' comments that he lacks style, that he is unformed, and that he has no sense of permanent values. These remarks need various qualifications. One notices, however a consistent hesitation or, indeed, refusal on the part of this poet to enter into the totality of his own selfhood in the poetry. He doubts the selfhood, perhaps. "Supposing I am nothing," says Geoffrey, the main character of *The Backward Son,* whom we may safely associate with the author. "All I am is a voice which says 'here'. . . . " The poet questions, certainly, the integrity of the great man: the great man who manifests any humanity is necessarily fragmented: "humanity seems to begin where eccentricity appears, when they think or act in a way which is inconsistent with being general, statesman, or big-game hunter."[42] In the early poem, "An 'I' can never be great man," Spender suggests that greatness cannot contain all the facets of the composite self:

> Central 'I' is surrounded by 'I eating',
> 'I loving', 'I angry', 'I excreting',
> And the great 'I' planted in him
> Has nothing to do with all these
> Can never claim its true place
> Resting in the forehead, and secure in his gaze.

Not to go into his personal psychology, one observes the poet fragmented throughout the poetry; and one suspects that wholeness, like the resolved conflict in "Darkness and Light," is a poetic

41.*Chaos and Control in Poetry: A Lecture Delivered at the Library of Congress, October 11, 1965* (Washington: Library of Congress, 1966), p. 8.
42. "Confessions and Autobiography," *The Making of a Poem* (London: Hamish Hamilton, 1955), pp. 63-64.

fiction: he had anticipated it, but he was never to arrive where it was to be had. He had expected, he says,

> Some brightness to hold in trust,
> Some final innocence
> Exempt from dust;
> That, hanging solid,
> Would dangle through all
> Like the created poem
> Or faceted crystal.[43]

There is a curious phrase at one point in an essay in which Spender is discussing the Auden group, including himself: "Their poetry often gives the impression that they stayed at the fringe of their own personalities and of the problems that obsessed them."[44] One of his early poems begins, "Never being, but always at the edge of Being."[45] The poet proceeds in it to say that he moves lips for tasting and hands for touching, but never comes nearer than touching

> Though the Spirit lean outward for seeing.
> Observing rose, gold, eyes, and admired landscape,
> My senses record the act of wishing
> Wishing to be
> Rose, gold, landscape or another—
> Claiming fulfilment in the act of loving.

The poem is an early expression of the sense of the fragmented self, which consists of the two parts that are later designated the still center and the self in the world of the will. The "Spirit" from the center leans outward to contact the other half of the self, which it can do no more than touch. It observes the self in the world, the poet's body, as a landscape with which it desires to be identified; and, so the poem implies, it is frustrated. But the act of loving (in later versions of the poem, the "fact of loving") establishes some

---

43. *Poems,* p. 25.
44. *Poetry Since 1939* (London: Longmans Green, 1946), p. 28.
45. *Twenty Poems* (Oxford: Basil Blackwell, n. d.), p. 2.

kind of integration and hence "fulfilment." It is significant that Spender made an exception to the chronological order of the poems in his first book so that he might set this one at the forefront of his published work[46] and that the phrase "edge of Being" should have remained with him to be used twenty years later as the title for a volume of poems. For if Being is the personality unified by will, then it is at the edge that the poet wishes to be, where his lyric abilities will not be injured or destroyed. And at the same time he wants to be no nearer than the edge to a world whose reality he thoroughly doubts. In sum, the claims of integrity and integration are opposed.

I believe that these three features of Spender give rise to and are part of his most characteristic poems: first, his tenuous engagement with the solid world; second, the conflict of the spirit and its lyric pastimes with the demands of the workaday life; and, third, the fragmentation of the self.

For forty-five years the poetry has been what these characteristics have made it: few poets have changed their styles less. Spender has been largely unswayed by passing planetary figures and fashions: not the word-glory of Dylan Thomas, the terse superior commentary of Graves, the brassy eruptions of the surrealists, the guarded modesty of the Movement, not even the enormous gravitational pull of Auden has noticeably drawn him from his proper orbit. Nor, for that matter, except on rare occasions, do we hear his voice in the work of others. He is original and independent.

46. Not counting *Nine Experiments*, printed on his own press in 1928. "At the Edge of Being" is number 1 in *Twenty Poems*. The volume is introduced by a note declaring that with the exception of the first, the poems are arranged "almost" chronologically.

# Selected Bibliography

Aiken, Conrad. "Back to Poetry." In *Collected Criticism*. Edited by Rufus A. Blanshard. New York: Oxford University Press, 1968.

Allott, Kenneth, *Poems*. London: Hogarth Press, 1938.

———. "Play for Puritans." *New Verse,* no. 30 (Summer 1938).

———. *The Ventriloquist's Doll.* London: Cresset Press, 1943.

———. *The Penguin Book of Contemporary Verse.* Harmondsworth, Middlesex: Penguin Books, 1950.

Auden, W.H. *The Orators.* London: Faber & Faber, 1932.

———. *Look, Stranger!* London: Faber & Faber, 1936.

———. "Psychology and Criticism." *New Verse,* no. 20 (April/May 1936).

———. *The Age of Anxiety: A Baroque Eclogue.* New York: Random House, 1947.

———. *Louis MacNeice: A Memorial Address*. London: Faber & Faber, 1963.

Barker, George. *Thirty Preliminary Poems*. London: Parton Press, 1933.

———. *Poems*. London: Faber & Faber, 1935.

———. *Calamiterror*. London: Faber & Faber, 1937.

———. *Lament And Triumph*. London: Faber & Faber, 1940.

———. *Eros In Dogma*. London: Faber & Faber, 1944.

———. *Collected Poems, 1930–1955*. London: Faber & Faber, 1957.

Bell, Julian. *Chaffinches (A Poem)*. Cambridge: Heffer & Sons, 1929.

———. *Winter Movement and Other Poems*. London: Chatto & Windus, 1930.

———. *Work for the Winter and Other Poems*. London: Leonard and Virginia Woolf, 1936.

———. "The Proletariat and Poetry: An Open Letter to C. Day Lewis." *Essays, Poems and Letters*. Edited by Quentin Bell. London: Hogarth Press, 1958.

Blackmur, R.P. "The Audience and Politics." *Twentieth Century Verse*, no. 18 (June/July 1939).

Blakeslee, Richard C. "Three Ways Past Edinburgh: Stephen Spender's 'The Express'." *College English* 26 (April 1965).

Blunden, Edmund. *Poems 1930–1940*. London: Macmillan & Co., 1940.

———. *Shells By A Stream*. London: Macmillan & Co., 1944.

Borroff, Marie. "Computer as Poet." *Yale Alumni Magazine* 34 (January 1971): 22–25.

Bottrall, Ronald. *The Loosening and Other Poems*. Cambridge: Minority Press, 1931.

———. "XXX Cantos of Ezra Pound." *Scrutiny* 2 (September 1933): 122.

———. *Festival of Fire*. London: Faber & Faber, 1934.

————. *The Turning Path.* London: Arthur Barker, 1939.

————. *Farewell And Welcome.* London: Editions Poetry, 1945.

————. *Selected Poems.* London: Editions Poetry, 1946.

————. *The Palisades of Fear.* London: Editions Poetry, 1949.

————. *Adam Unparadised.* London: Verschoyle, 1954.

Breit, Harvey. "View of the World." *Poetry* 59 (December 1941): 160.

Brooks, Cleanth. "Poetry and Political Faith." *Poetry* 50 (August 1937).

Bullough, Geoffrey. *The Trend of Modern Poetry.* 3d rev. ed. London: Oliver, 1949.

Cameron, John. *The Winter House And Other Poems.* London: Dent & Sons, 1935.

Campbell, Roy. *Talking Bronco.* London: Faber & Faber, 1946.

Carpenter, Maurice. "We Ask For Life." *Left Review* 3 (February 1937).

————. "A Welsh Girl." *Left Review* 3 (July 1937).

Caudwell, Christopher. *Studies in a Dying Culture.* London: John Lane, 1938.

————. *Further Studies in a Dying Culture.* Edited by Edgell Rickword. London: Bodley Head, 1949.

————. *Poems.* London: Lawrence & Wishart, 1965.

————. *The Concept of Freedom.* London: Lawrence & Wishart, London.

————. *Illusion And Reality.* London: Lawrence & Wishart, 1966.

Charques, R. *Contemporary Literature and the Social Revolution.* London: Martin Secker, 1933.

Chisholm, Hugh. "Ode." *New Verse* 1 (January 1939).

Cockburn, Claud. *In Time of Trouble: An Autobiography.* London: R.H. Davis, 1956.

————. *I, Claud: The Autobiography of Claud Cockburn.* Harmondsworth, Middlesex Penguin Books, 1967.

"A Conversation with Claud Cockburn." *the Review,* no. 11/12, pp. 51–52.

Cornford, John. "Left?" *Cambridge Left* 1 (Winter 1933–34).

———. "Full Moon at Tierz: Before the Storming of Huesca." *Left Review* 3 (March 1937).

Daiches, David. *Poetry And The Modern World.* Chicago: University of Chicago Press, 1940.

———. "The Lyricism of George Barker." *Poetry* 69 (March 1947).

———. *The Present Age.* London: Cresset Press, 1958.

Dodds, E. *The Collected Poems of Lewis MacNeice.* Edited by E. Dodds. New York: Oxford University Press, 1967.

Dodsworth, M. "Bernard Spencer: The Poet of Addition." *the Review*, no. 11/12.

Draper, Colin. "Wanted! New Poets for Revolution." *Poetry and The People* 19 (July 1940).

Dyment, Clifford. *First Day.* London: Dent & Sons, 1935.

———. *Poems.* London: Dent & Sons, 1949.

———. *C. Day Lewis.* London: Longmans, Green, 1955.

Empson, William. *Poems.* London: Chatto & Windus, 1935.

Ewart, Gavin. "Journey." *New Verse,* no. 8 (April 1934).

———. "Two Views of a Play." *Twentieth Century Verse,* no. 10 (May 1938).

———. *Poems And Songs.* London: Fortune Press, 1939.

Ford, Hugh D. *A Poet's War: British Poets in the Spanish Civil War.* Philadelphia: University of Pennsylvania Press, 1965.

Foxall, Edgar. *Water-Rat Sonata and Other Poems.* London: Fortune Press, 1940.

———. *Poems.* London: Fortune Press, 1946.

Fraser, George S. *Vision And Rhetoric.* London: Faber and Faber, 1959.

Fuller, Roy. "Poems by Editors." *Twentieth Century Verse,* no. 17 (April/May 1934).

———. *Poems.* London: Fortune Press, 1940.

———. *The Middle Of A War.* London: Hogarth Press, 1942.

————. *A Lost Season*. London: Hogarth Press, 1944.

————. *Epitaphs And Occasions*. London: John Lehmann, 1949.

————. *Counterparts*. London: Verschoyle, 1954.

————. "Norman Cameron: Four Views." *the Review*, no. 27/28 (Autumn/Winter 1971–72).

Gascoyne, David. *Roman Balcony*. London: Temple Bar Publishing Co., 1932.

————. *A Short Survey of Surrealism*. London: Cobden Sanderson, 1935.

————. *Man's Life Is This Meat*. London: Parton Press, 1936.

————. *Poems 1937–1942*. London: Editions Poetry, 1943.

————. *A Vagrant And Other Poems*. London: John Lehmann, 1950.

Gide, André. *Back From the USSR*. Translated by Dorothy Bussy. London: Secker & Warburg, 1937.

————. *After Thoughts: A Sequel to Back From the U.S.S.R.* Translated by Dorothy Bussy. London: Secker & Warburg, 1937.

Gill, Eric. "Eric Gill On Art And Propaganda." *Left Review* 1 (June 1935).

Golfing, F.C. "Mr. Barker And His Critics." *Poetry* 72 (April 1948).

Goodman, Richard, and Spencer, Bernard. *Poems*. London: B. Blackwell, 1931.

Graves, Robert. *The Common Asphodel*. London: H. Hamilton, 1949.

————. *The Crowning Privilege*. London: Cassell, 1955.

————, and Hodge, Alan. *The Long Weekend: A Social History of Great Britain 1918–1939*. London: Faber & Faber, 1940.

Grigson, Geoffrey. "Two First Books." *New Verse*, no. 7 (February 1934).

————. "Two Poets." *New Verse*, no. 8 (April 1934).

————. "Nertz." *New Verse*, no. 15 (June 1935).

————. Review of *Poems Of Strife* by Julius Lipton. *New Verse* 21 (June/July 1936).

————. *The Crest On The Silver: An Autobiography.* rev. ed. London: Cresset Press, 1950.

————. "Remarks." *New Verse*, no. 28 (January 1938).

————. "New Poems by MacNeice and Prokosch." *New Verse*, no. 30 (Summer 1938).

————. "Lonely, But Not Lonely Enough." *New Verse*, no. 31/32 (Autumn 1938).

————. *Several Observations.* London: Cresset Press, 1939.

————. "Remarks on Painting and Mr. Auden." *New Verse* 1 (January 1939).

————. "Rum Tum Tum On A Broken Drum." *New Verse* 1 (May 1939).

————. *Collected Poems of 1924–62.* London: Phoenix House, 1963.

————. *A Skull In Salop And Other Poems.* London: Macmillan, 1967.

————. *Under Cliff And Other Poems.* London: Routledge, 1943.

————. *The Harp Of Aeolus.* London: Routledge, 1948.

————. *Poems And Poets.* London: Macmillan & Co., 1969.

Grubb, Frederick. *A Vision Of Reality.* London: Chatto & Windus, 1965.

Hamilton, Ian. Review of *Buff* by Roy Fuller. *London Magazine* 5 (June 1965).

Harper, Robert D. "Back to the Personal." *Poetry* 57 (October 1940).

Hawkins, A. Desmond. Review of *Calamiterror* by George Barker. *Twentieth Century Verse,* no. 4 (June/July 1937).

Hoggart, Richard. *Auden: An Introductory Essay.* London: Chatto & Windus, 1951.

Hope, Francis. "Then And Now." *the Review,* no. 11/12.

Hoskins, Katharine B. *Today The Struggle: Literature And Politics*

————. *In England During The Spanish Civil War*. Austin: University of Texas Press, 1969.

Isherwood, Christopher. *Lions and Shadows: An Education in the Twenties*. Original Edition Hogarth Press, 1938. London: Methuen, 1953.

Jacobs, Willis. "The Moderate Poetical Success Of Stephen Spender." *College English* 17 (April 1956).

James, R. Scott. "Editorial Notes." *London Mercury* 35 (February 1937).

Kenner, Hugh. *Wyndham Lewis: New Directions*. London: Methuen, 1954.

Larkin, Philip. "What's Become of Wystan?" *Spectator* 205 (July 15, 1960).

Leavis, F.R. *New Bearings In English Poetry: A Study of the Contemporary Situation*. Ann Arbor: University of Michigan Press, 1960. Paperback edition.

Lehmann, John. *A Garden Revisited And Other Poems*. London: Hogarth, 1931.

————. *The Noise Of History*. London: Hogarth Press, 1934.

————. *The Whispering Gallery: Autobiography*. London: Longmans, 1955.

————. *I Am My Brother*. London: Longmans, 1960.

————. Review of *A Poet's War: British Poets And The Spanish Civil War* by Hugh D. Ford. *London Magazine* 5 (November 1965).

Lewis, C. Day. *A Hope For Poetry*. Oxford: B. Blackwell, 1934.

————. "Revolutionaries And Poetry." In *Revolution In Writing*. London: Hogarth Press, 1935.

————. *A Time To Dance*. London: Hogarth Press, 1936.

————. *Collected Poems of C. Day Lewis*. London: Cape & Hogarth, 1954.

————. *The Buried Day*. London: Chatto & Windus, 1960.

Lewis, Wyndham. "First Aid For The Unorthodox." *London Mercury* 32 (May 1935).

———. *One-Way Song*. With Foreword by T.S. Eliot. rev. ed. London: Methuen, 1960.

Lindsay, Jack. "On Guard For Spain." *Left Review* 3 (March 1937).

Lowbridge, Peter. "The Spanish Civil War." *the Review,* no. 11/12.

MacNeice, Louis. *Poems*. London: Faber & Faber, 1935.

———. "To A Writer On His Birthday." *New Verse,* no. 17 (October/November, 1935).

———. *I Crossed the Minch*. London: Longmans, 1938.

———. "A Statement." *New Verse,* no. 31/32 (Autumn 1938).

———. *The Earth Compels*. London: Faber & Faber, 1938.

———. *The Strings Are False: An Unfinished Autobiography*. New York: Oxford University Press, 1966.

Madge, Charles. "Instructions." *New Verse*, no. 2 (March 1933).

———. "Poetry And Politics." *New Verse* 3 (May 1933).

———. "Poetic Description And Mass Observation." *New Verse*, no. 24 (February/March 1937).

———. "The Oxford Collective Poem." *New Verse* no. 25 (May 1937).

———. *The Disappearing Castle*. London: Faber & Faber, 1937.

———. *The Father Found*. London: Faber & Faber, 1941.

Mason, H.A. Review of *Calamiterror* by George Barker. *Scrutiny* 6 (1937–38).

———. "Mr. Spender's Play." *Scrutiny* 7 (September 1938).

Maxwell, D.E. *Poets Of The Thirties*. London: Routledge & Kegan Paul, 1969.

Muggeridge, Malcolm. *The Thirties*. London: Hamish Hamilton, 1940.

Muir, Edwin. *The Present Age From 1914*. London: Cresset Press, 1939.

Muste, John M. *Say That We Saw Spain Die: Literary Consequences Of The Spanish Civil War*. Seattle: University of Washington Press, 1966.

Nemerov, Howard. *Poetry And Fiction*. New Brunswick, N.J.: Rutgers University Press, 1963.

Nettlefold, W. R. "Remembrance Day." *Left Review* 3 (December 1937).

———. *Inside The Whale And Other Essays*. Harmondsworth, Middlesex: Penguin Books, 1962.

———. *The Road To Wigan Pier*. Harmondsworth, Middlesex: Penguin Books, 1967.

———. "The Frontiers Of Art and Propaganda." *The Collected Essays, Journalism And Letters of George Orwell. Vol. 2: My Country Right Or Left, 1940–1943*. Edited by Sonia, Orwell, and Ian, Angus. New York: Harcourt-Brace & World, 1968.

Parsons, Clere. *Poems*. London: Faber & Faber, 1932.

Orr, Peter, ed. *The Poet Speaks: Interviews with Contemporary Poets*. New York: Barnes & Noble, 1966.

"The Poet's Dilemma: The Impact of Events." *Times Literary Supplement*, May 6, 1939.

"Politics: And A Request." *New Verse*, no. 2 (March 1933).

Porteus, Hugh G. Review of *Thirty Preliminary Poems* by George Barker. Scrutiny 3 (June 1934).

———. "Reading And Riding" *Twentieth Century Verse*, no. 14 (December 1938).

Pound, Ezra. "The Coward Surrealists." *Contemporary Poetry And Prose*, no. 7 (November 1936).

Prince, F.T. *Poems*. London: Faber & Faber, 1938.

———. *Soldiers Bathing And Other Poems*. London: Fortune Press, 1954.

Read, Herbert. *In Defense Of Shelley*. London: Heinemann, 1936.

Replogle, Justin. *Auden's Poetry*. Seattle: University of Washington Press, 1969.

Rickword, Edgell. *Invocations to Angels*. London: Lawrence & Wishart, 1928.

———. *Scrutinies by Various Writers*. Vol. 2. London: Lawrence & Wishart, 1931.

———. *Twittingpan And Some Others*. London: Lawrence & Wishart, 1931.

———. "Who Is This Noah." *Left Review* 2 (April 1936).

———. "When Writers Unite." *Left Review* 3 (March 1938).

———. *Collected Poems of Edgell Rickword*. London: Bodley Head, 1947.

Rimbaud, A. *A Season In Hell*. Translated by Norman Cameron. London: John Lehmann, 1950.

Roberts, Janet. "Introductory Memoir," in *The Collected Poems of Michael Roberts*. London: Faber & Faber, 1958.

Roberts, Michael. *These Our Matins*. London: E. Matthews & Marrot, 1930.

———. *New Signatures: Poems by Several Hands*. London: Hogarth Press, 1932.

———. "Preface." *New Country: Prose and Poetry by Authors of New Signatures*. Edited by Michael Roberts. London: Leonard & Virginia Woolf, 1933.

———. *Critique of Poetry*. London: J. Cape, 1934.

———. *Poems*. London: J. Cape, 1936.

———. *Orion Marches*. London: Faber & Faber, 1939.

———. *Collected Poems*. London: Faber & Faber, 1958.

Ross, Robert H. *The Georgian Revolt 1910–1922*. Carbondale: Southern Illinois University Press, 1965.

Scarfe, Francis. *Auden And After: The Liberation of Poetry 1930–1941*. London: Routledge, 1942.

*Poetry of the Thirties*. Edited by Robin Skelton. Harmondsworth, Middlesex: Penguin Books, 1967.

Sloan, Pat. "The Two André Gides." *Left Review* 3 (May 1937).

Spears, Monroe. *The Poetry of W.H. Auden: The Disenchanted Island*. New York: Oxford University Press, 1963.

Spencer, Bernard. *Aegean Island And Other Poems*. London: Editions Poetry, 1946.

Spender, Stephen. *Twenty Poems*. Oxford: Blackwell, 1930.

———. *Poems*. London: Faber & Faber, 1933.

————. *Poems.* 2nd ed. London: Faber & Faber, 1934.

————. *Vienna.* New York: Random House, 1935.

————. *The Destructive Element.* London: J. Cape, 1935.

————. "Writers and Manifestoes." *Left Review* 1 (February 1935).

————. *The Burning Cactus.* London: Faber & Faber, 1936.

————. *Forward From Liberalism.* London: Gollancz, 1937.

————. "New Poetry." *Left Review* 3 (July 1937).

————. "Heroes In Spain." *New Statesman* 13 (May 1, 1937).

————. "Poetry." *Fact,* no. 4 (July 1937).

————. "Auden and Politics." *New Verse,* no. 26/27 (November 1937).

————. *Trial Of A Judge.* London: Faber & Faber, 1938.

————. "The Left Wing Orthodoxy." *New Verse,* no. 31/32 (Autumn 1938).

————. *The New Realism: A Discussion.* London: Hogarth, 1939.

————. *Poems For Spain.* Edited by Stephen Spender, and John Lehmann. London: Hogarth Press, 1939.

————. *The Still Centre.* London: Faber & Faber, 1939.

————. *The Backward Son.* London: Hogarth Press, 1940.

————. *Selected Poems.* London: Faber & Faber, 1940.

————. *Ruins And Visions: Poems 1934–42.* New York: Random House, 1942.

————. *Life And The Poet.* London: Secker & Warburg, 1942.

————. *Nine Experiments. Being Poems Written At The Age Of Eighteen.* Original Edition 1928. Reprint Cincinnati, Ohio: University of Cincinnati, 1944.

————. *Botticelli.* London: Faber & Faber, 1945.

————. *Citizens In War, And After.* London: Harrap, 1945.

————. *Poetry Since 1939.* London: Longmans, Green, 1946.

————. *Poem of Dedication.* London: Faber & Faber, 1947.

————. *Edge of Being.* New York: Random House, 1949.

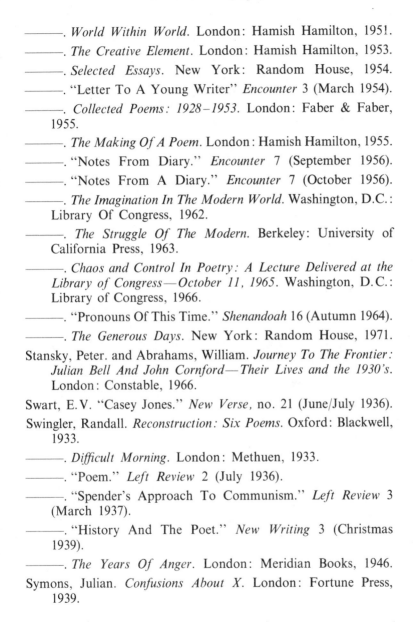

————. *World Within World*. London: Hamish Hamilton, 1951.

————. *The Creative Element*. London: Hamish Hamilton, 1953.

————. *Selected Essays*. New York: Random House, 1954.

————. "Letter To A Young Writer" *Encounter* 3 (March 1954).

————. *Collected Poems: 1928–1953*. London: Faber & Faber, 1955.

————. *The Making Of A Poem*. London: Hamish Hamilton, 1955.

————. "Notes From Diary." *Encounter* 7 (September 1956).

————. "Notes From A Diary." *Encounter* 7 (October 1956).

————. *The Imagination In The Modern World*. Washington, D.C.: Library Of Congress, 1962.

————. *The Struggle Of The Modern*. Berkeley: University of California Press, 1963.

————. *Chaos and Control In Poetry: A Lecture Delivered at the Library of Congress—October 11, 1965*. Washington, D.C.: Library of Congress, 1966.

————. "Pronouns Of This Time." *Shenandoah* 16 (Autumn 1964).

————. *The Generous Days*. New York: Random House, 1971.

Stansky, Peter. and Abrahams, William. *Journey To The Frontier: Julian Bell And John Cornford—Their Lives and the 1930's*. London: Constable, 1966.

Swart, E.V. "Casey Jones." *New Verse,* no. 21 (June/July 1936).

Swingler, Randall. *Reconstruction: Six Poems*. Oxford: Blackwell, 1933.

————. *Difficult Morning*. London: Methuen, 1933.

————. "Poem." *Left Review* 2 (July 1936).

————. "Spender's Approach To Communism." *Left Review* 3 (March 1937).

————. "History And The Poet." *New Writing* 3 (Christmas 1939).

————. *The Years Of Anger*. London: Meridian Books, 1946.

Symons, Julian. *Confusions About X*. London: Fortune Press, 1939.

————. *The Second Man*. London: Routledge, 1943.

————. *The Thirties: A Dream Revolved*. London: Cresset Press, 1960.

Tambimuttu. "First Letter." *Poetry* (London) 1 (February 1939).

————. "Mr. Symons In His Nursery." *Poetry* (London) 2 (April 1939).

Thomas, Hugh. *The Spanish Civil War*. 2d. ed., rev. Harmondsworth, Middlesex: Penguin Books, 1965.

Todd, Ruthven. *Ten Poems*. Edinburgh: Constable, 1940.

————. *Until Now: Poems*. London: Fortune Press, 1942.

Tomlinson, Charles. *Collected Poems of Ronald Bottrall*. London: Sidgwick & Jackson, 1961.

Treece, Henry. *Dylan Thomas 'Dog Among The Fairies*, London: Lindsay Drummond 1949.

*Twentieth Century Authors: A Biographical Dictionary Of Modern Literature*. Edited by Stanley. Kunitz, and Vineta. Colby, New York: Wilson, 1955.

Warner, Rex. Review of "Poems." *Left Review* 3 (July 1937).

————. *Poems*. London: Boriswood, 1937.

————. *Poems And Contradictions*. London: John Lane, 1945.

Warner, Sylvia Townsend. "In This Midwinter." *Left Review* 1 (January 1935).

————. "Red Front." *Left Review* 1 (April 1935).

Weintraub, Stanley. *The Last Great Cause: The Intellectuals and the Spanish Civil War*. London: Allen, 1968.

Winkler, R.O. "Ronald Bottrall." *Scrutiny* 8 (1939–40).

Wintringham, T.H. "Artists in Uniform." *Left Review* 1 (February 1935).

Wood, Neal. *Communism and British Intellectuals*. New York: University Press, 1959.

Woolf, Virginia. "The Leaning Tower." *Folios Of New Writing* 2 (Autumn 1940).

X. In *New Verse*, no. 28 (July 1938).

X. Review of "Trial Of A Judge." *Twentieth Century Verse,* no. 10 (May 1938).

Young, Andrew. *Speak To The Earth.* London: J. Cape, 1939.

———. *Collected Poems Of Andrew Young.* London: J. Cape, 1950.

# Index